International Federation of Library Associations and Institutions
Fédération Internationale des Associations de Bibliothécaires et des Bibliothèques
Internationaler Verband der bibliothekarischen Vereine und Institutionen
Международная Федерация Библиотечных Ассоциаций и Учреждений
Federación Internacional de Asociaciones de Bibliotecarios y Bibliotecas

About IFLA   www.ifla.org

IFLA (The International Federation of Library Associations and Institutions) is the leading international body representing the interests of library and information services and their users. It is the global voice of the library and information profession.

IFLA provides information specialists throughout the world with a forum for exchanging ideas and promoting international cooperation, research, and development in all fields of library activity and information service. IFLA is one of the means through which libraries, information centres, and information professionals worldwide can formulate their goals, exert their influence as a group, protect their interests, and find solutions to global problems.

IFLA's aims, objectives, and professional programme can only be fulfilled with the cooperation and active involvement of its members and affiliates. Currently, over 1,700 associations, institutions and individuals, from widely divergent cultural backgrounds, are working together to further the goals of the Federation and to promote librarianship on a global level. Through its formal membership, IFLA directly or indirectly represents some 500,000 library and information professionals worldwide.

IFLA pursues its aims through a variety of channels, including the publication of a major journal, as well as guidelines, reports and monographs on a wide range of topics. IFLA organizes workshops and seminars around the world to enhance professional practice and increase awareness of the growing importance of libraries in the digital age. All this is done in collaboration with a number of other non-governmental organizations, funding bodies and international agencies such as UNESCO and WIPO. IFLANET, the Federation's website, is a prime source of information about IFLA, its policies and activities: www.ifla.org

Library and information professionals gather annually at the IFLA World Library and Information Congress, held in August each year in cities around the world.

IFLA was founded in Edinburgh, Scotland, in 1927 at an international conference of national library directors. IFLA was registered in the Netherlands in 1971. The Koninklijke Bibliotheek (Royal Library), the national library of the Netherlands, in The Hague, generously provides the facilities for our headquarters. Regional offices are located in Rio de Janeiro, Brazil; Dakar, Senegal; and Singapore.

IFLA Publications 125

Library Management and Marketing in a Multicultural World

Proceedings of the 2006 IFLA Management and Marketing Section's Conference, Shanghai, 16–17 August, 2006

Edited by
James L. Mullins

u Ottawa

K · G · Saur München 2007

b30486877

IFLA Publications
edited by Sjoerd Koopman

Bibliographic information published by the Deutsche Nationalibliothek
The Deutsche Nationalbibliothek lists this publication in the Deutsche Nationalbibliografie;
detailed bibliographic data is available in the Internet at http://dnb.d-nb.de.

⊗

Printed on permanent paper
The paper used in this publication meets the minimum requirements of
American National Standard – Permanence of Paper
for Publications and Documents in Libraries and Archives
ANSI/NISO Z39.48-1992 (R1997)

Z
678
.I45
2006

Alle Rechte vorbehalten / All Rights Strictly Reserved
K. G. Saur Verlag, München
An imprint of Walter de Gruyter GmbH & Co. KG

Cover illustrations: Shanghai Library, photograph used with permission from the Shanghai Library;
Royal Palace, Seoul, Korea, photograph by James L. Mullins, used with permission.

Printed in the Federal Republic of Germany by Strauss GmbH, Mörlenbach

ISBN 978-3-598-22032-6
ISSN 0344-6891 (IFLA Publications)

Contents

II. How to Organize and Promote Library Services

III. Marketing Library Services to the General Public

Preface

The papers collected in this volume were presented at the 2006 IFLA M&M Shanghai Pre-Conference. The pre-conference, *Library Management and Marketing in a Multicultural World*, was held in Shanghai, China from August 16–17, 2006. It preceded the International Federation of Library Association (IFLA) World Library and Information Congress: 72nd IFLA General Conference and Council, *Libraries: Dynamic Engines for the Knowledge and Information Society*, held in Seoul, Korea from August 20–24, 2006. The pre-conference was presented under the auspices of the IFLA Marketing and Management Section. The Marketing and Management Section was pleased to collaborate with the Shanghai Library in the planning and organization of the pre-conference.

The Shanghai pre-conference would not have been possible without the following co-hosts: Library of China Executive Leadership Academy Pudong; Shanghai Pudong New Area Library; Shanghai Information Center for Life Sciences of the Chinese Academy of Sciences; Shanghai Society for Scientific Information. Generous support was provided for the pre-conference by China Hewlett-Packard Co., Ltd.

The articles in this volume address some of the latest developments in the marketing and management of libraries worldwide. The authors undertook different research methodologies to determine trends, opportunities and needs, as well as effectiveness and assessment. Several of the papers report on the success of programs designed to promote libraries within a community, nation, or academic community. Others report on trends and changes taking place within their user community and present a case study on their library's response to meeting the challenges and opportunities.

The scientific committee included: Jingli Chu (China); Jieyin Feng (China), co-chair; Dinesh Gupta (India); Haoming Lin (China); Àngels Massísimo Sánchez de Boado (Spain); and the editor of this volume, co-chair. In addition, the encouragement and support of Qihao Miao, deputy director of the Shanghai Library and member of the M&M Section was invaluable. We thank Jun Zhang, professor of economics at Fudan University for his keynote address; Ms. Àngels Massísimo, University of Barcelona, Library and Information Science and chair of the M&M Section, provided us with the inspiration to think locally as well as globally in her paper, *Think Globally,*

Act Locally—Manage Multiculturally; and Mr. Dinesh K. Gupta, V.M. Open University, Library and Information Science, who presented *Glimpses of the "Marketing Library and Information Services."* Attendees were also privileged to be addressed by Dr. Claudia Lux (Germany), IFLA president elect, 2007–2009, who presented her talk in both Chinese and English, acknowledging Chinese as one of the official languages of IFLA.

The editor wishes to extend special recognition to one individual, without whose help and leadership, this pre-conference would not have been possible: Jieyin Feng. Jieyin and I first met in Oslo in August 2005, where she presented the idea for the Shanghai pre-conference. As a result of her tireless efforts, the planning, review of papers, and logistical arrangements for the pre-conference were accomplished with outstanding ease and success. Questions about lodging, travel and more were answered in a timely, supportive and warm manner. Thank you, Jieyin Feng, for your hard work in making the pre-conference a success!

Finally, without the professional insight and hard work of several people at the Purdue University Press, this volume would have been delayed and of significantly lesser quality. Margaret Hunt, executive editor of the Press, coordinated the layout and design as well as supervising the work of Faris Habayeb and Amy Leigh Schutts, student editors, who formatted and corrected syntax and grammar.

Dr. James L. Mullins, Editor
Dean of Libraries & Professor of Library Science
Purdue University, USA

Library Management and Marketing in a Multicultural World—Program

16 August 2006

9:00-9:40

Opening Ceremony

Chair: Qihao Miao, Deputy Director, Shanghai Library
Claudia Lux, IFLA President-elect (2007-2009)
Endi Zhang, Vice-Mayor, Pudong New Area, Shanghai
Jianzhong Wu, Director, Shanghai Library

10:00-11:30

Keynote Addresses

Chair: Dr. James L. Mullins, Standing Committee Member, IFLA M&M Section

Jun Zhang, Professor of Economics, Fudan University

Ms. Angels Massisimo, Chair, IFLA M&M Section
Think Globally, Act Locally—Manage Multiculturally

Mr. Dinesh K. Gupta, Standing Committee Member, IFLA M&M Section
Glimpses of the 'Marketing Library and Information Services'

13:30-17:00

Session I: Marketing Library Services to Students

Chair: Teresa To, Senior Assistant Librarian, Run Run Shaw Library, The City University of Hong Kong, China

Bharati Sen
Marketing of Library Services to the Marginalized

Cuiying Mu
Marketing Academic Library Resources and Information Services to International Students

Lily Gao
Reaching Offshore—a Partnership Approach to Marketing
Australian University Libraries' Services to Offshore Students

Louisa McLam, Colin Storey & Teresa To
Target the Staff, then Target the Market—How Academic Librarians Can
Successfully Reach the Minds of New Generations of Students

Barbara I. Dewey
The University of Tennessee Libraries Transformation Plan: Realigning
the Research Library for 21st Century Students and Scholars

Questions & Answers

13:30-17:00

Session II: How to Organize and Promote Library Services

Chair: Sharon Karasmanis, Interlending and Document Delivery Librarian, La Trobe University Library, Victoria, Australia

Leonor Gaspar Pinto & Paula Ochôa
Dealing with Evidence Based Management: Roles and Dimensions of
Library Services Promotion

Dr. Grace Saw & Fei Yu
Different Strokes for Different Folks: Strategies in Promoting Library Services to International Customers, a Case Study

Li Zhang, Chunhua Yang & Guizhi Wang
Impact of Health Informatization on the Organization and Administration
of Medical Libraries in China

Sharon Karasmanis
From Australia to China Online: Delivery of Online Library
Services to Offshore Students in China

Questions & Answers

13:30-17:00

Session III: Marketing Library Services to the General Public

Chair: Wee Pin Wan, Acting Manager, National Library Board, Singapore

Maria Gental Morral
The Intercultural Dialogue in the Public Library: The Experience of the
District 2 Library in Terrassa (Barcelona)

Antonia Arahova & Sarantos Kapidakis
Globalization and Library Management: Practical Ideas for Effective Strategic Methods

Wee Pin Wan
Beyond Promotion—The Destination Library:
The National Library of Singapore Case Story

Questions & Answers

18:00–20:30
Reception Dinner

20:30–21:30
Boat Tour on the Huangpu River

August 17, 2006

9:00–12:00

Session IV: Changing Libraries in a Multicultural World
Chair: Dr. Marian Koren, Head, Research and International Affairs, Netherlands Public Library Association

Keqian Xu
Librarians' Professional Value and Perspective in the Era of the Digital Library

Dr. Marian Koren
Think Multiculturally, Recruit Nationally, Relate Locally: Library Campaigns in the Netherlands and Denmark

Xuemao Wang
Develop Future Library Leaders in the Context of Globalization with an Analysis on Cultural Intelligence

Ronghui Su & Qingming Yang
Impact of Globalization on Library Management and Marketing

Questions & Answers

9:00–12:00

Session V: Information Technology and Library Management
and Marketing

Chair: Dr. Christie M. Koontz, Committee Member, IFLA M&M Section

Liang Zhao
Performance Measurement of Metadata Management

Xiaowen Ding
Knowledge Society of Digital Librarians Blogging
Information Management

Jill Cousins
Using the Feedback Loop to Create a Marketing Campaign

Maja Coltura & Bart Vercruyssen
The Library: Mirror of Culture—Underlying Cultural Patterns
in Lending Statistics

Questions & Answers

14:00-17:00

Opening Ceremony of the 3rd Shanghai International Library Forum

Welcoming Address

Endi Zhang
Deputy Governor, Pudong New Area, Shanghai

Good morning, ladies and gentleman,

It's our great honor that IFLA Marketing and Management Pre-conference is held in the Pudong New Area. On behalf of the Pudong government, I'd like to say thanks to our guests from various libraries in the world, and welcome you to Pudong, the newly developed area in Shanghai.

Pudong is located at the east of Shanghai, separated by the Huangpu River from the old area of the city. There are four bridges across the Huangpu River and five tunnels running through the river for auto traffic. This area covers 570 square kilometers with a population of 2.6 million. It is becoming the business and commercial center of Shanghai. There is also a diversity of touring sights in this area, such as the Oriental Pearl TV Tower, Shanghai Aquarium, the central Greenland of Lujiazui, the Riverside Boulevard, the Century Park, and Sunqiao Modern Agriculture Development Zone.

The Pudong Public Library is one of the largest district libraries in Shanghai. It was opened in 2001, covering a space of more than 10,000 square meters. The library offers a rich variety of services to the general public, and is an information and cultural venue in Pudong New Area. We believe the IFLA M&M pre-conference will give librarians here an excellent opportunity to learn from the experience of colleagues from other countries and improve our own marketing and management of library services.

I wish this meeting every success and hope you enjoy your stay in Pudong. Thank you.

Welcoming Address

Jianzhong Wu

Director, Shanghai Library

It is my great pleasure to meet you here at Pudong Cadre College. On behalf of the Shanghai Library and Shanghai Library Association, I would like to express my warmest welcome and heartfelt gratitude to all our delegates from home and abroad.

I myself was involved in M&M in 1999, when I attended the Bangkok Pre-conference of M&M and also got a certificate issued by the section. Then I gave a talk at the Bangkok conference's M&M session at the invitation of Dr. Christie Koontz.

In the last twenty years Shanghai has seen a rapid development of libraries, especially public libraries. There are now 245 public libraries in the city. Each community has a library of an average of 50,000 books. But all these public libraries are independent. The Shanghai Library has no direct administrative link with all these libraries. To share resources among the local public libraries, the Shanghai Library developed an online circulation service in 2002. In 2005 all the 23 district libraries used the system. And starting in 2006 the system extended to community libraries; so far there have been 50 public libraries sharing the service. According to the Shanghai Library's plan, there will be 130 public libraries joining the system in 2010. That means a user can get the Shanghai Library's service at his or her nearest neighborhood library. The quantitative development is good, but the problem of the future development is quality. That is why we are interested in the theme of library management. We are so happy that you are bringing in your ideas and suggestions. Tomorrow you will go to the Shanghai Library to join a bigger audience at the opening ceremony of the Third Shanghai International Library Forum and to attend the cultural evening. I look forward to meeting you there.

Thank you very much indeed.

Keynote Addresses

Think Globally, Act Locally—Manage Multiculturally

Àngels Massísimo, Chair
IFLA Management and Marketing Section

Abstract

Welcome, on behalf of IFLA Management and Marketing Section, to all the delegates, sponsors and authorities attending our Satellite Meeting. Some reflections about what it means "to manage multiculturally", in relationship to the different sessions and contributions to the meeting and to the work of IFLA Management and Marketing Section—especially about multicultural issues and management.

Thank you so much for being here.

First of all, thank you to the authorities, because they are giving us the necessary support and encouragement to keep working in the enhancement of library services: they are here to give us their support, but also to share our worries, our successes, our experiences and reflections.

Thank you also to our sponsors: to the IFLA Management and Marketing Section (to our colleague and friend Jim Mullins, who took the responsibility at the level of organizing and scientific committees; and the local team of organizers, led by our colleague and friend Qhiao Miao, co-chair of our Satellite Meeting). Thank you to the Shanghai Pudong New Area Government, Shanghai Library, Shanghai Pudong New Area Library, Shanghai Life Sciences Library, and the Chinese Academy of Sciences. And to our special supporters: the Communication and Cooperation Committee, the China Society for Library Science. We are happy to have been able to rely on you all, on your help and collaboration, in order to launch this meeting.

This meeting would not be possible without the cooperation of our authors and contributors, and without the positive interest of our delegates and attendees. So, last, but not least, thank you to you all: you make it possible for us to be here today to see and listen, to discuss and evaluate, to learn from each other about multiculturalism and libraries.

And now, dear colleagues, I apparently ought to give you a keynote—a welcome speech. Let me start with a quotation.

In 1948, the world-known violoncello player Pau Casals was invited to give a lecture to the United Nations General Assembly. Mr. Casals, a Spanish exile born in El Vendrell (Catalonia, Spain), started his lecture with this phrase: "I am a Catalan."

I am a Catalan, too. I also am a Spanish citizen—a European citizen. And I also am a global citizen. Not in the usual, sometimes contested, economic sense, but in the geographical, cultural, "soul" sense. I am—as most of you also are—a multicultural product.

A global citizen. A product from centuries of cultural influences, demographic blends, mutual exchanges among regions—and also among continents, like most of you also are.

Spanish people went to America. They went to Asia and to Northern Africa, as well—not only as conquerors in the more distant past, but also as political exiles in very recent times. They also went to Europe as refugees, then as economic emigrants. And now, America's people, Asian people, African people, are coming to Spain—and to Catalonia as well. As they do to other European countries—past metropolises, a rich world—and to North America as well.

They are willing to give us back the visit. And they are not always attaining their goals.

Immigrant newcomers often "constitute" for the governments a logistic problem—we heard this kind of phrase sometimes in the recent years—it better would be said that they "create" a logistic problem, in any case. We are sure people never "constitute" a problem. The governments ought to do their best to organise the flow of humans, to receive newcomers, to suitably accommodate them, and to guarantee them, in their new country, a new life in humanly acceptable conditions, regarding work, home, education, health—and culture. Culture is one of the keywords in this context. Newcomers are born in a lot of different cultural contexts, have a lot of different cultural backgrounds. Usually they have a common characteristic: they know nothing about the culture receiving them. In that situation, immigrants become most vulnerable: they cannot find and use most social services; they need help for everything, and sometimes they are not even able to ask for it. Libraries and librarians have a word to say about that. Libraries and librarians can—and have to—offer services, resources, programs and staff in order to help newcomers to cope with their disadvantaged situation and to bridge as soon as possible the gap between them and their new society. Thanks to our contributors, we will learn a lot of examples of this kind of services, resources and programs from this meeting.

Let me say that, nowadays, in my country, people from 192 different nations are living and working together with us—speaking about 300 different languages. We are (only) 7 million people now in Catalonia, 42 million in the whole of Spain. One million people in Catalonia are born somewhere else in the world, and about one and a half million left, in more or less recent past, their homes in other regions of Spain, and came to Catalonia to start a new life. We now live altogether. We work altogether. We learn from each other. And this is a festival. As American former President Jimmy Carter said, "We become not a melting pot but a beautiful mosaic. Different people, different beliefs, different yearnings, different hopes, different dreams."

Every year Barcelona celebrates "The Week of Diversity"—and so do other cities. For a week, a lot of people born in different countries of the world let us know their musics, their languages, their traditions, their dresses, their crafts, their food, their beliefs. And so do we to them. We try to build altogether a beautiful mosaic. I won't say to you it always is easy. We all needed to adapt to the new context, to learn to live together—to work together. Problems arose, unfair situations had to be faced. But it was—it is—an exciting process, indeed. And encouraging.

Saul Alinsky, a U.S. political activist, said

Change means movement. Movement means friction. Only in the frictionless vacuum of a nonexistent abstract world can movement or change occur without that abrasive friction of conflict.

In building the new multicultural society, it is useful for us citizens to bear in mind that we all probably are—or were—newcomers at some moment of our history.

We sometimes fail. Our memory is so weak. We often don't remember the days when—not such a long time ago—our grandparents, our relatives, and our friends had to emigrate for one reason or another. Norwegian people went to the States in the 19th century—Irish people as well. British people were exiled in New England in the 17th century. Spanish and Portuguese people went across the oceans many times, and for different reasons, since the 15th century. Italian, Spanish, and Turkish people have travelled to Germany, Switzerland, etc. Chilean and Argentinian people went to Sweden, Denmark, etc. Latin people go to the States. A lot of people from everywhere went to Canada and to Australia. And from Australia to Southeastern Asia. People are moving.

People keep moving. We seek more freedom, a peaceful environment, better life conditions, more welfare, more and better education, more opportunities. And we certainly deserve all this. Immigrant people in every country have had to work in jobs "native people don't want to work in"—we always heard this. And we had to state this a lot of times. The French playwright Henry Becque wrote, "The defect of equality is that we only desire it with our superiors."

This is often our failure. We only look at the top—never at the bottom. But people keep moving. They keep seeking their opportunities. They are around us, near us, close to us. They become our neighbours. And they are asking for an answer. We as human beings have to give an answer to them. We as citizens have to demand a better organized and more humanitarian planned management of demographic migrations. We as librarians cannot accept working to help a few fortunate newcomers while every day we have to hear about a great deal of others dying anywhere in their quest of a better life. We as human beings cannot accept that things continue as they do now. Governments must certainly regulate and organize the human flows in their areas; we as citizens, however, cannot allow people to die in the 'cayucos', young men and women, and even little children, to give their lives in the desert, in the sea, in the river, in the borders of any nation. All this is inhumane, and it is certainly incumbent upon us as citizens, and upon our governments, to find a way to manage these situations in order to propose a solution convenient for all.

Finally, people are arriving to our country, to our city, to our district, to our neighbourhood. And they seek jobs. Immigrant people in every country have to work in jobs "native people don't want to work in." We as citizens cannot accept this, either. We cannot accept that qualified people have to work in non-qualified jobs—perhaps in slavery conditions—only because they are foreigners. We cannot accept that workers have to live alone, often in not so good conditions, far away from their families—only because they are foreigners. We as citizens—we as librarians—cannot accept this.

What can we citizens do?

There are a lot of expert people who could answer this pressing question much better than I can. Let me only share with you some reflections, let's listen together to the experts' voices.

Multiculturalism has to do with diversity: it involves respect for people's diversity—and respect for our own diversity, as well. Only from our social self-respect and cultural self-esteem, from the respect and love of our own culture and our own roots, will we be able to be respectful toward others' roots and culture. And to perceive them as a richness—to love them as an opportunity, not as a threat. Too often some people look at diversity as a threat. And that is not the way to progress. Without love for the differences, respect can be perhaps only a cold "politically correct" tolerance—perhaps insincere, perhaps even reversible.

Let's listen to UNESCO's voice:

> Given that cultures embrace literature and the arts as well as ways of life, value systems, traditions and beliefs, the protection and promotion of their diversity present special challenges: notably defending creative capacity through the multitude of its material and immaterial forms and ensuring that all peoples live together peacefully.
> (UNESCO, *Cultural Diversity: A New Universal Ethic*)

Defending creative capacity and ensuring that all peoples live together peacefully: an exciting program. But how to do it?

Again according to UNESCO's voice, two working lines would be essential for citizens in their developing a "peace culture":

- To ensure harmonious coexistence and willingness to live together peacefully means:
  - Respecting human rights,
  - Promoting intercultural dialogue,
  - Acting in favour of indigenous peoples,
  - Taking a cultural approach to HIV-AIDS.

- To defend diverse creativity and the multiplicity of cultural expressions means to protect and promote:
  - Tangible and intangible heritage,
  - Endangered languages,
  - Local indigenous knowledge on nature,
  - Contemporary cultural expressions: cultural goods and services,
  - Crafts,
  - Creative content for radio, television and new media,
  - Multilingualism in the Cyberspace,
  - Cultural and linguistic diversity in education.

(UNESCO—*Action in Favour of Cultural Diversity*)

UNESCO states that the Universal Declaration on Cultural Diversity represents a major step towards the recognition of cultural diversity as a key factor of sustainable development. However, it acknowledges that this Declaration will serve no purpose unless it is translated into action. Large actions, little actions: we as citizens definitely must act. As the U.S. political activist Jerry Brown said, "Inaction may be the biggest form of action."

What can we librarians do?

Let's go into action. Some of the points outlined above fall, totally or partially, in the field of libraries' competencies and duties. In recent years, a lot of librarians worldwide have become aware of the crucial role of libraries to help newcomers, and other disadvantaged persons, to fully integrate in their new society. Consequently they have started information services and programs to receive them, to help them with work-, home- or school-seeking, to inform them about public health administration, to help them in language learning, etc. They also have started measures to help foreign students, information illiterates, etc. Librarians certainly are engaged in a process of "bridging the gap"—not only the digital gap, but all the gaps which separate individuals from information access, thus from the opportunities they deserve.

Eldridge Cleaver, an African American writer and Black Panther leader, said, "You're either part of the problem or part of the solution."

So, let's go into action. Or, better said, let's keep in action. UNESCO's voice helps us again:

Missions of the public library

The following key missions which relate to information, literacy, education and culture should be at the core of public library services:

. . .

2. supporting both individual and self conducted education as well as formal education at all levels;
3. providing opportunities for personal creative development;

. . .

5. promoting awareness of cultural heritage, appreciation of the arts, scientific achievements and innovations;

. . .

7. fostering inter-cultural dialogue and favouring cultural diversity;
8. supporting the oral tradition;
9. ensuring access for citizens to all sorts of community information;

10. providing adequate information services to local enterprises, associations and interest groups;
11. facilitating the development of information and computer literacy skills;
12. supporting and participating in literacy activities and programmes for all age groups, and initiating such activities if necessary.

(*UNESCO Public Library Manifesto*, 1994)

Let's keep in action.

Multiculturalism has to do with diversity: racial diversity, ethnic diversity, gender and age diversity, as well; cultural, linguistic diversity, religious and spiritual diversity, physical and health conditions diversity. Managing multiculturally then probably means to cope with all these issues in the daily life of a library: with our staff, with our colleagues, with our users, with our (still) non-users. And with our authorities, as well.

Too often, somewhere in the world, individuals bearing the signs of one or more of these differences were—or still are—denied the opportunities they deserve exactly because of these differences: women, because they aren't men; old people, because they aren't younger; physically handicapped, because they aren't physically powerful; coloured people, because they aren't white; believers in one religion, because they aren't unbelievers, or because they aren't believers in any other religion; unbelievers, because they aren't believers; speakers of a native language, because they are; nonspeakers of a given language, because they aren't; political dissidents, because they are not following the way their authorities have decided; poor people, because they aren't rich; foreign people, because they aren't native; native people, because they are. Etc. They all suffered, or are suffering, discriminatory measures, and these measures often extend over decades—even over centuries.

At the end of the way, however, a more fair situation is restored, and a given society decides to enter in a situation of fair equal opportunities. It can then be perceived that some special, provisory measures are needed, if the formerly discriminated people are to be given back the normal opportunities to recover their pace. Sometimes, then, "equal opportunities" can mean that "non exactly equal" measures or policies are needed during a period, that "interim" measures are needed in order to rebalance society's unbalances and to finally be able to start from zero. Such policies or measures are called "positive discriminatory measures", and they obviously are not always perceived as useful, or good, by all the individuals in a society. And this is also a matter of conflict. Again.

In recent years, positive discriminatory measures were implemented in libraries in a number of countries all over the world. Some years ago, we had the opportunity to hear about measures put in place in South Africa with the aim of re-balancing the opportunities for library jobs among all the ethnic groups of the country.[1] We also heard about measures set up in German libraries, in order to rebuild a world of opportunities and to harmonise the working cultures of West- and East-German staff.[2] Somebody talked to us about measures developed in New Zealand for a more comprehensive and multiracial library society (workers, users).[3] Somebody else explained to us—and impressed us with—the story of services for immigrant populations in Swedish[4] cities. Last but not least, we heard about experiences with multicultural student communities in Thailand.[5]

I would refer you to all these cases as examples of managing libraries multiculturally. They all are speaking about libraries and librarians, about managing staff and users, about access to information and education resources—and finally about freedom of information. Because no freedom is possible without equal opportunities to all.

Librarians concerned with multiculturalism in the communities they serve have to be aware of the work done by UNESCO, IFLA and other entities and organizations in order to approach the diversity issues in libraries and other cultural and social institutions. In particular, we must remain aware of the work done by IFLA Sections of Libraries Serving Disadvantaged Persons and on Library Services to Multicultural Populations, which are both examples of the continuous effort to enhance the awareness of diversity issues in libraries, to study the barriers to information access for diverse minorities and to promote equal opportunity policies in libraries all over the world.

Once more, then, today and tomorrow, we will have the opportunity to hear about actions and policies being established by librarians from all kinds of libraries all over the world to bridge the gaps among people. We shall hear about actions and policies designed to facilitate cultural integration; to promote intercultural dialogue; to serve multicultural communities of users; to enhance communication with newcomers, etc. Again, today and tomorrow, we will have the opportunity to hear about measures and programs implemented by librarians in recent years all over the world. Marginalized students, offshore students, are being reached in different ways by smart and proactive librarians, and we will be able, today and tomorrow, to listen to their stories and to discuss their approaches. We will also analyze concerns about globalization and its consequences in libraries during this meeting. Library promotion methods among international customers will be discussed, as well as intercultural mediation patterns which have been developed in some countries—as in mine—in order to help foreign and native users to live together. We will enjoy learning and discussion about all these stories and best practices during the next two days.

Once more, then, today and tomorrow, we will to be given the opportunity to reflect together, and to learn from each other, about the possibilities and challenges we are facing in our beautiful multicultural world, in our definitely wonderful, "diverse" world. Let me wish you—let me wish ourselves—a most beneficial, enjoyable, worthwhile IFLA Satellite Meeting on Library Managing and Marketing in a Multicultural World.

Authorities, sponsors, dear colleagues: let me end my keynote address with a last quotation, most appropriate for today, from the English art critic Clive Bell:

> Only reason can convince us of those three fundamental truths without a recognition of which there can be no effective liberty: that what we believe is not necessarily true; that what we like is not necessarily good; and that all questions are open.

Thank you very much.

Notes

1   Heather Edwards, "Managing multicultural staff in a South African university library". *65th IFLA Council and General Conference: Bangkok, Thailand, August 20th-28th, 1999.* (025-106E). http://www.ifla.org/IV/ifla65/papers/ 025-106e.htm [12/07/06].

2   Claudia Lux, "Managing library staff from a different cultural background —the East-West conflict in Berlin". *65th IFLA Council and General Conference: Bangkok, Thailand, August 20th-28th, 1999.* (034-106E). http://www.ifla.org/IV/ifla65/papers/034-106e.htm [12/07/06].

3   John Mohi, "A New Zealand perspective on managing cultural diversity". *65th IFLA Council and General Conference: Bangkok, Thailand, August 20th-28th, 1999.* (095-106E). http://www.ifla.org/IV/ifla65/papers/095-106e.htm [12/07/06].

4   Maud Ekman, "To reach multicultural users in libraries—some reflections and examples from Sweden". *65th IFLA Council and General Conference: Bangkok, Thailand, August 20th-28th, 1999.* (008-106E). http://www.ifla. org/IV/ifla65/papers/008-106e.htm [12/07/06].

5   Tasana Saladyanant, "Meeting the needs of foreign student users in Chiang Mai University and Payap University libraries, Chiang Mai, Thailand". *65th IFLA Council and General Conference: Bangkok, Thailand, August 20th-28th, 1999.* (096-106E). http://www.ifla.org/IV/ifla65/papers/096-106e. htm. [12/07/06].

Glimpses of the "Marketing Library and Information Services"

Dinesh K. Gupta

Associate Prof. of Lib. & Inf. Sc., V M Open University, India

The Marketing of Library and Information Services

This presentation is to introduce the publication *Marketing Library and Information Services: International Perspectives,* which is published under the auspices of IFLA. I had the opportunity to coordinate this study with a team from the IFLA Management and Marketing Section (Dinesh K. Gupta, Christie Koontz, Angels Massisimo and Rejean Savard). This publication is to give insight into marketing library and information services.

Since its emergence in 1997, the Management and Marketing Section has regarded marketing library and information services as a focal point of its work. It has developed a marketing glossary, instituted an international marketing award, organized an annual satellite meeting/program to discuss marketing/management issues of interest to library and information professionals, along with undertaking projects, and creating publications international in scope.

Through discussions at annual meetings of the Standing Committee of the Section, it was determined that there was a need to publish a comprehensive review of the literature of marketing of library and information services. During the Berlin conference (2003), the publication was proposed and the project was approved with the following aims:

- Tracking the various stages of LIS marketing at the international level;

- Systematizing the marketing of library and information services and presenting it in a more useful manner;

- Identifying areas where further study and research were needed in the marketing of library and information services;

- Setting an example to pool best practices;
- Encouraging inter-sector collaborations regarding theory and best practices of marketing of library services.

The team started working in early 2004 and submitted the manuscript in mid-2005 to IFLA headquarters for publication. The book was published in February 2006 and was released during the mid-year meeting of the Section at Munich on 24 February 2006.

This publication is a treasure trove on LIS marketing comprised of forty contributions divided into six sections with stimulating ideas and viewpoints, endeavors, case studies, and country reports. The first section begins with a conceptualization of marketing, highlighting its relevance to modern libraries. The next section offers a detailed analysis of activities, efforts and programmes of marketing library and information services in various countries. The third section reviews the value of library associations in marketing libraries. The fourth section emphasizes the importance of the addition of marketing into library and information science curricula. The fifth section details the awarding of "best practices" of marketing in libraries in different countries. The last section reviews databases of marketing information and literature.

Forty-seven contributors from more than 20 countries contributed to this book. Contributors include IFLA Governing Board Members, Presidents (elect) of the Special Library Association and Canadian Library Association, a former President of the American Library Association, Officers and Members of many IFLA Sections Standing Committees, Jury Members of the IFLA International Marketing Award, Award Winners, professors from some leading business schools, library schools, practitioners, consultants, researchers, etc.

What Is Marketing All About?

What marketing is and what it is not is an issue that is discussed time and again in library and information circles, but this has never resulted in a definitive conclusion. Changes in marketing are taking place at a faster pace, and each mainstream marketing text requires a new edition within three years' time. Obviously, there can be no single acceptable definition of marketing. But at the core of any marketing definition are the following concepts:

- There are individual needs, wants, and demands for the product or service;
- The product or service has the ability to satisfy customer needs;

- The exchange of the product or service is the primary activity for payment;
- There is always a need to edge out other competitors;
- The identification of favorable marketing opportunities;
- Resources must be utilized shrewdly to maximize business market position; and
- The aim to increase market share in prime target markets.

These themes are important, but there has been great change during recent years, particularly in regard to consumers' buying behaviour, consumption patterns, delivery mechanism, quality criteria, and so forth. Such changes have affected marketing substantially and necessitated a redefinition of marketing. An alternate paradigm of marketing is widely discussed and accounts for continuous disagreement among marketing proponents. The new information technologies are key enablers to this end. The new definition of marketing by the American Marketing Association, which was adopted in August 2004, addresses such a concern:

> Marketing is an organizational function and a set of processes for creating, communicating and delivering value to customers and for managing customer relationships in ways that benefit the organization and its stakeholders.

Interestingly, this definition has changed greatly from the definition that was adopted more than 20 years ago on March 1, 1985: "Marketing is the process of planning and executing the conception, pricing, promotion, and distribution of ideas, goods, and services to create exchange that satisfy individual and organizational goals". The marketing concept has become an *organizational function* together with the value-added processes. The new definition does not have the word 'exchange' but has incorporated '*relationship*'; does not talk of 'satisfying' individual and organizational goals but *benefiting* the organization and the *stakeholders*. The use of the term 'stakeholder' is wider and includes customers as well as advocators, focus groups, fund providers and even employees. This shift of focus marks a new epoch in the field of LIS marketing.

But definitions do little if we don't develop a process and culture to actually 'do' marketing. Most of us do not fully understand the place of marketing in library and information services or how marketing is useful in our day-to-day work and helps in managing libraries efficiently. Marketing must be seen as a natural sequence of what we do, how we do it, for whom we do it, and how the nature of our services is changing. We must see 'how much of marketing' exists in these acts of ours. The book includes twenty-three observations of library professionals on marketing as they appeared in literature, summarized as *Marketing is mindset, a management style, a set of techniques, and a customer focus approach.* Often marketing is equated with advertising, promotion, public relations, or advocacy, but marketing is an umbrella concept which includes promotion, public relations, publicity, advocacy, and campaign.

There is always a greater need for appreciation and a good understanding of marketing and what it can do for us. Such understanding often brings better results than the hard-core marketing always defined in marketing terminologies and the marketing mix. The marketing mix is commonly referred to as the four P's of marketing—*product, price, place* and *promotion.* Some more P's have been added over the years, e.g. *process* and *people* and *physical evidence.* The mix still provides a useful framework for thinking about ways in which an organization's marketing strategy is implemented. The mix also considers a range of aspects concerning marketing and reflects on how they interact with each other. However, there is a continual debate whether the marketing mix is relevant in the present day. The marketing mix can be taken with some flexibility and open-ended approach while applying it to libraries.

Marketing today is growing as an important area within library services and is described in new categories such as relationship marketing, internal marketing, interactive marketing, technological marketing, emotional marketing and experiential marketing, etc. Interestingly many of these theories are evolutionary in nature, but at the same time the old theory has not vanished and been replaced by a new one. In such a situation most of the time we are caught in some of these theories. But before we are inclined to any particular theory/theories, we must understand that the following are intrinsic to our work:

- We work in not-for-profit situations,
- We are essentially service providers,
- We are in the information business, which has tremendously changed with the Internet, and
- We have to establish relationships with users, advocates, focus groups, fund providers, proponents, and other agencies which help us fulfill our mission.

As such not-for-profit marketing, services marketing, relationship marketing and Internet marketing have direct bearing on our marketing efforts.

These theories have gradually entered into library and information literature and have affected the marketing approaches in libraries. An integrated framework of marketing needs to be employed in libraries.

Marketing Is Everywhere . . .

Marketing is growing throughout the world in all types of libraries. The book *Marketing Library and Information Services: International Perspectives* offers a detailed analysis of activities, efforts and programmes of marketing library and information services in various countries, from Norway to Kenya. Following are some concepts discussed in the book.

The concept of marketing formally originated in the US. In US libraries, marketing is defined as the integration of a wide variety of disciplines, such as market research, public relations, advertising, promotion, publicity, and customer service into a single plan which creates the action that draws consumers into the library, creates patrons out of them and keeps them coming back.

In Denmark the concept of marketing is diffused and diversified. Often marketing is considered as a part of strategic planning of an organization directed toward increasing the customers' knowledge of its products and services. Marketing has become a hot topic in the UK, dominating conferences, workshops, and professional publications.

In Finnish libraries campaigns and outreach activities occurred in the 1960s, and more active public relations and communication activities were developed from 1970 onwards. In the present decade libraries are more inclined towards marketing, as can be seen through various campaigns, conferences, discussions, and research.

In France, the integration of marketing in libraries and documentation is about two decades old. At the end of the 1980s the first French written work appeared. The movement of library and information professionals towards marketing has been slow. Many reservations about marketing still reside in the minds of librarians and archivists.

Twenty years ago marketing was a strange thing in China. In 1986 the first paper appeared on library marketing and that has gradually increased over the years. Marketing practices in libraries are superficial, even distorted, with only a few exceptions.

Libraries in Norway had neither the tradition nor the knowledge of how to market their services until 1990. Library and information professionals were eager and idealistic at that time, but lacked the ability to have clear priorities.

They looked more internally rather than having a focus externally. Public libraries are most advanced in marketing and promotional activities.

In Africa, libraries created solid, dynamic marketing strategies and plans commensurate with current marketing practices. The effort was dominated by the promotional mix aspect of marketing processes. Brochures, circulars, newsletters, posters, and leaflets are used in some libraries. Workshops, meetings, exhibitions, etc. are also organized. Education and training avenues in marketing are still not available.

LIS in Kenya are at the initial stage of implementing and developing marketing as an effective strategy for quality information service provision and delivery. Marketing is more prevalent in university and special libraries than in the public, college and school libraries. In Kenya, marketing is still equated with advertising and beyond that promotion, distribution and public relations are done by special libraries.

In Australian university libraries, during the last few years, the products and services have changed considerably. Marketing is considered as basic, as the whole business is seen from the client's perspectives, due to changes in educational approaches, impact of technology and new methods of information provision and decline in budgetary provisions. LIS professionals need to know their clients and understand their needs, plan for products and services, brand the products and services, and integrate promotional strategies.

Library marketing is a well-known concept in Romanian literature, dealing, more in *abstracto*, and unfortunately rather as an unapplied *desideratum*, however, it is understood that there is a necessity to introduce marketing concepts and practices in daily activities of Romanian libraries. There are still many obstacles against implementing marketing techniques and practices in libraries, e.g. time barriers, mental barriers, and institutional barriers.

LIS Marketing on the March . . .

Since the early 1970s, when the literature about library and information services marketing surfaced, it has been growing over the years. But there are limited numbers of outlets for research library and information services marketing. *The Marketing Treasure* and *Marketing Library Services (MLS) Newsletter* are important newsletters. However, many academic journals and newsletters have brought out special issues on the subject. The *MLS Newsletter* started in 1988 and provides information professionals in all types of libraries with specific ideas for marketing their services in an easy-to-understand way. There are a number of texts, bibliographies, and web resources available. The subject has also attracted the attention of researchers, and doctoral dissertations have been undertaken to assess the present marketing scenario and find new marketing avenues for the future. Some interesting cases of LIS marketing have been included in *Marketing Library and Information Services: International Perspectives*. The *ProSeBiCA1* (this is an abbreviation of the German translation of "Prospective control of the services of academic libraries by means of Conjoint Analysis") is an ongoing study at the Bielefeld University in Germany. The project brings together the existing rudiments of marketing methods in libraries and pursues the aim to define a spectrum of future relevant academic library services, using the methods of Conjoint Analysis. 'Research for design and testing of information products' is a study which was undertaken at the IIM, Ahmedabad with the support of IDRC to design and test the product *Information Bulletin on Management (IBM)*. A study of marketing culture in Finnish libraries is underway. Marketing culture refers to the unwritten policies and guidelines, which provide employees with behavioral norms, to the importance the library as a whole places on the marketing function, and to the manner in which marketing activities are executed.

There are other projects which mainly concentrate on creating databases for promotional literature, literature on marketing LIS, etc. which provide a sound basis to interpret data for new research and outcomes. 'MatPromo' is the name given to the on-line image database of library promotional materials that is currently being developed as a project of IFLA's Management and Marketing Section. It aims at creating a database of images of objects and documents designed for promoting all types of libraries. Promotional material includes posters, bookmarks, postcards, logos, membership cards, flyers, claim notes, a full range of library merchandizing objects, images of libraries and books, etc. 'Database on LIS marketing literature in India' is a bibliographical database on Indian literature on Marketing of library and information services. The scope includes documents in the form of papers in journals, conference proceedings, edited books, books, encyclopediae, research reports, theses, monographs, etc. published in India and by Indian authors abroad on this theme.

Marketing has been identified as one of the areas of competency that is important for professionals in library and information science in the US and Canada. However, marketing is not a major area of focus in graduate LIS education. It is certainly the case that library and information science programs must fulfill the role of graduate programs in general, with regard to presenting the theoretical and practical in a range of content areas. In Canada, marketing/advocacy/public relations courses are offered in all seven information science schools. The content of five LIS Marketing courses is comparable to a great extent. However, pertaining to objectives, readings, and assignments, there are some distinctive priorities. One course pertains to the inclusion of an advocacy course, granting, "advocacy is essentially the marketing of an issue." Finally, the development of a "public relations and advocacy" course in the seventh LIS school is underway. In UK, management is still strongly represented in the curriculum, with marketing sometimes mentioned as one of the topics covered in a management module. A few specific marketing modules exist. There have been some changes during recent years within the marketing curriculum, reflecting developments in the field. For example, Customer Relationship Management, Relationship Marketing and aspects of Internet marketing are now more likely to be taught. CILIP conducts short-term training programmes on different aspects of library marketing. In India, the need for education in marketing LIS was felt in the early 1980s. Though marketing was considerably discussed in literature, conferences, and many training programmes started during the 1980s, the inclusion of the marketing theme in the curriculum was slow, as the UGC Model Curriculum did not lay much emphasis on marketing.

It is welcomed that some universities and institutions have recognized the need for inclusion of the topic in their syllabi. University of Bangalore has a major paper on Marketing LIS whereas University of Delhi has a short paper on marketing LIS and in NISCAIR, the topic of marketing of information products and services is covered under the paper on Information Products and Services. However, the role of IIM, Lucknow in training of library and information services is significant. It offers short-term courses for top and middle level librarians of all kinds of libraries. In Pakistan, only a few large public, special and university libraries make use of some of the public relations tactics. A course on marketing was first introduced in 1995 by the Course Revision Committee of the UGC, but till 2002 books on LIS marketing were not included in the list of recommended books. In the year 1999 Islamia University implemented the curriculum recommendations. University of Punjab introduced the elective course in Marketing of LIS and was made a core course in 2002. In 2001, Sindh University of Hyderabad also started a Marketing of LIS course as a core course in 2001. Another university, Bahaudin Zikriya University in Multan, has adopted the curriculum of University of Pakistan in 2004. In France, though the theme is present in the syllabi of most of the universities, there are insufficient study hours and it is taught many times by faculty other than library science. The theme of marketing is almost never of-

fered in continuous training given to professionals of libraries or documentation. Of course ENSSIB's online training on marketing strategy is available
for heads of libraries and documentation services. In Estonia, among the institutions that prepare information professionals in Estonia, library marketing
is currently being taught both in the curricula of Department of Information
Science in Tallinn Pedagogical University and the curricula of Department of
Librarianship and Information Studies in Viljandi Culture Academy. In Norway, the marketing component in library syllabi is different from university
to university. There is less part of 'marketing' or 'public relations' or 'communication' in the curriculum.

Library associations, both at national and international levels, have
played a vital role in popularizing and promoting the role of libraries, their
present and potential services, resources and facilities for the benefit of the
community at large, and also in developing their members' marketing skills,
and providing them with support for the campaign. Rigorous efforts have
been made by international, national and regional associations for popularizing marketing through establishing separate sections, e.g. Management and
Marketing Section at IFLA, Advertising and Marketing Section at SLA, Public Relations and Marketing Section at ALA, Publicity and Public Relations
Section at CILIP. These associations organize various programmes/activities
and bring out publications, recognize the best practices through awards, etc.
The IFLA Management and Marketing Section is a forum of discussion for
all aspects of management and marketing in all type of libraries the world
over.

The IFLA Public Libraries Section's *Public Library Services: IFLA/
UNESCO Guidelines for Development* is a seminal work which has been
translated in about 20 languages and offers guidance, information and examples on how to build and develop a public library service. It gives due importance to marketing and communication, as one of the six chapters is 'The
management and marketing of public libraries'. Chapter 1 talks about mission,
role and purpose, which must be understood clearly, and chapter 3 pays considerable attention to helping the reader find the right words for that most important definition of the public library service in a local context. The mission
of the American Library Association— *'to provide/ leadership for the . . . promotion . . . of library and information services'*—played a vital role in marketing, promotion and advocacy, through national campaigns and annual events
that focus on libraries, marketing tools that libraries can use, graphic materials
that libraries can use to assist their marketing, programs on marketing at conferences, awards for marketing excellence, books and articles in marketing.

'Campaign for America's Libraries' "@ your library" started in 2001 has been continuing for five years and was made international as the 'Campaign for the World's Libraries' during the Boston IFLA conference in the same year. CILIP sees marketing as a key skill for library and information professionals, as marketing is vital in an increasingly competitive and performance-managed world. CILIP's Publicity and Public Relations Group was established in 1983 and works to raise awareness of the value of marketing and PR to library and information professionals and offers a platform for sharing ideas and experiences. It has produced various publications and organizes an annual conference, training and other events, produces publicity and promotional material, and rewards excellence in libraries through its Public Relations and Publicity Award. 'National Library Week in Lithuania' is an integrated campaign to promote libraries, to demonstrate their value and to provide their potential to innovate, to change and to make a difference in a knowledge-based society.

Really, Marketing Is Rewarding!

There are many excellent activities taking place in different types of libraries. Though marketing may differ from one library to the other, as marketing is flexible and adaptable, it requires a lot of creative thinking. Some interesting cases of library marketing have been presented in *Marketing Library and Information Services: International Perspectives*, and many of these have received recognition at the international level through various awards, such as the IFLA International Marketing Award and the CILIP Public Relations and Publicity Award. The other awards in the area include the John Cotton Dana Library Public Relations Award, Best Practices in Marketing Academic and Research Libraries @ Your Library Award, ALL/West Excellence in Marketing Award, etc.

"Power Card Challenge: A Long Term Marketing and Public Relations Plan to Increase Library Card Registration and Use by the Children of Houston", with the Power Card Challenge, Houston Public Library, USA created a 3-year programme that redefined library card campaigns, gave the library a branded identity in the community through a new library card design and graphics, ran a well-defined marketing/publicity campaign, and provided a model for other communities to replicate. The membership soared threefold during the three-year campaign.

"The Marketing Campaign: Literary Pathways" by Concorci de Biblioteques de Barcelona (CBB) Spain transformed non-users into users through the programme "Literary Pathways". This program featured actors or guides, leading tour participants and reading selections of works, into neighborhoods in which famous authors lived, or were portrayed in their writings.

"I came, I saw, I read" marketing initiatives for refugee children, by the school library of Australian Islamic College, located in Kewdale, WA, Australia used library resources to promote reading and computer literacy to 300 refugee children from Afghanistan, Iraq and Somalia. This programme transformed the perception of libraries from a boring place to a learning space, serving as a catalyst for learning and doing.

"We miss you" by the Public Library of Spijkenisse, in the Netherlands, is a simple but efficient marketing campaign of sending a postcard as a reminder to patrons, particularly to non-users, and significant growth was noted.

Oxford Brookes University Library's "Inspiration" programme involved branding and re-branding through a new logo, which was consistently used for the website and all library activities and everything the library produced.

"Teens for the Teens" is a marketing initiative at the Rijeka City Library, a public library in Croatia, which has taken place recently to serve teenagers and young adults. The *Teens for Teens presents a special kind of library* study trip is a new and innovative feature of the project. Personal involvement in crafts, design, painting, creative writing, and surfing are important ways to bring intimacy and ultimately lead to developing trust for the services of the library. This mutual understanding, intimacy and trust will lead to developing relationships between the library and users. Furthermore, the habits and interest developed during this age continue through life. It was considered the best poster at the IFLA 2004 conference.

The symbolic and effective attempt at the "Lucian Blaga" Central University Library of Romania interestingly started the publication of a library bulletin "Philobiblon" in 1996, a product meant to be sold from the very beginning. The publication was conceived for international exchange (as exchange is a market operation, a transaction). Another publication, the review 'ab initio' for exchange, was published in English with funding from an outside agency. This review brings a 200% profit to the library, as indispensable books and periodicals—which due to lack of funds could not have been bought—are acquired through exchange. There is also a symbolic profit, for the image of the library.

LIS Marketing to Grow . . .

I am fully convinced that the need for marketing in libraries will continue to increase. More and more LIS people will be adding a marketing agenda to their 'to-do list'. New forms of marketing will be emerging and, of course, new resources will be brought out to meet the challenges. I foresee that a time will soon come when a librarian would prefer to be called 'info-service marketer' rather than a scholar or a manager or a scientist or a technologist. With this optimism, I close my paper with a desire to see our work find a deeper echo in the hearts of all devotees of library science and uncover new ground for further interpretation.

Part I

Marketing Library Services to Students

The University of Tennessee Libraries Transformation Plan: Realigning the Research Library for 21st Century Students and Scholars

Barbara I. Dewey

University of Tennessee, Knoxville, USA

Abstract

This paper examines the leadership processes and resulting actions leading to the transformation of the University of Tennessee Libraries. Transformation is needed to address the massive changes experienced in higher education, scholarly communication, and the characteristics of the current generation of students and scholars. The paper documents why the changes are necessary, the process of developing study groups to examine specific areas needing change, and major initiatives implemented thus far in the transformation process.

1. Why Transformation and Why Now?

Why is transformation so critical today in higher education? We have huge responsibilities not only for educating young people but also for providing them with the appropriate social, cultural, and intellectual spaces to thrive. Transformation must occur in order to create spaces, physical and virtual, that are relevant to today's "born digital" students. Transformation must be done to better connect these students with scholarship across the ages in all forms in order for them to take their place as future creators of knowledge and change agents to improve the world.

Libraries, as the central gathering place of students and the repository of scholarship, are at the core of higher education's transformation. At the University of Tennessee we recognized that a strategic approach to change was needed, and quickly, to address a number of known factors about the world of scholarship, information seeking behavior of students, and opportunities afforded by marrying technology with the pursuit of knowledge in creative ways. The nature and format of scholarship is changing rapidly as well as the way people access information. If libraries are to support teaching, learning, and research we need to find ways of linking people to the world's knowledge applying what we know about their behavior to position facilities, services, collections, and virtual spaces.

2. Net Generation Students

OCLC's study, *College Students' Perceptions of Libraries and Information Resources*, provides important data to consider. The study included data from 396 college students from six countries. Selected key findings include the fact that over half of the respondents do not seek assistance from a librarian or staff member. Of those who seek assistance 52% consider the quality of assistance as equal to the search engine experience. Over half use their library's website to stay current with library resources but over 25% do not keep up with library resources at all.[1] Fifteen percent never use electronic resources provided by the library. The 2002 Pew Study Internet Goes to College found that 73% of students use the Internet more than the library for research while only 9% use the library more than the Internet.[2]

Millennial or net generation college students have certain characteristics that define the way they approach study, work, and fun. Generally they like to communicate and collaborate physically and virtually often working in formal and informal groups. They like to be around people even when working on a solo project. They are used to 24/7 virtual environments and expect the same for physical environments. They want to be treated as "one stop shoppers" and co-creator/critics such as on Amazon.com and Wikipedia. They expect personalization and customization. Lippincott notes these trends and encourages libraries to develop relevant "Net Gen environments (that) will:

- Provide individual and group learning spaces
- Support access to and creation of information resources
- Offer staff and faculty development and training
- Provide staff with a range of technology and information skills
- Effectively market services to all groups of potential services
- Integrate physical spaces and services with virtual spaces and services
- Build community[3]

Students and faculty also need new services and spaces to support the creation of knowledge and new ways of learning using print and digital materials with the assistance of ever emerging new tools, technologies, and gadgets. Faculty and graduate students particularly need physical and virtual spaces appropriate for research intensive contemplation and knowledge creation.

Scholarship is increasingly becoming digital and hence, the campus digital library is emerging rapidly and includes collections as well as services. Journals, course reserve systems, the ability to link resources within course management sites, digital special collections, chat and electronic reference, and instant messaging are all emerging. And, of course, many institutions around the world now incorporate digital libraries. This collective wealth of information combined with emerging retrospective mass digitization projects implies a very different use for existing campus library space and underscores the importance of the research library's unique special collections and archives.

3. The Study Group Transformation Process

The University of Tennessee Libraries,[4] recognizing the trends previously noted, began a strategic process to examine how we could transform our services, collections, and spaces to meet the needs of 21st century students and faculty for a campus of 27,000 students, 1,350 faculty, and 6,950 staff. The University of Tennessee Libraries is the 45th largest ARL (Association of Research Libraries) member.[5] The Hodges Library, the main library is a relatively new facility opening in 1987. The library is well known for excellent service and innovative uses of technology to support teaching, learning, and research. The University of Tennessee was one of the first large research university campuses to become wireless.

The Library Management Group (LMG) is the primary policy-making administrative group for the library and consists of 12 team leaders who head major departments or are part of the library administration. LMG began, in the fall of 2004, to identify and then examine key areas ripe for change. These areas were transitioned into the following study groups, four of which are discussed in this paper:

- Services and Spaces
- Digital Production
- Access to Content—User Interface/User Awareness
- Periodicals Management

- Collection Management/Technical Processes
- Special Collections and Archives

A designated convener led each study group in examining the respective areas and reports were developed with recommendations for change over the next several months.

Guiding principles were developed for the work of the study groups:

- Keep an open process.
- Failing is okay. Take a risk—most things can be undone.
- Be willing to try new things.
- Be willing to let go of old things (and practices).
- Create many opportunities for evaluation and feedback.
- Reach out to technically savvy users.
- Focus on user needs.
- Include everyone (library employees, faculty, and students) in the process.
- Streamline tasks and eliminate overlap across groups.
- Respect all opinions and hear all voices.
- Encourage cross-functional working groups.
- Go forward, not back.
- Widely distribute progress reports.
- Process should be efficient, but is not as important as the outcome.
- Identify clear decision-making processes. Align authority and responsibility.
- Maintain humor and perspective. Remember what is really important.
- We are all in this together.
- Change for the sake of service and improvement, not change for the sake of change.
- We serve each other.

Study groups tried to keep these principles in mind during the analysis, reporting, and implementation phases of the transformation. Study groups met with librarians and staff in affected departments, gathered information about operations and processes, and did research related to the topic of the group.

4. Services and Spaces

The Services and Spaces Study Group charge was to conduct an analysis of public service points in terms of the needs of the 21st century research library including efficient and effective use of human resources and space. The context of this group's work included the physical changes needed to make a 1987 library building more relevant, functional, and user friendly. When opened the building featured "wow factor" grand hallways and atria with services located in the interior of the building out of view of users. Also, large areas such as the Reserve Book Room needed repurposing since electronic reserves and full-text journals reduced the need for print reserve space dramatically. Additionally, the library had experienced positive collaboration with the Office of Information Technology (OIT) through implementation of the Digital Media Services, a drop off production facility to digitize faculty course-related materials in all formats,[6] and implementation of VolPrint, a system of pay-for-print, jointly developed by the library and IT.[7] Other areas of collaboration include innovative strategies for integrating scholarly resources and tutorials to embed library resources within the University's course management system (Online@UT)[8] using The Teaching Library@UT website.[9]

Recognizing this context, as well as the key characteristics of net generation students and younger faculty, the Services and Spaces Study Group recommended that an information commons be developed in partnership with OIT in high profile space currently occupied by the Reserve Book Room and expanding into other areas of the Hodges Library second floor. Complimentary services already existing on the floor include a 24 hour Starbucks and CyberCafe, the Studio and Media Services (multimedia digital authoring/production lab for students and faculty to produce digital work), and a Welcome Center area visible to users entering a high traffic door to the library. The group noted that "this collaboration will combine expert service and library resources in a technology-rich environment suited to both group and individual work." The group recommended that a popular computer lab operated by OIT and located on the ground floor of Hodges Library be incorporated into the information commons.

Other recommendations included moving periodicals and microforms to the first floor enabling the information commons to encompass much of the second floor. Further phases would include renovation of the Media Services area to expand multimedia computing and other technologically rich user space. Print government documents and low use microfilm/microfiche collections would be moved out of the first floor location to make room for periodicals.

5. The Commons

Obviously, the groundbreaking recommendation was to create an information commons and work began in earnest in April 2005. An information commons steering committee was created comprised of key library and OIT members to plan the facility. Initial work included creation of a vision for the facility and guiding principles, cultivation of support from students, faculty, and campus administrators, building a new "circle of service" model, blending differing IT and library cultures, proving the concept through "bootstrapping" resources, and using the results as a model for campus-wide information services. The name "Commons" was selected for the new area.

Vision: The Commons is a collaborative partnership between the Office of Information Technology and the University Libraries to connect students and faculty with the tools and information they need to be successful learners and teachers in the 21st century.

Guiding Principles—The Commons:

- is a true partnership of the Libraries and OIT
- is a physical and virtual environment
- leverages joint expertise of Libraries/OIT faculty and staff
- focuses on the needs of undergraduates, but also serves graduate students and faculty
- will increase services, access to content, and technology for users
- will be a 24/7 environment
- will be developed in a phased approach
- will be flexible, innovative, and appealing
- will be developed with advice from students and other key campus groups

The Commons, phase one, opened for the fall semester 2005 and features the "circle of service" philosophy addressing students' desire for one stop shopping. Services included information/reference, laptop checkout, login/netID assistance, 24 hour book retrieval from the stacks, Digital Media Service pickup point, printing/copying/scanning, statistical consulting, wireless access, and computer technical support. Faculty and staff from the library and OIT provided desk services. A modest marketing plan was developed and the students immediately embraced the facility from the very beginning of fall semester. Indicators of success included dramatic increases in gate count (December 2005 gate count was up 46%) and circulation (December 2005 circulation was up 79%), large numbers of students (i.e. 400) mid-week at midnight in the Commons and the adjacent Periodicals Room., and a minimal decrease in the ground floor OIT computer lab. Clearly, the students wished for even more workstations and study capacity.

The student perspective is well represented by two quotes. Kristen, a sports management student, noted that "every time I have been in the library after hours, the Commons has been packed full of students. Some students were finishing assignments, some were doing group projects, and some were just relaxing with friends. The group study areas are of the perfect number and size, and the computers have all the programs I could need on them. I cannot wait until the whole Commons project is complete." Mark, a business student comments, "The Commons is a great addition to the library. Students can study in groups or study alone, check out laptops, use computers, get help and find all the information they need in one room. The Commons has become the one stop shop at the library making it user friendly."

Phase one was developed without additional funding but through reallocation and modest one time investments. The Dean of Libraries and the Chief Information Officer then sought additional funding from the Chancellor and Vice Chancellors for phase two of the Commons. Initial funding was approved and designers were hired to develop plans and a more realistic budget for the expanded Commons. An ambitious design resulted, incorporating flexible furnishings for group and individual work, counters and stools for quick email, soft furnishings for more comfortable study and collaboration, and areas for tutorial and instructional purposes.

The expanded Commons will feature more services in a 24/7 mode, an information kiosk, course management software assistance, additional fully loaded workstations, group workstations with large monitors, computer repair and triage, mobile audio-visual conferencing services, additional conference and presentation practice rooms, tutoring services, and sound-proof media suites.

Phase three will include incorporation of additional second floor space through renovation of Media Services, expansion of the Studio, a digital multimedia authoring space, renewal of the Starbucks and Cybercafe, and a newly designed entrance to the building.

6. Digital Production

Transformation of this magnitude required the work of other study groups. The Digital Production study group's charge was to analyze and make recommendations for staffing configuration and locating digital production, duplication, and other Access and Delivery Services units. The group recommended that duplication would no longer serve the public given their preference for computer printing, scanning, or self service duplication services. All Reserve, Library Express, and Interlibrary Lending scanning would be managed centrally in one location, all Reserve public services moved to the former duplication room, and Reserve circulation would move to the main Circulation Desk.

7. Periodicals/Documents/Microforms

The Periodicals/Documents/Microforms study group charge was to review suggestions outlined in reports from the Periodicals Management study group and the Services and Spaces Study group. The context for this group's recommendations included:

- The University's success in increasing number and quality of students
- Increase in digital resources and a decrease in print documents and periodicals (i.e. during fiscal year 05 print periodicals were reduced by 350 titles)
- Decision to move to newspapers to all electronic print-on-demand format
- More storage available for remaining lesser used print materials with the installation of compact storage in the old Hoskins Library across campus
- Student demand for more learning spaces and more diverse spaces
- Transformation will provide opportunities for public and technical services reallocation

The group's recommendations, based on this context, included merging the Periodicals and Documents/Microforms services, collections and processing and locating them together on the Hodges library first floor. The move places these research collections in close proximity to the Reference Room and reference librarians, the content experts. The group also recommended maximizing high profile, high traffic space in Hodges Library by transferring selected, low use micro-formatted periodicals and research sets, print government documents, and print reference indexes/abstracts to library storage. Movement of additional materials to storage required improved online and physical retrieval services so that the materials can be retrieved and delivered quickly to users.

8. Special Collections and Archives

The Association for Research Libraries (ARL) Task Force on Special Collections prepared a report for ARL membership, "Research Libraries and the Commitment to Special Collections," recommended increased visibility of and access to special collections. In particular, the report noted that "Special Collections represents not only the heart of an ARL library's mission, but one of the critical identifiers of a research library."[10] The Special Collections and Archives Study Group agreed and came together to explore ways of establishing UT's Special Collections and Archives as a cornerstone of primary-source research and curriculum support for the University.

The study group recommending that change be made in three areas—organization and staffing, collection support, and facilities. The group recommended that the unit's organizational structure be modeled by service rather than format thereby creating a Research Services Unit and a Processing Unit. This model is intended to:

- Make collections available quickly
- Assist researchers in their use
- Integrate the unique research collections into the curriculum

Specific steps taken, based on the recommendation and further discussions with study group members, included the decision to merge digital library initiatives staff with Special Collections staff to operationalize digitization of as many special collections as feasible. This groundbreaking concept allowed the UT Libraries to increase access to special collections and archival material through online access, support digitization grants, further develop a Scholar's Archive for the campus, and create a sustainable workflow for digital production. An archivist and programmer were added to the staff through reallocation. To date hundreds of formerly "hidden collections" have been processed and several new digital collections created.[11]

9. Issues of Staff Reallocation

The transformations and reconfigurations summarized in this paper required repositioning librarians and staff to different assignments and, sometimes, different departments. Five principles were communicated to guide this challenging process:

- No layoffs
- No reductions in salary

- Match skills and experience with position assignments
- Affected staff given an opportunity to participate in the selection of future assignments
- Affected staff reallocated before entertaining requests to post positions externally

All affected staff were successfully placed in other positions and, in many cases, were promoted to higher pay grades. Open meetings were held to discuss the reallocation process and any other issues, questions, or concerns about the transformations.

10. Summary

The UT Libraries' transformation plan continues to unfold. Transformation and change is recognized as an ongoing process and should always follow the needs of changing generations of students and faculty and the way they work. The University of Tennessee's experience is an example of a strategic and broad approach using the creativity and expertise of librarians, faculty, staff, and students to lead the way.

Notes

1 College Students' Perceptions of Libraries and Information Resources. A Report to OCLC Membership. Dublin, OH: OCLC Online Computer Library Center, Inc. 2006. http://www.oclc.org/reports/perceptionscollege. htm.

2 Jones, Steve. *The Internet Goes to College: How Students are Living in the Future with Today's Technology.* Washington, DC: Pew Internet & American Life Project. September 15, 2002. http://www.pewinternet.org/ report_display.asp?r=71.

3 Lippincott, Joan. "Net Generation Students and Libraries," in *Educating the Net Generation* edited by Diana G. Oblinger and James L. Oblinger. Boulder, CO : EDUCAUSE. c2005 http://www.educause.edu/educatingthenetgen.

4 University of Tennessee Libraries, Knoxville, Tennessee, USA www.lib.utk. edu.

5 Association of Research Libraries Annual Statistics 2003-2004. Membership Criteria Index. http://www.arl.org/stats/factor.html.

6 University of Tennessee Digital Media Service, http://digitalmedia.utk. edu/.

7 University of Tennessee VolPrint Service, http://volprint.utk.edu/.

8 Online@UT (Blackboard) course management system, http://online.utk. edu/.

9 University of Tennessee Libraries. The Teaching Library@UT, http://www. lib.utk.edu/refs/teachinglib/index.html.

10 Association for Research Libraries. ARL Task Force on Special Collections. *Research Libraries and the Commitment to Special Collections.* Washington, DC: ARL. December 17, 2002. http://www.arl.org/collect/ spcoll/principles.html.

11 University of Tennessee Libraries Digital Library Center Collections. http://www.lib.utk.edu/eresources/digitalcollections.html.

The Marketing of Library Services to the Marginalized

Bharati Sen

SHPT School of Library Science, SNDT Women's University, Mumbai

Abstract

Students who do not consider libraries to be relevant to their academic endeavors have to be persuaded/attracted through targeting them as individuals and developing services that are a mix of information and entertainment.

The present paper is based on the perceptions of some academic librarians, the findings of a number of studies conducted over a period of three to four years and the assessment of the library scenario of the university under study.

1. Background

The university in which the study was conducted is special in a number of ways. It is a women's university. Postgraduate degrees are offered in a number of local languages. Additionally a number of subjects such as economics are taught in local languages as well as in English. However, English is the only medium of instruction for all professional courses, including nursing, engineering, management, and library and information science.

The Library has a good collection of books and journals in local languages as well as in English. Library orientation is given to all students. Separate groups are made of the students according to their language orientation so that the students do not have any difficulty.

Data had accumulated through a number of studies conducted over the last five years on non-use of the library services, use of OPAC, searching the Internet, library user need survey etc. All this data was scrutinized to discover if any pattern existed.

2. Objectives

The earlier studies conducted in 2002/3 did show that students who were studying in local languages did not like to use computers. They were not comfortable with OPAC. Also few accessed the Internet or sent e-mails. Most of these students did not have a computer at home. This was in contrast to the students who were studying through English medium, especially if they were doing some professional course. Even though orientation was for all students the gap in the use of library services by the students studying in English medium and in a local language persisted.

Therefore the specific objectives of the study were

1. To identify the characteristics of students who do not avail themselves of the services of the library

2. Design services through which these students could be drawn to the library. This of course would have to be done keeping in mind the resource limitations of the library.

3. Literature Search

The author did consult some books in library and information science but they did not have much that was new. Therefore books in management were checked for new ideas in service marketing. Kotler (1994) became the starting point for the search of new ideas. His stress on bringing the well-being of society into the equation and leaving out the profit motive appeared to be suitable for the current situation.

Gronroos's (1994) article on relationship marketing proved to be very useful as it provided a new perspective. Peters (1995) also spoke of relationship marketing. This focuses on developing a close relationship with customers, and appeared to be particularly important in the information and library sector.

4. Methodology

The researcher decided to probe more closely the characteristics of the students who did not avail themselves of the services offered by the library. Other than the data provided by the various studies mentioned earlier, she has taken the help of her own students doing their master's degrees in Library & Information Science, her colleagues both in the department and in the library as well as librarians in other academic libraries.

The process of research has been iterative and non-linear, that is, at various points of the study, the researcher has gone back to the students and colleagues to reconfirm her findings. When some data has not reflected the common perception, it has been rechecked with the persons concerned. The researcher has held discussion with some of the teachers as well as students. These discussions have been unstructured, as the idea was to get an insight and not play with numbers.

The students and library professionals who participated in the study were chosen on the basis of their availability, familiarity with the researcher and willingness to give their time and share their opinions. The students were met outside the library to ensure that the participants in the study came from both categories, namely users and non-users. Separate discussions were then held with the non-users. Scientific sampling technique was not followed.

5. Findings

Definitions of marketing have changed over the years from satisfying consumers' requirements profitably to participating in the society's well-being. The societal marketing concept puts even more emphasis on identifying the needs of the clients, and on providing a service or product that is of the required quality.

The first objective of defining the characteristics of the non-users had to be achieved in order to provide service or product suitable for the target group. This was a process of culling out the underlying problems of the non-users.

5.1. Identification of non-users

The services of the library were categorized under the following heads:

1. Reading room
2. Magazines
3. Storybooks
4. Newspapers
5. Subject periodicals
6. Subject books
7. Reference services
8. Internet
9. Databases
10 Library orientation

At first no student admitted to not using the library. Probing had to be done with a lot of care using nonjudgmental language. Here the data collected by the LIS students on library use and the study on user needs proved useful to frame questions and delve deeper.

This initial probing identified a group of students who rarely or did not use any of the above-mentioned services. This focus group of about ten students became the source of model building of non- user characteristics.

5.2. Characteristics of non-users

Closer interaction with these students identified the following explicit characteristics to be common in more or less all cases. All of them were from vernacular medium, poor in English, did not score good marks in their examinations, and came from economically weaker sections. They were pursuing post-graduation in the faculty of arts. Most of these students were first-generation learners. The majority earned through giving tuitions and had home responsibilities with more than one sibling. All of them had long traveling hours. Two of them said that they had to struggle with their parents to be able to pursue further studies. As college students during their undergraduate days they had not used their college libraries. Half of these students had done a certificate course in Microsoft Office. Caste did not figure in the findings.

The non-obvious characteristics were that these students were not ambitious, or to rephrase it, for them reaching this level was an achievement by itself. Generally mental ceilings was found where they had set their standards and were content as long as they achieved the levels set by themselves. For these students, notes from the teachers and their seniors handed down to them were sources of their studies. Few books were also available in their departments. They did not feel the need to read additional books or consult periodicals.

The library was felt to be a drab place where many rules had to be maintained. They did not feel by using the library they would gain much academically. The library and its services were associated with studies and passing exams, at the most reading newspapers and borrowing magazines. As a source of entertainment they would have liked to borrow film magazines and magazines on fashion but did not want to end up paying fines for being late. As these students spent time in traveling, giving tuitions and fulfilling home responsibilities they did not want the further tension of coming to the library in time to take or return library material. Also they had access to such magazines from their friends who utilized these facilities from the library.

These students knew about the Internet but felt it was for English medium students, as everything was in English. They had not really made any effort to use the Internet or find out what it could offer them. They were not sure what was meant by database. These students had not participated in library orientation, as they knew from their seniors that to pass their examinations it was not necessary.

6. Non-use or Marginalization

At the time of interacting with the students it was normal to find that many students did not avail themselves of the various services offered by the library. These students however had alternative means of access to literature and information. They had the resources to buy books and borrow from their friends and relations. The Internet was well utilized for e-mail, recreation and information work, albeit rarely. Most of them had a computer with Internet connectivity. These students were categorized as non-users by the researcher.

The focus group of students were considered to be marginalized, as they did not have an alternate source for material/literature/information other than the library, which they were not able to utilize even if the reasons could be personal. A postgraduate student has to develop the ability for independent studies. The library is also responsible for capacity building of the students in information literacy. Without such skills these students would be severely handicapped to join the mainstream of the educated workforce.

7. Services for the Marginalized Students

For the planning of the services for the marginalized the 4 Ps of marketing that were considered were the *product,* which is the services to be offered, and how to *package* these services and the means of *promotion* that would be attractive to the potential users and *persuade* the marginalized and non-users to use the services. *Placement* is another P that is often used, but here "persuade" was chosen as the more relevant concept. As this was social marketing the *pricing* element of the services was not considered.

When conversing with the students the researcher spoke about the necessity in the real world for individuals who could handle literature/information independently. The role of the Internet in the present society as a means of access to information very relevant to opportunities in life was pointed out. Students from the focus group were asked for suggestions by which they could become users of the library and avail themselves of the facilities.

The students did not want to be marked out as a special group requiring special attention. For borrowing books and journals they did not feel they needed any special facility. There was some bantering about payment of fines but this was not a major roadblock in the use of the library. The facet of the service that the students discussed at length was the Internet/computer facilities. They wanted sites in Hindi/local language. They would "love" to visit sites giving film, fashion, cookery and such information in Hindi/local language. For them English created a barrier for the use of the Internet. When suggested by the researcher the students were willing to use computers for typing their assignments in local language.

The basic plan was to evolve services that would attract the students and not intimidate them. After discussion with some library professionals the plan that evolved could be distinguished as macro-level and micro-level.

7.1. Services at the macro level

From the above opinions and suggestions it was felt that the library must initiate facilities by which students who are not able to use the electronic information revolution must be mainstreamed.

The need for an Internet café and facilities to use local language in word processing and other activities was paramount. Grants were sought for setting up a modest center for students to access the Internet and are currently being finalized. For facilities in local languages a government agency was contacted. They have developed a pack which allows more or less all the activities of word processing to the Internet searching, e-mailing etc. As this has been developed using Linux it is extremely economical. The café facilities would be for non-academic purposes.

7.2. Services at the micro-level

The focus group students associated the library with formal studies only. Recreational reading was a minor aspect. The library was not associated with information needs or personal development at all.

The services that should draw the students to the library will be setting up a job corner where all notices regarding jobs will be put up. The agencies have to be contacted to send their fliers. From the newspapers relevant sections can be highlighted and put up.

The students taking part in competitions, whether debates, speeches or 'rangoli' and 'mehendi,' should be made aware of how the library can help them. The Dean of Students could be made an ally in this.

The library should encourage students who have used the library and benefited from it to write in the students' magazines. The scheme of bringing a friend to the library where a user student brings a non-user friend to use the library is to be encouraged by assigning points. The user student must be awarded points on the basis of use made by the friends whom she has brought. At the end of the year the highest scorers could be awarded prizes and their names published in the university newsletter or other relevant publications.

The government sites have a Hindi version. These sites give information on the programmes of the government, some of which will be relevant to the students or their families. The students have to be made aware of such sites.

The CDs attached to magazines have games and movies that can be lent to the students or viewed in the café.

The library has to establish itself as an "infotainment" center to attract students who would otherwise sidestep the facilities that the library can offer. Otherwise the library will not be able to fulfill its role in developing information-literate students essential for a knowledge society.

8. The 4 Ps Revisited

The *product* to be offered was information access through the Internet. Facilities to do word processing, e-mailing and other personal work would be additional benefits. As the students gain confidence in working with e-information they will join the mainstream of information-literate students.

The *packaging* would be in the form of infotainment, that is information and entertainment together in Hindi/local language. It is believed that students trying to access information for recreation will learn the nuances of searching and retrieval.

The *promotion* would take place through the write-ups in the university newsletters, magazines. Through the Dean of Students the extracurricular activities would also be used to promote the library.

Persuasion as a concept was borrowed from "Relationship Marketing". The relationship marketing process is usually defined as a series of stages, and there are many different names given to these stages, depending on the marketing perspective and the type of services. The stages that fit with the current persuasion concept were:

Awareness → Comparison → Transaction → Reinforcement → Advocacy

These steps essentially identify and communicate with the students as individuals. Such recognition instills confidence in the marginalized. Using the relationship marketing approach, programs are customized for individual user groups and the stage of the process they are going through as opposed to some forms of orientation where everybody would get virtually the same information, with perhaps a change in the subject. The idea of students bringing their friends to the library was a relationship concept.

As the library becomes fully automated (currently it is not so) tracking individual students would become possible. That is when relationship marketing concepts will be fully exploited. The library will be able to track the members to find out who is using the services of the library. All permutation and combination of services and utilization by individual students will be apparent. The students not using the library or using the services infrequently could then be approached individually and induced to come to the library.

9. Conclusion

The marketing process is cyclical, with the stages being:

1. Mission for the library/information service
2. Assessment of current situation, and identify opportunities, using techniques such as SWOT and PEST
3. Formulate marketing objectives
4. Undertake market research
5. Modify marketing objectives
6. Formulate strategies, balancing various components of the marketing mix
7. Implement marketing strategies.
8. Monitor success
9. Reassess strategies and objectives and mission if necessary

The present paper was developed keeping in mind the stages delineated above. Since the micro-level programmes are yet to be implemented, their inherent capability is yet to be tested. The library professionals consulted felt that focus on individuals would definitely encourage marginalized students to utilize the library services. The success of the strategies will be determined by whether the students develop their capacity to maneuver in the information jungle.

References

1   Bhabal, Jyoti (2006) Library user need survey 2006: To analyze the user needs of Post-Graduate Students of SNDT Women's University. (currently the data is being analyzed).
2   Chinchure, Dipali, Jadhav, Kalpita,, Patil, Mangala, & Jain, Vasundhara

(2004). Internet use by SNDT Women's University students (MLISc. dissertation, SNDT Women's University, 2004).

3   Gokhale, Pradnya, Mane, Pratibha, Madhavi, Sarvari, & Gadkari, Shraddha (2006). Marketing and publicity of library services for Music Department (MLISc. dissertation, SNDT Women's University, 2006).

4   Gronroos, Christian (1994). From marketing mix to relationship marketing: towards a paradigm shift in marketing. *Management Decision.* 32 (2): pp. 4-20.

5   Kotler, Philip (1994). Marketing management: analysis, planning, implementation and control, 8th ed. New York: Prentice-Hall.

6   Kurup, Dhanya, Chauhan, Kirti, Desai, Rupal, & Shinde, Sarita (2006). Marketing and publicity of periodicals department: A survey project (MLISc. dissertation, SNDT Women's University, 2006).

7   Naik, Krupali, Rahalkar, Snehashree, & Gond, Manju (2006). Marketing and publicity of Reference Service (MLISc. dissertation, SNDT Women's University, 2006).

8   Peters, Tom (1995). The pursuit of Wow! Every person's guide to topsy-turvy times. London: Macmillan.

Marketing Academic Library Resources and Information Services to International Students

Cuiying Mu

Central Library, University of Canterbury Christchurch, New Zealand

Abstract

The paper examines the problems and challenges that international students meet in a western academic environment. Included in the discussion are strategies for marketing academic library resources and information services to international students and the challenges faced by information librarians dealing with these students. The paper also looks at what information literacy programs and activities are suitable to accommodate the information needs of international students and what teaching methodology should be used to teach them.

1. Introduction

In the last seven years, the New Zealand tertiary education sector has attracted hundreds of thousands of students from countries around the world to study at its institutions. From 1998 to 2004, there was rapid growth in the number of international students studying in New Zealand higher institutions. The total number of international students studying in publicly funded tertiary education organisations increased from 9,293 in 1998 to 50,455 in 2004, a greater than five fold increase (Education Counts, 2005).

Asian students compose 82.14% of the international students in New Zealand tertiary institutions. Those Asian students are mainly from China, Japan, South Korea, India, Malaysia and Thailand (Education Counts, 2005). As the number and diversity of international students increase on the campuses, the need to understand and to work effectively with this population becomes more important for academic librarians who are responsible for providing effective information services to those students. Since the majority of the international students are from Asia, my paper was written with a bias towards dealing with Asian international students.

There is a considerable body of literature which discusses the problems of international students in a western academic environment in the area of culture, language, social and personal uncertainties. To supplement this literature, I conducted interviews with fifteen international students at University of Canterbury. The interviews were to provide personal insights from the perspective of international students. The purpose of the interviews was to find out if they were aware of the resources and information services provided in a western academic library; and if they have the basic library skills essential in their academic study in a western educational system. The interviews were not intended by any means to be a scientific survey. The students interviewed have got either a bachelor or master degree from their home countries. They were in New Zealand to pursue a master or a PhD degree in engineering, commerce or law. The results differed little from the findings of other research cited in this paper.

2. The Problems, Difficulties and Challenges Faced by International Students

The difficulties and characteristics of students from developing countries, especially Asian students are recognized by Liu (1993). These are identified as language barriers, especially use of library terminology and difficulty in understanding the presentation during library orientation tours. In addition, most international students face potentially difficult adjustments to cultural, linguistic and academic environments, including the library (Curry & Copeman, 2005). International students' main problems were recognized as shyness, loneliness, language, social and personal uncertainties (Burns, 1991), insufficient study skills associated with fear of failure, and in some cases, library anxiety (Baron & Strount-Dapaz, 2001; Brown, 2000; Jiao & Onwuegbuzie, 1999) and communication problems (Brown, 2000; Burns, 1991).

International students face many challenges when they pursue their studies in a western country. One of the biggest challenges is to adjust to a western academic environment. The western essay-based learning styles—active involvement in class, creative thinking and evaluation of information—are challenges for international students who come from non-western educational systems in which emphasis is placed on teaching methods that include memorisation, observation and imitation (Roberston, 1992; Grarcha and Russell, 1993; Helms, 1995, as cited in Varga-Atkins & Ashcroft 2004).

Plagiarism has posed a great challenge to international students (Robertson, 1998, cited in Varga-Atkins and Ashcroft, 2004). International students have been described as "persistent plagiarisers" by Western Academic Institutions (Park, 2003). Ryan (2000) says that international students do not know that they must acknowledge the ideas and findings of other scholars because they are not familiar with the concept of plagiarism.

Library use is a big challenge for international students as most of them had little or no experience with the use of an academic library. Many international students suffer from a lack of experience with library-specific technology and resources, which compounds anxiety and difficulty in the use of sources (Allen, 1993). Though some might have experience, language barrier, cultural shock and the unfamiliarity of the library system make those international students experience a high level of library anxiety and cause barriers to effective use of the library (Patton, 2002). Some Asian students avoided using reference desk as they were afraid of asking stupid questions; afraid of their English not being good enough; afraid of not understanding answers well; some never think of asking reference questions or don't know what a reference librarian does (Liu & Bernice, 1997).

3. The Need for Marketing Library Information Services for International Students

Critical to the academic success of international students is their ability to use a research library and its databases for the purposes of fulfilling a variety of academic reading-to-writing tasks, such as writing library research papers and scientific papers (Hale, 1996, as cited in Kamhi-Stein & Stein 1998). Culture and communication differences make international students uncertain about the subject resources and services available in a library. For instance, services such as interlibrary loan, librarian reference-by-appointment, and live online reference are new concepts to international students (Jackson, 2005). The reference/information librarian's role is unclear to most international students because they don't know that a reference librarian's primary responsibility is to answer questions (Kumar & Suresh, 2000). Some Asian students even consider individual consultations to be a disruption of the librarian's regular work because in most Asian cultures, academic libraries do not provide individual subject consultation service. As a result, most students from Asia may not be fully aware of the readily available professional assistance on information-related issues and view the library as a place to study and librarians as book-keepers rather than information providers.

The main focus of every library is customer service, which is not another term for marketing (Nims, 1999). Marketing is vital to the success and continued existence of a library (Siess, 2003, p. 16). Effective marketing provides the means by which users are made aware of the services of the library and their value (Martey, 2000). Information librarians need to market their services and resources actively to create awareness of their library's value for international students. According to Sáez (2002, p. 82), significant sectors of the potential market for the library or information centre's services are probably not aware of all the services available or have no understanding at all of what is on offer.

4. Whose Role Is It to Do the Marketing?

Who should do the marketing? The answer is simple. It is reference librarians who should do the marketing because reference theory states that it is the librarian's task to ensure that all users and potential users of libraries have easy access to library resources and information services. The librarians need to be an active promoter of the use of information and libraries (Ajileye-Laogun, 2004). According to Low (1990, as cited in Ajileye-Laogun 2004), reference/ information librarians can be referred to as the image booster to the library she/he is working for because of his/her duties, which deal directly with the users. Information librarians are responsible for encouraging the use of the library resources and services they provide; for ensuring that those students are aware of what resources the library has in their subject area and how their subject information librarians render their services.

5. Marketing Strategies

To market a library's resources and information services is not difficult. Wolfe's (2005) *Library public relations, promotions, and communications: A how-to-do-it manual* is a very useful guide for your library marketing. Here are a few suggestions for marketing your library to international students:

1. Create a library web page for international students. A web page is a good way of promoting library information services and resources. Beyond simply providing students with information, the pages serve as a library welcome mat, assuring the international students population that the library is committed to understanding international students and meeting their needs (Jackson, 2005).

2. Use an email list. Emails are a preferred method of communication

by most international students. An email including a welcome message, introducing your services could be sent to all new international students. Emails containing new library resources and tips on finding information are of great value at the critical stage.

3. Use library wall space. The library can display different language study tools such as bilingual dictionaries, English thesaurus, dictionary of synonyms and antonyms, subject-related dictionaries and encyclopaedias. Displays of information librarians' photos help international students to know whom to contact in his/her subject.

4. Attend academic lectures if your liaised department has a prominent number of international students. Information librarians can meet international students to discuss and gather information about their information needs as well as to promote the information services offered.

5. Links to "Help" services from all appropriate library web pages, where assistance may be needed.

6. Visit your departments and talk to the student advisor or academic coordinator. At the beginning of each semester, please go to see the academic coordinator from your departments for a list of international students enrolled and send them a welcome message, introducing yourself and the services provided.

7. Cooperate with staff from the international students' support centre. This is the first place that international students visit whenever they experience problems. If the support centre staff know the library staff, they will refer the students to the appropriate subject librarian when those students need help in finding information.

International students contribute greatly to an institution's financial income. As information librarians, we should ensure that those students' information needs are adequately and timely met so that they can successfully complete their study in a western academic culture.

6. Information Literacy Programs for International Students

A number of LIS literature recommend offering a separate introduction session or program for international students with more printed material, less complicated and slower-paced speech, and a deliberate acknowledgement of special challenges that might be encountered by international students (Bilal, 1990;

Cope & Black, 1985; DiMartino & Zoe, 2000; Hoffman & Popa, 1986; Liu, 1993, as cited in Patton 2002). Separate instructional sessions were needed because of differences in language skills, level of familiarity with the library system and with library resources (Lafon, 1993). Helton and Esrock (1998) also believe that it is not wise to lump together all the potential users of your library and promote services to this mass audience in exactly the same way, as each group in our society has different wants, needs, values, motivations, influences, language, slang terms, etc. It is acknowledged that international students have specific characteristics and difficulties, therefore, the academic libraries need to design a program suitable to this most disadvantaged group to help improve their academic achievements.

A coordinated program of orientation to the library, teaching research skills, and instruction in critical thinking can assist international students to reduce academic stress and increase the likelihood of success (Patton, 2002). The following information activities and programs should be included to develop those students' information literacy skills which are essential to their academic success:

1. **Library orientations**

   Jackson's (2005) survey found that international students repeatedly note the need for more orientation and introduction to the library and even requested that the library orientation information and changes in library policies be sent to all students via email.

2. **Physical library tours**

   Library tours are especially important to international students. It is a good chance for those students to familiarize themselves with the library environment, resources and contact staff. Tours should be done by a professional librarian because the information librarians are the experts of the information services and the library resources in his/her subjects.

3. **Library resource introduction**

   A session introducing resources should be made compulsory to all new international students as a number of research articles recognize that international students are not aware of what is available in the library. Only when a student knows what resources the library has for their subject can they make good use of them. It is acknowledged that knowing and using library resources effectively will help international students to improve their academic achievements.

4. Searching the catalogue

Searching the library catalogue and especially reading the search results is very difficult for some international students since the terms such as "library classifications", "call numbers", "status of the books", "item held", "in process", "on order" are jargon to them.

5. Locating information for their research

Locating information is a big challenge for international students since they grow up in a culture where a library collection is mainly made up of printed books and journals; where their assignments are mainly based on their text books. It is shocking that none of the students interviewed used an online database before coming to New Zealand. If we fail to teach them where to get quality information for their research, students will turn to other sources of information, especially the Internet. They should be taught where to search for information in a western academic library, where library resources are electronically-dominated and their assignments are essay-based.

6. Information retrieval skills

Having learned to find information, most international students still find database searching is very complicated as it is found that the use of synonyms, a necessity in keyword searching, is a difficult skill to master, especially for students with limited English vocabulary (Jacobson, 1988; DiMarting & Zoe, 2000, as cited in Patton 2002). When teaching international students database searches, subject or topic keyword search is a good place to start, as it does not involve as much use of synonyms, Boolean connectors or truncation.

7. Evaluating information critically

The critical skill of information evaluation is more important for international students since they grow up in a culture where they did not need to judge information for themselves. And due to the popularity of the Internet, they can retrieve large quantity of information over the computer without coming into the library. For instance, two students interviewed failed their research thesis as most of their references were from .com web sites. One of the most important literacy skills for international students is to learn to differentiate information from web sources like .com, .org, .govt, .ac, .edu, and to distinguish between articles from popular magazines, trade magazines, newspapers, academic or peer-reviewed journals. Kappoun (1998, as

cited in Patton 2002) calls for faculty and librarian alike to give instruction and experience in critical evaluation of web sites as well as
printed materials.

8. Citing information

It is known that international students' plagiarism annoys many western lecturers. To teach them why and how to cite information is an
essential part of information literacy program. Ryan (2000, p. 56)
suggests that the following should be included in any program aimed
at reducing plagiarism among international students:

- Discuss what is meant by plagiarism and give real examples
- Explain the difference between paraphrasing and plagiarism
- Demonstrate to students how to paraphrase, synthesise and
  weave other sources into their own work
- Show students how they are supposed to meet referencing re-
  quirements and why they are required
- State where syndication is not permitted, describing what it is
  and why it is unacceptable
- Explicitly state the consequences of not complying with rules
  against plagiarism and syndication.

9. Providing follow-up sessions

Most confirmed that although some international students had received some kind of instruction on catalogue or database searching,
the sessions included too much information, and they still had problems with the skills. Curry and Copeman (2005) say that follow up
procedures in reference interview/ instructional services would be of
great importance to an international student. Thus, the need for individual practice, not only during or following an instruction session,
but individual practice with individual assistance was desirable since
each international student is an individual, regardless of the student's
specific culture (DuPraw & Axner, 2002).

7. Challenges Faced by Academic Librarians

A great number of research articles have discussed the challenges and difficulties faced by international students, but it is also very important to consider
the challenges to information librarians. Here are some major challenges faced
when dealing with international students.

7.1. Create a positive image

One of the biggest challenges faced by information librarians is to create a positive image as most students including international students hold negative attitudes towards librarians. For decades, people though of librarians as "trained" or "skilled" but not necessarily as "professionals" and have no idea of the qualifications or training requirements (Heron, 1977; Rothwell, 1990, as cited in Ajileye-laogun, 2004). In some Asian countries, librarians are simply retrieval clerks or have low social status, so master's students may consider themselves more competent and more knowledgeable than library staff and regard it unnecessary to approach a librarian for help. Knealle (2002) asserts that many people still tend to think of librarians as people who do not necessarily hold college degrees, let alone a master's. Therefore, we librarians need to demonstrate that we have got both qualifications and a variety of skills; we are information experts who teach, assist, develop search strategies and offer access to knowledge.

7.2. Be proactive

Language problems may hinder international students from seeking help and thus from receiving and benefiting from the assistance offered by the library (Patton, 2002). Accordingly, some international students have to rely on friends rather than librarians for information or instruction. Therefore, Jiao and Onwuegbuzie (1999) encourage librarians to be proactive in approaching and reaching international students—to look for verbal and nonverbal clues of lack of understanding. All professional librarians have got to talk with international students about their services because exchanges between the service agent (librarians) and the customer (international students) can elicit information about customer requirements, and also permit the services agent to explain the organization's products and how these can meet the customer needs (Rowley, 1998).

7.3. Build good relationships

There is no real shortcut to providing good information services to international students. According to Mendelsohn (1997, as cited in Curry & Copeman 2005), quality reference service involves a relationship between the user and librarian within a "Cycle of Dimension of Service": willingness to assist user; knowledge (how to assist user); assessment (of user's need), and action (physically moving with the user).

7.4. Create a welcoming environment

Mellon (1986, as cited in Patton 2002) mentioned that 75% to 85% college freshmen viewed the library as scary, overpowering and confusing. Therefore librarians need to develop the ability to create a welcoming environment, to be patient, and to build confidence in the students. When librarians are friendly, and welcoming and helpful, users are encouraged into the library, while in a library where the librarians are unfriendly and lazy, users are driven away. It is reported the personality of the librarian determines the rate of utilization of the library by its users. If she/he is friendly and professional, the user will be convinced that there is an approachable and reliable information expert in that library. If they are drawn to the library by the mien of the librarian, they will then be able to browse through the books and thus become aware of the availability of materials relevant to their studies and research, and the use of the collections increases (Ajileye-Laogun, 2004).

7.5. Know how to communicate well with students from different cultures

Information librarians need to learn ways of international students' communications styles because the way people communicate varies widely between different cultures. One aspect of communication style is language usage. Across cultures, some words and phrases are used in different ways (DuPraw, 2002). For instance, I had one student who had huge fines for a book he borrowed because he misunderstood the concept of returning a book. To him, "return" a book means putting it back on the shelf. Don't assume that the way you are behaving is the "right" way of doing things. Consider a variety of approaches to a procedure.

7.6. Respect cultural differences

One of the significant barriers in cross-cultural communication is the use of language. Curry (2005) finds that in most cases reference librarians are not changing their style because of international students' communication difficulties; they are unaware of the jargon used and of the need to provide definitions or demonstrations of "peer reviewed", "call number" "full-text", "subject heading" or "Boolean search". Wang & Frank (2002) recommend that information services in libraries that are sensitive to and encompass differences in culturally influenced styles are more likely to be responsive to the information needs and interests of international students. As information librarians become more aware of cultural differences, they will become good listeners and communicators and could communicate better with students from different cultural background.

8. Teaching Methodologies

We frequently hear international students complaining that Westerners speak too fast and use too many colloquialisms, idioms, and technical terms (Badke, 2002). Therefore, when teaching international students, it is important for instructional librarians to understand and incorporate second-language learning theories, such as innatist and interactionist (Conteh-Morgan, 2002). A basic understanding of teaching second language theories is essential to improving information librarians' abilities to teach international students information literacy skills better and to help them learn more effectively. Some advice for teaching international students is: avoid complex sentences, don't use slang or jargon and use a clear, slow, but normal speech pattern. Check often for comprehension, use repetition and synonyms and elaboration to enhance understanding.

To enhance international students' comprehension, it is more advisable to use longer pauses between semantic groups so that students can process the whole meaning and not spend too much time deciphering individual words or sentences (Blau, 1990, as cited by Monteh-Morgan 2002). When international students listen to their lecturers, they still mentally translate languages, but the linguistic patterns of their native language may affect their ability to construct effective search statements in English. For instance, the Chinese language does not use plurals, nor do they use connectors such as "and" and "or," so truncation and Boolean searching are especially difficult concepts to grasp for Chinese-speaking students. As already stated, the use of synonyms, a necessity in keyword searching, is a difficult skill to master, especially for students with limited English vocabulary (Jacobson, 1988 cited in Patton 2002).

To teach information literacy effectively for international students, the following six principles suggested by Kamhi-Stein and Stein in 1999 are very useful:

- **Principle 1**: Library instruction should provide students with comprehensible input. Strategies include using gestures, graphic illustrations, and questions; using expansions, rephrasing, and simplification; decreasing speech rate and increasing volume; and defining new terminology and recycling it in different contexts.

- **Principle 2**: Library instruction should provide students with scaffolds. Scaffolding procedures in the library include: breaking down library tasks into subtasks, modelling the strategies needed to complete the tasks, and engaging students in activities that ensure a gradual shift in responsibility from the reference librarian or subject specialist to the students.

- **Principle 3**: Library instruction should be "adjuncted" to content courses, namely course-related.

- **Principle 4**: Library instruction should be relevant to the students' academic needs as instruction that focuses on subject matter relevant to the academic needs of foreign students is perceived to increase motivation, and is conducive to more effective learning.

- **Principle 5**: Library instruction should integrate information competence strategy training. In this program, library instruction-related activities focus on what search strategies students need to use, why the strategies have to be used, and how to use them.

- **Principle 6**: Library instruction should be hands-on to allow students to engage actively in learning. A workshop approach to online database instruction is most appropriate to provide students with hands-on activities aimed at learning how to employ the databases.

In short, when teaching international students, you need to consider these learners' characteristics, language proficiency, learning styles and their subjects of interests so that the teaching methodology and examples you use are attracting their attention. It is known that most international students are not used to independent learning, thus information librarians need to design activities that encourage students to conduct searches and reflect on the whys and hows of results to develop their independent learning, which is critical to their academic success in western academic study. You need to demonstrate different modes of searches and get them to practice. Subject guide/topic search seems much easier for international students than basic key words search since they have difficulties in finding synonyms and understanding Boolean connectors which are essential in key word searches.

9. Conclusion

Information/reference librarians must be able to identify and work with the unique information-related issues associated with international students. Information librarians serve a special role as information providers and can play a significant part in ensuring the academic success of those international students (Kumar & Suresh, 2000). Without being given specialized information services, those students can't be expected to succeed in their academic study in a western country, a system totally alien to them.

Communicating effectively with international students is of great importance in reference services or information literacy teaching. Positive contact with international students increases their social adjustment, relaxed contact with library staff contributes to lowered library anxiety and enhances the ability to acquire skills for effectively using the university library (Mosley, 1997).

As students' level of success in using the library is related to their English proficiency, frequency of library use, and frequency of reference desk inquiry (Liu & Redfern, 1997), information /reference librarians should continue to exploit ways of promoting the library resources and their reference services for international students. Besides, new approaches should be developed to make them feel more comfortable about coming into the library, asking reference questions and using the library resources so that they can achieve better grades in their study.

References

1   Ajileye-Laogun, J. O. (Summer 2004). Reference librarian/user relationship at the Obafemi Awolowo University Library [Electronic Version]. *Information for Social Change),*19. Retrieved 15/02/2006 from http://libr.org/isc/articles/19-Laogun-1.html.

2   Allen, M. B. (1993). International students in academic libraries: a user survey. *College & Research Libraries, 54*(July), 323-333.

3   Badke, W. (Winter 2002). International students: information literacy or academic literacy. *Academic Exchange Quarterly, 6*(4), 60-65.

4   Brown, C. C. (2001). Reference services to the international adult learner: understanding the barriers. *The Reference Librarian, 33*(69/70), 337-343.

5   Burns, R. B. (1991). Study and stress among first year overseas students in an Australian university. *Higher Education Research and Development, 10*(1), 61-67.

6   Conteh-Morgan, M. (2002). Connecting the dots: Limited English proficiency, second language learning theories, and information literacy instruction. *The Journal of Academic Librarianship, 28*(4), 191-196.

7   Curry, A., & Copeman, D. (July 2005). Reference service to international Students: A field stimulation research study. *The Journal of Academic Librarianship, 31*(5), 409-420.

8   DuPraw, M. E., & Axner, M. (2002.). Working on common cross-cultural communication challenges. Retrieved 09/03/2006, from http://www.pbs.org/ampu/crosscult.html.

9   Education Counts. (December 2005). International students enrolled in tertiary education. Retrieved March 20, 2006 from http://educationcounts.edcentre.govt.nz/indicators/engagement/tspar12.html.

60

10 Helton, R., & Esrock, S. (April/May 1998). Positioning and marketing academic libraries to students. *Marketing Library Services (MLS)*,12(3). Retrieved 13/02/2006 from http://www.onlineinc.com/mls/apr98/howto. htm.

11 Jackson, P. A. (February 2005). Incoming international students and the library: a survey. *Reference services Review, 33*(2), 197-209.

12 Jiao, Q. G., & Onwuegbuzie, A. J. (1999). Library anxiety among international students [Microfiche]. (ERIC Document No. ED437 973).

13 Kamhi-Stein, L. D., & Stein, P. S. (1999). Teaching information competency as a third language: A new model for library instruction. *Reference & User Services Quarterly, 38*(2), 173-179.

14 Knealle, R. A. (2002). You don't look like a librarian. Retrieved 10/03/2006, from http://www.librarian-image.net/perc.html.

15 Kumar, S. L., & Suresh, R. S. (2000). Strategies for providing effective reference services for international adult learners. *Reference librarian,* (69-70), 327-336.

16 Lafon, F. S. K. (1992). *A comparative study and analysis of the library skills of American and foreign students at the University of Michigan.* Unpublished Ph.D., University of Michigan, United States.

17 Liu, M., & Redfern, B. (1997). Information-Seeking Behavior of Multicultural Students: A Case Study at San Jose State University. *College & Research Libraries, 58*(4), 348-354.

18 Liu, Z. (1993). Difficulties and characteristics of students from developing countries in using American libraries. *College & Research Libraries, 54*(1), 25-31.

19 Martey, A. K. (2000). Marketing products and services of academic libraries in Ghana. *Libri, 50*, 261-268.

20 Mosley, P. A. (1997). Assessing the comfort level impact and perceptua value of library tours. *Research Strategies, 15*(4), 261-270.

21 Nims, J. K. (1999). Marketing library instruction services: Changes and trends. *Reference Services Review, 27*, 249-253.

22 Park, C. (2003). In other (people's) words: Plagiarism by university students—literature and lessons. *Assessment & Evaluation in Higher Education,* 28 (5), 471-489.

23 Patton, B. A. (2002). International students and the American university library [Microfiche]. (ERIC Document No. ED469810).

24 Rowley, J. (1998). Promotion and marketing communications in the information Marketplace. *Library Review, 47*(8), 383-387.

25 Ryan, J. (2000). A guide to teaching international students. Oxford: Oxford Centre for Staff and Learning Development.

26 Sáez, E. E. d. (2002). *Marketing concepts for libraries and information services.* (2nd ed.). London: Facet Publishing.

27 Siess, J. A. (2003). *The visible librarian: Asserting your value with marketing and advocacy.* Chicago: American Library Association.

28 Varga-Atkins, T., & Ashcroft, L. (2004). Information skills of undergraduate business students—a comparison of UK and international students. *Library Management, 25*(1/2), 39-55.

29 Wang, J., & Frank, D. (2002). Cross-cultural communication: Implications for effective information services in academic libraries. *Portal: Libraries and the Academy, 2*(2), 207-216.

30 Wolfe, L. A. (2005). *Library public relations, promotions, and communications: A how-to-do-it manual.* New York: Neal-Schuman Publishers.

Reaching Offshore: A Partnership Approach to Marketing Australian University Libraries' Services to Offshore Students

Lily Gao

School of Information Studies, Charles Sturt University, Australia

Abstract

The continuing development of information communication technology is having a profound impact on every facet of cross border education amongst participating nations. Education is becoming a "globalization" issue which necessitates the providers to move into the "marketing" arena to be able to successfully meet the needs of their clients. Statistics from the Australian Education International organization (2005) showed a 314% (from 8,431 in 1994 to 34,905 in 2000) increase in offshore student enrolments with Australian educational programs offered via satellite and Internet across nations in Asia, Africa, America, Europe and Oceania. Along with this development comes the provision of offshore library services, which presents a unique services opportunity as well as challenges to Australian university libraries in developing library marketing and communications in a multicultural environment. Traditional library marketing plans and strategies have been formulated with a focus on the local market. A new marketing approach is needed in providing library services to meet the different requirements of clients located in a range of diverse multicultural locations.

In the current climate of budget constraint, compounded with language and culture barriers, as well as geographical differences, Australian university libraries have adopted a collaborative approach in developing partnership relations with stakeholders in promoting their library services to offshore students in many countries, such as China, India, Singapore and Vietnam.

This paper examines the ways in which Australian university libraries engage with major stakeholders in developing marketing strategies that fit within local operating environments. The benefits and constraints of the partnership marketing approach in the multicultural environment will also be discussed.

The discussion will be based on the traditional marketing principles of five P's—product, place, price, position and people and their implications for offshore library services management and marketing in both the information technology environment and the overall global context.

1. Introduction

The continuing development of information communication technology is having a profound impact on every facet of cross border education amongst participating nations. Education is becoming a "globalization" issue which necessitates the providers to move into the "marketing" arena to be able to successfully meet the needs of their clients. Statistics from IDP (2005) show that there are an estimated 54,460 transnational students, of whom approximately 11,944 (22 percent) are studying off-campus (distance/online) and an estimated 42,516 (78 percent) students are studying at offshore campuses. Along with this development comes the provision of offshore library services, which presents a unique services opportunity as well as challenges to Australian university libraries in developing library marketing and communications in a multicultural environment. Traditional library marketing plans and strategies have been formulated with a focus on the local market. But a new marketing approach is needed to provide library services to meet the different requirements of multinational clients located in a range of diverse cultural locations.

In the current climate of budget constraints, compounded by language and culture barriers, as well as geographical differences, Australian university libraries have adopted a collaborative approach in developing partnership relations with stakeholders to promote their library services to offshore students in many countries. This paper examines the ways in which Australian university libraries engage with major stakeholders in developing marketing strategies that fit within local operating environments. It will look at the marketing variables (Product, Price, Place, Position, Promotion and People) from the transnational information delivery perspectives and the applications of partnership approaches in promoting and communicating Australian library resources and services to offshore students in a transnational library services context. The advantages and constraints of the partnership approaches will also be discussed.

2. Marketing Concept in the Library World

Library marketing is about understanding user needs, and identifying better ways to meet those needs. The marketing concept in the library world can be traced back to the early 18th century marketing activities such as the librarian reading books to children, by means of his horse-drawn wagon, to reach dwellers in the back country (Renborg, 1997, p. 6). The other terms and activities related to this effort include advertising, extension work, outreach, publicity, public relations and publication. These traditional forms of marketing strategies, be they formal or informal, continue to bear their marks in the electronic library environment of today, but with new contents centred upon the concept of "offering the right product, in the right place, at the right price, with the right promotion for the right person" (Greiner, 1990, cited in Roy, 2002, p. 217). To achieve this requires a more coherent and systematic approach, which is what we now term "marketing process".

A definition of marketing provided in the IFLA Glossary of Marketing Definitions (IFLA, 1998, p. 11) describes marketing as "the process of planning and executing the conception, pricing, promotion, and distribution of ideas, goods and services to create exchanges that satisfy individual and organizational goals." Owens (2002, p. 26) suggests that library marketing is to demonstrate the value of library information services to its users, to help an organization see the big picture, to help to build user allegiance, respect and trust, to help gain organizational support and enhance visibility and build market share and shape public perception.

2.1. Marketing mixes in library and information science

The application of marketing in the library world was conceptualized by Weingand (1998, pp. 1-2), which describes:

- Products = those programs and services that the library provides to its customers

- Price = what it costs to produce its product plus any user fees that are assessed

- Place = How products and customers (or patrons) are connected, distribution channels

- Promotion = how the library communicate with its customers, relating details on how customer needs have been identified and what responses have been developed to meet those needs."

However, these concepts have been developed largely based on the printed world with a focus on the physical collection of books, etc. from the libraries. Fisk and Summey (2004, p. 81) remark that many authors write about marketing principles and strategies in the context of libraries with four walls. In the electronic environment, libraries' resources and services are competing with other electronic resources widely available on the Internet (Adams & Cassner, 2001, p. 5). Dillon (2002) stresses that the need to reposition and project libraries as leaders in offering value-added, quality information to their potential users becomes paramount. He further stresses that it is even more of a challenge to promote electronic resources to users who have grown up with printed books and journals. For Australian university libraries, the task of introducing and promoting the concept and services of virtual libraries to offshore students who are accustomed to traditional physical libraries will be even more challenging and rewarding. With today's electronic information environment and user-centred services, it is important to "position" the library in the mind of our "people" (two Ps), as the very existence of our libraries lies with our people.

3. Library Services for Australian Offshore Programs

3.1. Offshore programs

A working definition offered in a discussion paper released by the Hon. Dr. Brenda Nelson MP, the Australian Government Minister for Education, Science and Training (2005, cited in AEI, 2005, p. 3), states that

> Definition of Australian transnational education and training, also known as offshore or cross-border education and training, refers to the delivery and/or assessment of programs/courses by an accredited Australian provider in a country other than Australia, where delivery includes a face-to-face component. The education and/or training activity may lead to an Australian qualification or may be a non-award course, but in either case an accredited/approved/recognised Australian provider is associated with the education/training activity.

In 2003, there were thirty-eight Australian institutions (Appendix 1) offering a total of 1,569 offshore programs, with majority at masters and undergraduate course levels (Figure 1), and 70% of the offshore programs were located in China, Singapore and Malaysia (Figure 2).

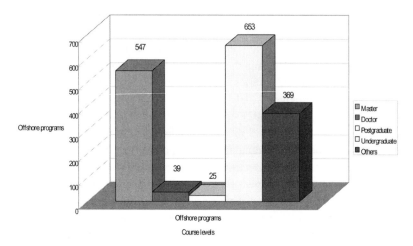

Figure 1. Offshore programs by course levels.

Data source: AVCC (2003), Offshore programs of Australian universities, May 2003

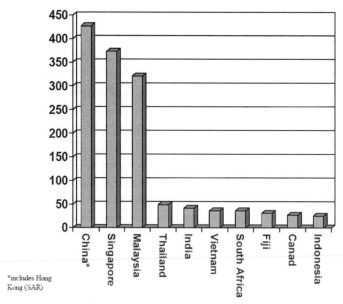

Figure 2. Offshore programs of Australian Universities, 2003

Source: AVCC, Australian Universities Offshore Programs, May 2003., p.5

Education and training services delivered offshore may take many different forms (Table 1). Different offshore programs also entail varying requirements for library resources pending an arrangement with partners in the hosting countries (AVCC, 2005, p. 14). While Australian university libraries provide most of the library services to offshore programs via online platform, there are also library services arrangements with offshore partner institutions and agencies (Table 2).

Types	Forms of operations
Offshore Campus	Wholly owned by an Australian institution
On Campus Courses /programs	Offered in partnership with local providers
Twinning arrangements	Where an Australian university curriculum is delivered as part of the Australian university's relationship with an offshore provider and where students are not formally enrolled as Australian university students until their transfer to the Australian university program.
Franchising of curricula and/or courseware	Where an accredited Australian provider remains an identifiable partner
Distance education programs	Programs contain a component of face-to-face instruction (by local and/or Australian instructors)
Education and training activities	Conducted on behalf of an Australian entity (i.e. training tailored for an offshore organization.

Table 1. Types of offshore programs

A CAUL survey of library support for offshore students and staff also indicates that library support varies depending on course, context, location and mode of delivery (CAUL, 2004b, p. 4). Hence, traditional marketing variables bear different connotations in the transnational information delivery context.

Provider	Delivery to offshore students
Australian university libraries	Via online platform
Offshore campus libraries	Operated by offshore campus, with collection development and training support to local librarians offered by Australian university libraries
Partner institutions offshore	Library services in offshore partner institutions
Information resource centre	Collaborate with offshore partner institutions in collection building and services support

Table 2. Library support arrangements for Australian offshore programs

4. Marketing Mix in Transnational Context

4.1. Product

Following CAUL's (2004) Principle for Library Services to Offshore Students, Australian universities' libraries strive to offer resources and services to offshore students' equivalent to that of onshore students (Table 3). However, it is also noted that not all Australian university libraries' electronic resources are accessible from offshore locations due to infrastructure constraints or copyright and legal issues (McSwiney and Parnell, 2003; CAUL, 2004 and VU, 2005).

Also, in the global information resource environment, the concept of product (resources and services) extends beyond what one's library could offer, embracing those available to the global learners in their own locations. The University of Wollongong (UoW) Library's web site for offshore students is a good example, which includes sources and resources within and outside of the Australia home library. Among the services available to offshore students, links are provided to offshore partner institutions' library sites (Figure 3).

Resources	Services
Catalogue	Literature (subject) search
Databases	Online interactive library orientation
E-Journals	Information literacy training Online/CD-ROM
E-resources	Online reference enquiries
E-Reserve	Online technical assistance
E-Book	Document Delivery Services (web, email, fax)
Online tutorial Web-ezy	Inter Library Loan
FAQ	Online chat
Information technology support	Blackboard services
Software download	Subject portals

Table 3. Australian university libraries' Online Resources and Services to Offshore Students —a brief summary (not exclusive)

Source: extracted from 2004 CAUL Survey of Library Support for Offshore Students and Staffs: Summary of Response.

4.2. Place (distribution mechanism)

Among other traditional distribution methods, such as postal delivery, fax, email and CD ROM, Australian library resources and services to offshore students are largely distributed over the online platform, supported by authentication systems and innovative information and telecommunication technologies. In this regard, different information technology infrastructures and bottlenecks in telecommunication transmission cross the continents and between countries may present challenges to transnational information access and delivery.

4.3. Price

In defining price, the IFLA glossary states that for a library user the price may come in the form of time the library users must expend to obtain library materials or services. In the online information environment, the price may include the components such as computing cost, online cost, and printing cost and downloading cost borne by the offshore students. For example, an interactive online library orientation session may require a proper speaker headphone which may not be retainable for some offshore students, which makes the promotional services difficult.

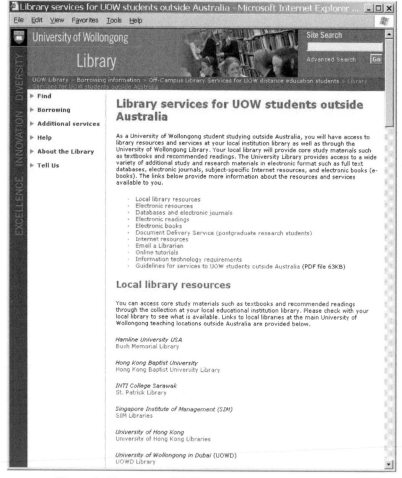

Figure 3. University of Wollongong Library web page for students outside Australia

Source: University of Wollongong Library, http://www.library.uow.edu.au/services/ offcampus/overseas.html

4.4. People

Offshore students, viewed as a new user group, are defined as those enrolled in an Australian higher education course and taught offshore by the home institution's staff, or a student located offshore studying, researching or being taught by local staff employed by, or employed in consultation with, the home institution (CAUL, 2004a). They are spread around the world, with the majority of them being based in Asia Pacific regions, such as China, Singapore and Malaysia (Table 4). They study in various fields of education with the majority being in the field of Management and Commerce (Table 5 and Figure 4). They can be young or mature students from all walks of life with multicultural backgrounds. They could be newly graduated high school students, professional workers, or executive administrators. They could be foreigners themselves in the countries of their studies (Chapman & Pyvis, 2006, p. 239). These are the students that our librarians may never see and never talk to. Cultural, physical and language barriers present challenges to the effort of promoting and communicating the value of library services to offshore students.

Country	PRE - 2000	2000	2001	2002	2003	Total (a)
China	98	30	22	24	24	200
Hong Kong (SAR)	154	21	26	23	16	227
Indonesia	15	3	2	1	3	25
Malaysia	174	59	28	24	29	321
Singapore	194	43	30	58	53	375
Other	260	62	39	43	18	421
TOTAL	895	218	147	173	143	1569

Table 4. Current Offshore Programs of Australian Universities (by year of first intake), Pre 2000 – 2003

Source: Australian Vice-Chancellors Committee, Australian Universities Offshore Programs, May 2003.

Notes (a) The total may not add due to expected 2004 programs being included.

Field of Education	2001	2002	2,003	2,004
Management & Commerce	16,251	34,306	37,199	39,695
Health	3,753	4,670	4,322	4,485
Information Technology	3,655	5,983	6,631	7,896
Society & Culture	1,297	295	2,436	3,060
Creative Arts	933	1,217	1,429	1,718
Engineering & Related Technologies	782	2,442	3,265	3,491
Education	625	1,133	1,251	1,466
Architecture & Building	419	659	792	639
Natural & Physical Science	386	656	791	1,152
Non-Award Courses	139	2,004	347	491
Agriculture, Environment & related studies	21	54	50	53
Food, Hospitality & Personal Services	5	-	-	-
Total Off-Shore Overseas Students	**28,266**	**53,419**	**58,513**	**64,020**

Table 5. Offshore students by Field of Education, 2001 – 2004
Source: DEST Selected Higher Education Student Statistic s (unpublished table)

4.5. Position

In the global information resources environment, library online resources and services are no longer enjoying their monopoly position in providing information services as users have a variety of options available to meet their needs (Adams & Cassner, 2001; Ewers & Austen, 2004). The concept of library as "information gateway" may be alien to offshore students as the role of the academic libraries varies significantly between countries (McSwiney, 2001). Distant from the Australian universities, offshore students have no physical proximate reminder of Australian library resource and services. They may not be aware of library services available to them from the home universities as most of them may have limit or no exposure to the Australian university library systems (Hughes, 2005). Their previous experience of library services is an ongoing influence on their perception of Australian university library services (McSwiney, 1995, p. 132).

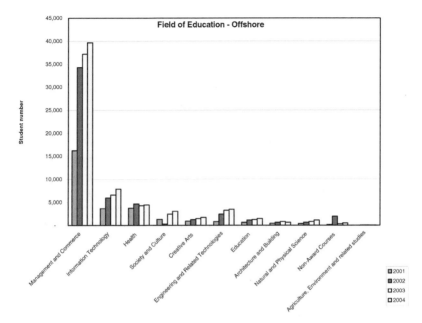

Figure 4. Offshore students by Field of Education, 2001 – 2004

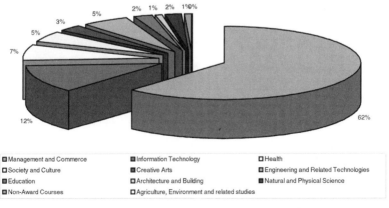

Figure 5. Distribution of Offshore students by Field of Education, 2004

4.6. Promotion/Communication

Most of the traditional promotion techniques, such as subject-specific hand-out, pamphlets, mail-outs, library user handbooks, emails, user orientation, and user surveys have been deployed by Australian university libraries (Ewers & Austen, 2004). Web pages designed for offshore students are heavily used to web cast ranges of offshore library online resources and services with online library tutorials, multiple access points linked through faculty pages, student portals, international students services pages as well as library home pages. However, due to infrastructure difficulties, online tutorials may not be accessible for offshore students in countries where infrastructure is still developing. Dillion (2002, p. 126) also expresses concern that these library market tools are ineffective in linking users with the contents they needs, but drowning them in a mass of unhelpful trivial information. Recent offshore students' survey (McSwiney and Parnell, 2003; UoW, 2004; VUL, 2005) identified that, among other issues, offshore students have a low awareness of the range of Australian university library information resources, possess under-developed information literacy skills and seek easy access, point-of-need support and provision of information resources relevant to their local context. Cross-border/cross-country marketing needs more proactive personal interaction and communication.

5. Challenges

The above analysis indicates that promoting and communicating library services to offshore students require an appreciation of the local context, user knowledge and their specific information needs, but which are currently beyond the knowledge of the majority of Australian university libraries (AUQA, 2004; Ryan, 2006). Challenges are many:

A. Budgetary constraints prevent large scale, intensive library marketing campaigns or sending visiting librarians to each offshore program location, especially where offshore students are not centrally located;

B. Knowledge of local information environment in host countries is lacking;

C. Knowledge of diverse user information needs for individual research projects or customized offshore programs is needed;

D. More effective communication channels adapting to local culture and learning style are needed to disseminate library messages to the offshore students.

In response to these challenges, the traditional partnership marketing approach used by Australian university libraries is re-deployed with new dimensions and applications in the transnational marketing arena.

6. Partnership Approach in Library Marketing

Advocating partnership approach in library marketing, Weingand (1998, viii) states:

> Partnerships provide for the division of responsibilities; increase the amount of energy and expertise available for problem solving and doing necessary work; create communication linkages to promote information exchange; stimulate an interactive environment in the which the existence of the partnership is actually greater than the sum of its individual and independent parts.

Australian university libraries have long recognized the importance in building and maintaining close relationships with faculty members in order to provide responsive library services to academic teaching and learning information needs (Schmidt, 2000). The partnership approach is even more critical in offshore operations in the transnational context as revealed from recent AUQA audit (Cooksey, 2004). Many Australian university libraries are actively seeking and building close partnership relations with major stakeholders, such as visiting lecturers, partner institutions and offshore librarians, through communication, consultation, presentation and training (VUL, 2005; and VU, 2005)

6.1. Partnership with visiting lecturers

- Communication: engaging in active communication with visiting lecturers before, during and after their offshore mission, by
  - o Proactively seeking visiting lecturers' input on specific information requirements for the on-coming mission;
  - o Engaging visiting lecturers' assistance in distributing and disseminating library publications and fliers offshore;
  - o Maintaining 24/7 open line email communication with visiting lecturers during their offshore mission;
  - o Responding promptly to information needs and support required from visiting lecturers;
- Consultation
  - o Preparing course packs for tailored offshore programs in close consultation with visiting lecturers;

- o   Actively seeking feedback on any concern relating to off-
      shore library services from visiting lecturers and their stu-
      dents;
- Presentation
  - o   Arranging presentations to inform visiting lecturers of po-
        tential resources and services available in support of off-
        shore teaching and learning;
- Training
  - o   Provide information skills training to visiting lecturers on
        using library resources and services;
  - o   Updating visiting lecturers on changes and/or deployment
        of new information technologies in the library.

The new offshore library services lead to closer collaboration between Australian university libraries, faculties and staff in their efforts of promoting library services to offshore students to facilitate teaching and learning in transnational education. However, there is both advantage and constraint to such
an approach.

6.1.1. Advantages

In transnational information delivery, visiting lecturers are part of the delivery
of library information services as they often carry excessive baggage containing library promotional fliers, course materials, and reference papers for their
offshore students (NTEU, 2004). During teaching and consultation sessions,
visiting lecturers often find themselves being called upon to assist with online access and problem solving when using Australian university libraries resources. Orava (1997) also suggests that natural infiltration is a more successful strategy than an aggressive campaign. Teaching information skills at the
point-of-need can be very effective in changing offshore students' perceptions
of library services. Visiting lecturers are in a better position in influencing offshore students' orientation to Australian university libraries services through
their teaching and assessment techniques (Ewers & Austen, 2004), and they
can be more effective in communicating and promoting relevant Australian library resources and services to offshore students, due to

- their knowledge of information requirements for offshore programs;
- direct contact and face-to-face interaction with offshore students;
- opportunity of assessing the usability of library resources and services from offshore locations;
- knowledge of their offshore students' desire, capabilities and local
  constraints.

While visiting lecturers could reach out to offshore students and share with them the advantages of library resources and services, there is also constraint in such strategies.

6.1.2. Constraints

Visiting lecturers are often under pressure with overloaded and time-intensive teaching schedules (VU, 2005, p. 18). Consequently finding time to fit in an extra session promoting library services can be all but impossible. There is also concern that short briefing or "training" sessions for offshore students and staff are not enough to develop a common understanding of terms like "plagiarism," for example; the Chinese reference is quite different from the Australian one and this impacts on explanations of plagiarism (VU, 2005, p. 10 & p. 21). Visiting lecturers may lack the depth and breadth of library information resources and services knowledge; as one professor stated, "at the end, Aiya, I am not an expert on the library system anyway" (paraphrase from an anonymous visiting professor's email). On many occasions, the information skills session is offered on request either by offshore students or offshore coordinators in an ad hoc manner resulting in piecemeal training rather than systematic skills training, as students may not get the most out of their experience. Depending on the particular offshore program, visiting lecturers may not have access to local technical and technological support in running library information sessions (NTEU, 2004, p. 17). In the effort of marketing library services to offshore students, it is important to gain collaboration from offshore partner institutions.

6.2. Partnership with partner institutions

In collaboration with offshore partner institutions, many Australian universities are providing short study tours, professional development training or teacher exchange to offshore teaching staff to improve their awareness of the practices of Australian universities, including library resources and services. For example, the University of Wollongong trains Dubai academics to teach the Wollongong way (UoW, 2003). Course managers from Singapore Institute Management visit Australian universities periodically to become familiar with these systems (McLean, 2005, p. 7). The University of South Australia develops induction packages for offshore tutors/lecturers to improve their understanding of teaching and learning policies, library services and practices in the University of South Australia (UniSA, 2005). Offshore staff of partner institutions attended the Victoria University's professional development program in Melbourne to become familiar with Australian academic services. The

CAUL (2004b, p. 11) survey reveals that some Australian university libraries collaborate with offshore partner institution librarians in information literacy facilitation. The University of Wollongong engaged partner institutions in designing a web page dedicated to offshore students. It is also worth noting that these relationship-marketing activities have been integrated with other aspects of Australian university services, not just for library services.

6.2.1. Advantages

Collaboration from partner institutions is invaluable in publicising library resources and services to increase the presence of Australian university libraries offshore. Partner institutions' assistance in organizing library skill training events, securing venues and providing necessary technical and technological support is critical in facilitating the promotional efforts (UoW, 2004, p.16). It is also important to have local advice from offshore partner institutions to avoid cultural conflicts or potential legal problems, such as Internet censorship issues.

Involvement of offshore partner institutions with the information skills training could allow the flexible delivery of training modules at a time, place and level that is suitable for the offshore students without confining them to a particular time block in line with the visiting Australian lecturers' tight schedules. They could also contribute valuable input to the training program with culturally relevant examples to facilitate learning and continue interaction with offshore students with follow-up sessions. In the case where the offshore partner institution is hosting several offshore programs for different Australian universities, it may be more cost-effective for the offshore partner institution to coordinate the library and information literacy training and reduce the cost and duplication of effort from individual Australian university libraries.

6.2.2. Constraints

Different cultures may have different interpretations and standards on the roles of library services and information literacy. Offshore partner institutions or agencies may not be familiar with the standard of information literacy and its relation to the effective use of Australian university library resources and services. Ongoing communication and training is needed to keep offshore partners and staff informed of Australian university libraries' services and practices, so that they can integrate the knowledge into their teaching programs (UoW, 2003; UniSA, 2005). The development of information literacy skills and offshore librarians are indispensable in this endeavour in interacting and coaching offshore students in using library resources and facilities.

6.3. Partnership with offshore librarians

In the case where the library services are supported through offshore campus libraries, the offshore librarian is our front-line services staff. In order to provide effective library services to offshore students, offshore librarians visit Australian university libraries regularly to receive training and familiarize themselves with the standard and the range of Australian university libraries' resources and services. For example, offshore librarians from Swinburne Sarawak Information Resources (Library) visit Swinburne University of Technology Melbourne campus library regularly to update their knowledge of the Australian university library systems and the range of library resources and services.

6.3.1. Advantages

Every reference and enquiry session is a library services marketing opportunity. Offshore librarians have first-hand accounts of user knowledge by observing offshore students' information-seeking and attending to their enquiries. They appreciate more the feeling and culture value of the offshore students from their day-to-day interaction with the students. They could provide point-of-need assistance to offshore students to solve their immediate problems. They have established local contacts to tap into local library information resources and arrange local access for the offshore students.

6.3.2. Constraints

While encouraging offshore students to use Australian university library resources and services, offshore librarians often need to maintain students' expectations. Some of the local information resources may not be properly stocked and the online resources may not live up to the expectation and information needs of the offshore students (McSwiney & Parnell, 2003). Or parent libraries may not have the knowledge to develop a library collection in users' languages or relevant to their local context as most of the Australian university libraries' collection and resources are Western oriented (Dimatteo, 2004; McLean, 2005). Therefore, offshore librarians may not be in a favourable position to promote and recommend library resources and services to offshore students without a sound infrastructure and resources foundation.

7. Conclusion

In summary, the partnership approach facilitates collaboration between Australian university libraries and stakeholders in communicating the value of library services and reaching out to the offshore students, although there may be disadvantages or "danger" in doing this. In Chinese, "danger" comes with two words: "opportunity" and "risk". When we explore new opportunities and new ways to market library services, we also prepare to take the associated risk. By evaluating the strength and weakness of various partnership approaches and options, Australian university libraries will be in a better position in leveraging their marketing efforts to achieve more with less.

Library marketing is our mission, but it is also the common interest of our stakeholders. In the marketing process, it needs concerted efforts from every stakeholder—and not just the visiting lecturer, offshore partner institutions, and librarians (onshore/offshore), but also offshore students and top-level senior management in charge of funding. A more integrated marketing activities and coordinated collaboration arrangement could see more effective marketing results. It is worth further efforts in exploring different marketing partnership models as Australian university libraries strive to reach out to their invisible offshore students. The paths and approaches may be different, but the goal is the same: to enhance the image of Australian university libraries in the minds of offshore students, and to raise the awareness of Australian university libraries' resources services in order to maximize their potential benefit to our offshore students.

References

1   Adams, K. E. & Cassner, E. 2000. "Marketing Library Resources and Services to Distance Faculty." In *The Ninth Off-Campus Library Services Conference Proceedings*: Portland, Oregon, April 26-28, 2000, compiled by P. Steven Thomas. Mount Pleasant, MI: Central Michigan University, pp. 1-12. Reprinted in *Journal of Library Administration* 31, no. 3/4 (2001): 5-22.

2   Australian Education International (AEI), 2005. *Analysis of responses to the discussion paper: A national quality strategy for Australian transnational education and training.* http://www.dest.gov.au/aei [accessed 1 November 2005].

3   Australian University Quality Agency, 2004. *Commendations & Recommendations from AUQA Audit Reports*, 2004, http://www.adm.monash.edu.au/cheq/reviews/reviews_docs/   auqa_coms_recs_for_twenty-one_unis.doc [accessed 15 February 2005].

4   Australian Vice-Chancellors Committee (AVCC), 2003. *Offshore programs of Australian universities*, May 2003, Canberra.

5   Australian Vice-Chancellors' Committee (AVCC) 2005. *Provision of Education to International Students, Code of Practice and Guidelines for Australian Universities*, April 2005, http://www.avcc.edu.au [accessed 1 August 2005].

6   Chapman, A. & Pyvis, D, 2006. "Quality, identity and practice in offshore university programs: issues in the internationalization of Australian higher education", *Teaching in Higher Education*, 11(2), April 2006, pp. 233-245.

7   Cooksey, R.W., 2004. *Interim analyses of commendation and recommendations in Australian University Quality Agency (AUQA) Audit Reports*. Paper presented in ANZAM, 2004, http://divcom.otago.ac.nz/mgmt/ANZAM2004/CD/papers/abstract55.htm [accessed 25 April 2006].

8   Council of Australian University Librarians, 2004a. *CAUL Principles for Library Services to Offshore Students*, 11 May 2004. http://www.caul.edu.au/best-practice/OffshoreLibrary Services.doc [accessed 30 May 2006]. [accessed 1 May 2005].

9   Council of Australian University Librarians, 2004b. *CAUL 2004 Survey of library support for offshore students and staff: summary of response*. http://www.caul.edu.au/ [accessed 3 May 2006].

10 Department of Education, Science and Training (DEST), 2004. "3.8 Overseas students, Table 55. All Overseas Students by Country of Permanent Home Residence, Mode of Attendance, Type of Attendance and Gender, 2004" in *Higher Education, Offshore Student Statistics*. Higher Education Statistics, DEST, D http://www.dest.gov.au/NR/rdonlyres/ 6637C897-F927-47C0-BE1F-6772FDF545E0/4214/08Overseas.xls [accessed 23 May 2006].

11 Department of Education, Science and Training (DEST), 2004. "3.8 Overseas students, Table 56. All Overseas Students by Country of Permanent Home Residence and BroadField of Education, 2004", in *Higher Education Statistics*, DEST, http://www.dest. gov.au/NR/rdonlyres/6637C897-F927-47C0-BE1F-6772FDF545E0/4214/08Overseas.xls [accessed 23 May 2006].

12 Department of Education, Science and Training (DEST), 2004. "3.8 Overseas students, Table 57. Commencing and All Overseas Students by State, Institution and Onshore/Offshore Status, 2004", *Higher Education Statistics*, DEST, http://www.dest.gov.au/NR/ rdonlyres/6637C897-F927-47C0-BE1F-6772FDF545E0/4214/08Overseas.xls [accessed 23 May 2006].

13 Dillon, D. 2002. "Strategic marketing of Electronic Resources", In *Stra-*

tegic marketing in library and information science, edited by I. Owens, Hawthorn Press, pp. 117-134.

14 Dimatteo, D. 2004. "Passport required, librarians conducting information literacy sessions overseas", Paper presented at *ALIA 2004 Biennial Conference Challenging ideas* Gold Coast Australia 21-24 September 2004. http://conferences.alia.org.au/alia2004/pdfs/dimatteo.d.paper.pdf [accessed 2 May 2005].

15 Ewers, B. & Austen, G. 2004. Marketing orientation: a framework for Australian university library management, http://www.eprints.qut.edu.au/ archive/00000469/01/Ewers_Market.pdf.

16 Fisk, J. & Summey, T.P. 2004. "Got distance service? Marketing remote library services to distance learners", *Internet Reference Services Quarterly*, 9 (1/2), pp. 77-91.

17 Hughes, H. 2005. "Cultural diversity and educational inclusivity: international students' use of online information", paper presented at the *23th International Conference on Learning*, Granada, July 2005.

18 IDP, 2005. *International students in Australian, Higher Education,* http:// www.idp.com/ research/fastfacts/article406.asp [accessed 1 May 2006].

19 IFLA, 1998. *Glossary of marking definition,* IFLA Section on Management and Market, http://www.ifla.org/VII/s34/pubs/glossary.htm.\ [accessed 20 May 2006].

20 McLean, S.V. 2005. *Auditing transnational programs*, AUQA Auditor Training Program, Melbourne, October 2005, http://education.qut.edu.au/ about/dean/public/Auditing%20 Transnational%20Programs%203%20N ov%2005.pdf [accessed 23 May 2006].

21 McSwiney, C. 1995. *Essential understandings: international students, learning, libraries*. Auslib press, Blackwood, SA.

22 McSwiney, C. 2001. *Internationalisation of the university: implications for the academic library*, PhD Dissertation, Monash University, Clayton, Vic.

23 McSwiney, C.M. & Parnell, S. 2003. "Trans-national expansion and the role of the university library: a study of academics and librarians in an Australian university." *The new review of libraries and lifelong learning*, 2003, pp. 63-75. http://www.library.unisa.edu.au/about/papers/McSwiney-transnational.pdf [accessed 11 August 2005].

24 National Tertiary Education Union (NTEU), 2004. *Working offshore: Guide for Australian University Staff Working Overseas*, NTEU National

Office. http://www.netu.org.au/ publications/overseas [accessed 23 May 2005].

25 Orava, H. 1997, "Marketing is an attitude of mind". In *Adapting marketing to libraries in a changing and worldwide environment*, pp. 84-89. Paper presented to 63rd IFLA Conference, Copenhagen, September 1997.

26 Owens, I. 2002. "Marketing in library and information science: a selected review of related literature", in *Strategic marketing in library and information science,* edited by I. Owens, Hawthorn Press, pp. 5-31.

27 Renborg, G. 1997. Marketing library services. How it all began. In *Adapting marketing to libraries in a changing and worldwide environment*, pp. 5-11. Paper presented at 63rd IFLA Conference, Copenhagen, September 1997.

28 Roy, L. 2002. "Marketing in public libraries", in *"Strategic marketing in library and information science"* edited by I. Owens, Hawthorn Press, pp. 215-235.

29 Ryan, Y. 2006. *Borderless education: has it been 'good business'?* Speech presented at Canberra University, 27 March 2006. http://www.canberra. edu.au/__data/assets/pdf_file/30126/y-ryan-notes.pdf [accessed 10 May 2006].

30 Schmidt, J. 2000. "Unlocking the Library: Marketing Library Services: a case study approach". *AVCC Staff Development and Training Programme. University Libraries in the 21st century: Threats? Challenges? Opportunities?*, Melbourne, June 2000.

31 Swinburne University of Technology, 2004. Pocket statistics, http://www. swin.edu.au/ corporate/spq/docs/statistics/pctstats04_fin.xls.

32 Swinburne University of Technology, 2005. 2005 Annual Report, http:// www.swin.edu.au/ corporate/spq/reports_annual.html [accessed 25 May 2006].

33 University of South Australia (UniSA), 2005. "Induction packages for offshore tutors", *Learning Connection.* http://www.unisanet.unisa.edu.au/ learningconnection/staff/practice /transnational-induction.asp [accessed 25 May 2006].

34 University of Wollongong, 2003. "Dubai academics train to teach the Wollongong way", *University of Wollongong Latest News*, 17 February, 2003, http://media.uow.edu.au/ news/2003/1702f/index.html [accessed 25 May 2006].

35 University of Wollongong Library, 2004. *Review of library services at off-*

shore teaching locations, report. University of Wollongong Library, April 2004.

36 Victoria University Library (VUL), 2005. *Library operational plan*, http://w2.vu.edu.au/ library/info/files/LibraryOperationalPlan2005.pdf [accessed 25 May 2006].

37 Victoria University, 2005. "*Improving language and learning support for offshore students*", AVCC Project Report, June 2005. http://aei.dest.gov.au/AEI/GovernmentActivities/ QAAustralianEducationAndTrainingSystem/VU_pdf.

38 Weingand, D.E. 1998. *Future-driven library marketing*, American Library Association, Chicago.

Appendix 1: Commencing and all offshore students by state, institution, 2004

State/Institution	Commencing students	All students
New South Wales		
Avondale College	4	17
Charles Sturt University	1,808	5,428
Macquarie University	307	890
Southern Cross University	672	1,684
The University of New England	282	922
The University of New South Wales	136	377
The University of Newcastle	720	1,514
The University of Sydney	258	672
University of Technology, Sydney	267	766
University of Western Sydney	867	3,222
University of Wollongong	1,030	2,807
Total New South Wales	**6,351**	**18,299**
Victoria		
Deakin University	424	1,394
La Trobe University	566	1,162
Monash University	2,304	6,035

Royal Melbourne Institute of Technology	3,284	7,931
Swinburne University of Technology	518*	647**
The University of Melbourne	23	80
University of Ballarat	788	1,350
Victoria University of Technology	968	2,286
Total Victoria	**8,357**	**20,238**
Queensland		
Bond University	246	905
Central Queensland University	516	1,338
Griffith University	239	465
James Cook University	240	311
Queensland University of Technology	100	190
The University of Queensland	12	116
Total Queensland	**1,353**	**3,325**
Western Australia		
Curtin University of Technology	3,105	7,461
Edith Cowan University	666	1,600
Murdoch University	473	671
The University of Western Australia	345	823
Total Western Australia	**4,589**	**10,555**
South Australia		
The Flinders University of South Australia	415	906
The University of Adelaide	418	717
University of South Australia	2,103	6,790
Total South Australia	**2,936**	**8,413**
Tasmania		
Australian Maritime College	6	6
University of Tasmania	967	1,539
Total Tasmania	**973**	**1,545**

Northern Territory

Charles Darwin University	12	32
Total Northern Territory	**12**	**32**
Australian Capital Territory		
The Australian National University	161	449
University of Canberra	380	1,022
Total Australian Capital Territory	**541**	**1,471**
Multi-State		
Australian Catholic University	101	142
Total Multi-State	**101**	**142**
TOTAL	**25,213**	**64,020**
TOTAL 2003	23,315	56,261
% Change on 2003	8.1%	13.8%

Source: Extracted from Department of Education, Science and Training, 2004, Higher Education Statistics, 3.8 Overseas Students, Table 57, Commencing and All Overseas Students by State, Institution and Onshore/Offshore Status, 2004.

*Swinburne University of Technology, 2005. Annual Report

** Swinburne University of Technology, 2004 Pocket Statistics, http://www. swinburne.edu.au/corporate/spq/docs/statistics/pctstats04_fin.xls

Target the Staff, Then Target the Market: How Academic Librarians Can Successfully Reach the Minds of New Generations of Students

Louisa McLam

Li Ping Medical Library, The Chinese University of Hong Kong

Colin Storey

The Chinese University of Hong Kong

Teresa To

Run Run Shaw Library, City University of Hong Kong

Abstract

This paper discusses the essential prerequisite for a state-of-the-art academic library in marketing and promoting its services today and into the future: library staff with particular personal and professional attributes. Using the experiences of The Chinese University of Hong Kong (CUHK) and City University of Hong Kong (CityU) libraries, the authors describe in what practical ways library management can prepare and support staff to market the library product effectively.

Libraries are facing unprecedented change. Two trends in particular are highlighted in this paper, since they directly affect the physical and virtual usage of libraries. First, there is a new generation of computer-literate young people who always resort to the Web for any first, and indeed last, search for information. Second, this generation seems to have developed new study habits, and is now more interested in sharing together in an interactive and informal environment.

To be able to adapt continuously to the changing environment and attract new generations of readers, library staff members not only need to offer a wider range of facilities, but also need to engineer a fundamental change in their approach to service delivery. Librarians need to be effective and proactive in marketing. It is posited here that marketing is not the same as publicizing; it is not simply telling their communities how good their libraries are, and hoping people will come. The right people are crucial in making any implementation a success. Professional librarians and library assistants need to be recruited and promoted to ensure the future place of the library in the hearts of its community of readers. Library management needs to work hard at supporting outgoing and lively staff in this profound cultural shift, by developing and honing their marketing skills. In focusing on ever-evolving interaction with, and surveys of, users, in constantly re-engineering provision, and learning from service outcomes, any library will secure its place and its brand name as a dynamic learning engine for both its readers and its staff.

1. Introduction

In his controversial article "The Deserted Library", Carlson (2001, p. A35) presented a gloomy picture of academic libraries: "One Thursday afternoon at Augusta State's Reese Library, the computer labs are packed, but the reading areas are sparsely populated—and Reese isn't the only college library that's empty. . . . Here in Augusta this afternoon, for instance, there are more Medical College of Georgia students packed into the tiny cafes of the local Borders and Barnes & Noble than there are in the college's sprawling library." Undeniably, the rapid emergence of advanced computing technologies in the past two decades has called into question the value of the academic library as the intellectual and social heart of a university. The Internet has bred a new species of student who prefers Google to library resources. The ubiquitous access to computers anywhere anytime provides them with the means to enter "libraries not through turnstiles but through phone lines and fiber optic cables" (Carlson, 2001, p. A35). Growing up with a wide array of computer gadgets, this generation of students is nurtured with a more diversified learning pattern that is vastly different from the past. How can we, the aging librarians, successfully reach the minds of the younger students? While many library experts emphasize the need of being innovative in packaging library services and designing facilities, this paper further argues that in addition to enhancing the tangible hardware, it is more important to develop and nurture the intuitive software, the brand itself—the library staff. The experiences of the University Library System (ULS) of The Chinese University of Hong Kong (CUHK) and the Run Run Shaw Library (RRSL) of City University of Hong Kong (CityU) are examined to describe in what practical ways library management can prepare and support staff to market the library services effectively.

2. Changing Needs and Learning Patterns of the New Generation of Students

The current student body of the universities is made up of people born in the late 1980s or early 1990s, when the World Wide Web caught world attention. These youngsters, coined as the "Net Generation", "Generation Y" or "the Millennials" (Jackson, 2005), were raised amid computers and various digital media such as video games and cell phones. Compared with their older siblings, they do not see computers as a 'technology', which is somehow separate from themselves, and are accustomed to multimedia tools and environments. In the study conducted by the Pew Internet & American Life Project, Jones (2002) reported that many college students incorporated the Internet into their school, personal and social lives. Being digital natives, these students exhibit distinct learning styles and information-seeking habits, which bring new challenges to academic libraries.

The Internet is often cited as their primary source of information. Again in Jones's survey (2002), 73% of the college students relied on the Internet for information more than the library. The same phenomenon was echoed in Outsell's study (Friendlander, 2002, p. 16). The research findings also support the view that most students use Google-like search engines as their first point of entry to information rather than searching the library Web site or catalogue (Lippincott and Kyrillidou, 2004, p. 57).

In OCLC's study (2002), the students admitted that their heavy reliance on Google was in part due to the difficulty of searching and navigating the library Web pages and its resources without being an expert. In fact, they are accustomed to independent navigation of the Net and figuring things out themselves (Lippincott, 2005, p. 57) as they learn from playing video and interactive games to develop skills based on their experience. They are not particularly interested in reading lengthy instruction, nor do they have much patience or time to attend formal instruction classes to learn the use of library resources. In addition, most library Web sites and catalogues cannot provide what Google is providing. The search results from the catalogue and the databases are not integrated. Despite the extensive use of Z39.50 protocols in library catalogues, users consider it time-consuming to search one library resource after another—in contrast to the global search of Google. Not all searches are linked to full text information, and once available, they are limited to text only. The students prefer information in all formats: print or media. Google, which aggregates all types of materials in all formats and just requires one click, looks more appealing. With a 'fast food mentality of scholarship', the new generation demands for instant gratification of answers with zero delays. It is hard for traditional libraries to meet their needs without undergoing a fundamental paradigm shift.

The young undergraduates display a strong preference towards collaborative teamwork, and expect nomadic communications. The technology allows them to interact with multiple persons in multiple simultaneous activities and conversations in playing Web games, and engaging in chat rooms and IM. They are also more skilled in multitasking than previous generations. Carlson (2005, p. A34) described their behaviours vividly. "They are able to juggle a conversation on Instant Messenger, a Web-surfing session and iTunes playlist while reading *Twelfth Night* for homework. Whether or not they are absorbing the fine points of the play is a matter of debate." It is important for them to access multimedia tools anywhere anytime. As such, they expect the technologies to be mobile and the devices portable.

Another fast-growing trend in teaching and learning is the yearning for liberty and freedom of choice. With many more alternatives in services and products available to them than any previous generation, they already "accept as their right the ability to make choices and customize the things they choose" (Carlson, 2005, p. A35). They desire to have diverse educational environments that accommodate different learning styles. They prefer a place where they can eat, drink, discuss, listen to music, check e-mails and read books, all at the same time. In this regard, are librarians posing too many use restrictions on our young undergraduates? It is not their habit to get information from a specific physical location during specific opening hours and following specific rules and regulations.

Yet, there are other users, mostly graduates and faculty members, who still need a more traditional service. They need a quiet place where they can immerse themselves in their own study and not be disturbed by computer keyboards, printer sounds and mobile phones (Demas, 2005, p. 29).

3. Marketing Concepts and Libraries

In face of the heterogeneous needs of a versatile group of young adults growing up in a technologically diversified Web environment, it is no longer viable for academic librarians to assume that libraries are the natural places to which users would turn to fulfil their information needs. Instead, we must reach out to lure students into the physical and virtual library. Marketing is a need rather than a luxury.

The UK Chartered Institute of Marketing defines marketing as "the management process which identifies, anticipates and supplies customer requirements efficiently and profitably" (Kavulya, 2004, p. 118). It is not simply promotion, which is the organized effort of convincing the customers how good the products and services in question are through public relations, advertisement and other publicity means. Marketing is broader in scope and encompasses the entire activities of planning, pricing, promoting, and distributing goods and services that satisfy customers' needs and organizational goals. Applied to libraries, it entails establishing users' needs, investigating which library products and services will satisfy those needs, and packaging, promoting, branding and distributing them so that they are in the right place at the right time.

Any effective library marketing strategy requires the identification of a perfect marketing mix. According to de Saez (2002, p. 51), it is "the planned package of elements that makes up the product or service offered to the market. It is aimed at supporting the library and information service to reach target markets and specified objectives". The tools of the marketing mix are a set of controllable variables that the library utilizes to fulfil the needs of a specific user group. The traditional approach incorporates the four 'Ps' of *'product'*, *'place'*, *'price'*, and *'promotion'*. In this paper however, we replace *'price'* with *'people'* to reflect that library marketing should focus more on *people*.

In the library environment, 'product' refers to various services that the library is offering or could offer which are of value to users and potential users. On top of the core services, different clientele will be provided with different types of services in order to cater for their specific needs. 'Place' refers to the efforts the library makes to deliver its services to the target user groups. It includes the channels of distribution, physical and virtual environment and locations. 'Promotion' is "all the activities undertaken by the library to communicate its resources and services to the target user groups through advertising, public relations and direct selling" (Kavulya, 2004, p. 119). Here we suggest that 'people' may refer to the library users and specifically to the library staff who deliver services to the users.

4. Product—Public Services

New challenges demand new thinking. The traditional library services should undergo reformation and transformation to give way to modern services that embody enabling technology, media-rich content, convenient access and customized features.

4.1. Enabling technology

Library Web portals present great potential in providing personalized value-added services that a techno-savvy generation expects. In a single interface, users are allowed to access a wide array of electronic resources both within and without the library on multiple platforms including PCs, PDAs, and cell phones; to collaborate with others through chat, IM, e-mails, discussion groups and blogs; to select their own preferred information resources and to customize the look and feel of the layout. MyLibrary@CUHK is the portal developed by the ULS to provide one-stop user-centered information. For the RRSL, the university e-portal serves to present the right dynamic information to users at the right time.

Delivering library services to portable devices the young students use frequently, such as PDAs, cell phones and iPods, and developing Blogs with RSS feeds are promising trends of service delivery. These measures not only make library resources available to students at the point of need, but also update them with new information resources and communicate with them interactively. Both the ULS and the RRSL are aware of these technologies and are exploring their applications in their own libraries.

4.2. Diversified searchable content

While most library OPACs have included not just text but also a number of digital collections, they could be further expanded to integrate more multimedia resources like images, sound, movies, maps, streaming media and 3-D objects so that the students can search across all displays, and have a wider selection of resources. There is no need to limit the searchable content to library-subscribed resources; the open Web resources should be included (Lippincott, 2005, p. 58). It is imperative to provide the one-stop shopping experience that students are so accustomed to in searching Google if we are to bring them back to the library. In recent years, the ULS has started to provide on-demand viewing of videos of local TV programmes in the library OPAC as well as in its Web pages. It also launched the WebBridge service in 2006 to provide one-stop federated search of selected resources. In the RRSL, the link server SFX is adopted to help generate service links, including full text links, bringing more convenient access to users.

It is now not simply enough to have media-rich information resources; the new generation likes integrated and seamless access to all resources in order to save time. Lippincott (2005, p. 57) suggests that libraries should "find ways to increase their presence in general Web search engines". One of the means is to collaborate with Google Scholar so that relevant library resources could appear in the search result of Google Scholar. Libraries can also add Google Scholar to their Web sites for free, or embed a Google search box into the library catalogue search so that the library information is "harvestable and accessible through Google (or its successor)" (Sweeney, 2005, p. 173). CityU's Web site search is already powered by Google.

4.3. Convenient access

4.3.1. Online chat reference service

Compared to a digital reference service using e-mails such as "Ask a Reference Librarian", it is more convenient for today's students to have a live chat reference service that can be available 24 hours. The chat software allows reference librarians to interact directly with users, search the information with them together and the users to personalize the information needed. The service can also make use of digital media with which the young students are comfortable. The QuestionPoint collaborative virtual reference service developed by OCLC in partnership with the Library of Congress embraces all these benefits. The ULS is one of the first libraries in Hong Kong to subscribe to the service in 2002. In the initial implementation, not all the features of the software. such as online chat and 24-hour availability, were utilized. Now, recognizing the need of the young to have personal and direct interaction with librarians, the ULS is planning to migrate to the new flash chat interface to provide online chat reference service in July this year.

4.3.2. Continuing information literacy instruction with new methods

In the Internet environment, there is a more pressing need than before for students to learn information literacy (IL) skills in order to develop effective search strategies and critical thinking, and to evaluate quality information of reliable provenance. They also need to be aware of the critical issues surrounding intellectual property and privacy. However, the Net generation is not as interested as their older siblings in attending traditional IL instruction courses. How to enhance their interest in 'learning the library' is a great challenge.

Instead of singling out the IL course as a separate class, librarians should incorporate IL elements into the curriculum of large-enrolment courses by partnering with other academic departments. It is also worthwhile to create self-paced interactive Web-based tutorials to enable students to learn at their own time and speed. The ULS was successful in this regard in transforming one of the mandatory courses of the University's Improving Postgraduate

Learning programme, "Observing Intellectual Property and Copyright Law during Research", into a WebCT course in 2004 and since then, all research postgraduates are required to go through this course and pass the online assessment before they can graduate from the University. A more interactive Web-based IL tutorial with online exercises is now in development. In CityU, the RRSL also provides and manages the Library and Information Skills Programme online courses to be accessed via the University's e-learning portal on Blackboard. It consists of six self-paced interactive online learning modules for learners who need a flexible learning schedule. In addition, there is also an online tutorial on searching databases.

To further reach out to students who opt not to attend courses at scheduled times and places, librarians can offer to teach at late hours at locations convenient to students, instead of asking them to come to the library. In both the ULS and the RRSL, many instruction classes are arranged in the evenings. Some branch librarians will also go to student hostels on request.

4.3.3. Eliminate the limits of physical locations

Last but not the least, there is a need to eliminate the limits of physical location in service delivery. Flexibility is of paramount importance to the Net generation. The ULS does allow students to borrow and return their loans in every branch library. Both the ULS and the RRSL also join the Hong Kong Academic Library Links to allow their own students to borrow the circulating items of other local universities without the need of travelling to those libraries.

5. Place—Environment and Facilities

The above user-centered services could not reach the young generation without an effectively designed environment. Dove (2006, p. 28) rightly states, "Design offers libraries one of their greatest marketing opportunities. Excellent design provides a vision through inspirational spaces, which embody the values and qualities of the service, attract and retain the public, and can be responsive to their changing needs."

5.1. Diversified needs

As already mentioned, current library users have diversified needs. To attract both the traditional as well as the new 'Net Generations' readers, the traditional paradigm of library building as a more controlled environment is already shifting. The library is no longer just a study hall. Although many users may still prefer the library to be a quiet place to read and study, other users would welcome zones where chatting, discussion and the use of cell phones are allowed. The library therefore needs to retain facilities for independent study such as quiet areas or even totally silent zones and, at the same time, provide informal and group study spaces where noise can be more tolerated. Single study carrels that suit only certain types of users are now not the only popular facility. Instead, students need more space to work in teams, not only because they prefer working with friends but also many teaching faculties encourage group assignments. Group study / discussion rooms are of much higher demand.

Many more new functions are expected from the library in response to technological advancement. To cater to the need of using computers and other high-tech facilities, libraries are now offering wire and wireless access space as well as 24-hour remote access to their resources. Some libraries have also established areas to provide a designated space to facilitate e-learning activities, such as the 'Information Commons' in the ULS and the 'Information Space' in the RRSL.

To accommodate the multitasking characteristic and fast-food mentality of the young generation, the library needs to provide new technology to upgrade service efficiency, and extra space will be needed for these new facilities. For example, the RRSL is the first library in Hong Kong that has a Self-Check system installed. Users can check out books at their own pace. Besides, both the ULS and the RRSL are seriously considering using RFID for security, sorting and stocktaking. To incorporate the system into the whole library operation, specific spatial designs and organization of zones will be required.

As the new generation prefers easy access and some find the library classification system quite off-putting, libraries are trying to organize their collections in more effective ways. Subject libraries may be able to facilitate the use of the specific collections and services. Libraries may also make use of space design to enable the 'zoning of subjects'. This will help amplify the concept of subject clustering and allow easy identification and more efficient browsing. For example, in the ULS, a designated floor in the main library is assigned for the Law Library while another designated floor in a branch library is assigned for the Fine Arts collection. In the case of the RRSL, a specific zone has been designated for the Pearl River Delta & Yangzi River Delta Collection.

5.2. Cultural and social space

As quoted by Albanese (2003), "Today's campus library is more than just a place to get resources. It's a destination that supports new, technology-driven teaching, learning, and research patterns, offering everything from books to digital databases to a social space for students to gather". To meet the new needs of the new users, libraries should no longer just provide a quiet space with books and study carrels but a lively place to encourage and enhance collaboration and interactive learning activities. It should also be a social sphere for informal and socializing attractions, which help create a common culture.

Learning can indeed take place in a more informal, social situation of this kind. Students need community and places that offer a casual atmosphere, such as a comfortable lounge, information commons, informal seating, and a coffee bar where they can enjoy a snack and each other's company during study breaks. The casual reading areas with vending machines in the ULS branches have proved to be very popular and the RRSL has already put the cyber café in its overall renovation plan in the coming year.

Apart from a place for learning, the library should be a cultural venue promoting art and cultural sense. Art exhibitions can help enrich the library's atmosphere and draw users' attention to what else is happening around them. Thus, both the ULS and the RRSL have designated areas for their art exhibits and often organized art and cultural events in the libraries.

Like many of their counterparts, both the ULS and the RRSL have committed to major renovation and spatial reorganization projects in recent years. They understand that what users need most are an effectively designed space with desirable facilities and efficient workflow. Both libraries also get students involved in the planning of the library renovation projects.

6. Promotion

Promotion is a part of the marketing process. Both the ULS and the RRSL have carried out promotional activities in order to make the Libraries more visible to their customers. These include events such as seminars, conferences and exhibitions, which help publicize the services and images to the public. All the library 'publications' such as the Web homepage, library handbooks, library brochure, leaflets and booklets on specific topics and issues allow the public to know more about the Libraries.

Face to face meetings with the customers is also a highly effective means of communication. Both the ULS and the RRSL assign subject librarians to all teaching and research departments. Apart from communicating with teaching faculty regarding their subject collection development, librarians also take the opportunity to help promoting library services and activities to the whole community on all levels.

Technology has changed the learning and research patterns of library users. Our real challenge is not just trying to attract users to get inside the libraries but also marketing our services outside the libraries to create better awareness of library services. The ULS has organized a semi-formal Library Users Group to encourage more interaction between the Library and users while the RRSL staff also meet regularly with the Committee of Information Services and Technology, of which both teaching faculty and student representatives are members.

7. Inside Marketing

We have so far discussed three aspects of the marketing mix—products, place and promotion. They are the important hardware to draw and retain users in the library. Once they get in, they will be able to discover the treasures that cannot be found elsewhere. However, we also need the software: the people, who are crucial in making any implementation a success. As Sass (2002) suggests, "we should remember to market the value of what is the largest percentage of most library budgets—the staff".

Huczek & Socha (2002) have also pointed out that inside marketing "focuses on the importance of the human potential as factor in the successful strategy of an institution". Marketing of libraries is the responsibility of all the staff who interact with users, that is, both professional and supporting staff. Both the ULS and the RRSL are committed to train their library staff as marketers to implement marketing plans and strategies.

8. Preparing Staff

Most information is offered online in recent years. So what is the role of libraries in such an age of easy access? What makes us different from the search engines on the Internet? The answer is: it is the personal encounters and human connection that make us unique. That is, it is our own library people who help *brand* the library for potential customers.

Even with excellent space design and user-focused services, libraries need to have the right people with the right attributes and skills to market our strengths. The key success of the implementation of inside marketing depends largely on the professional expertise and knowledge as well as the right personality and attitude of the staff members. Libraries need staff to recognize the institutional mission and goals and be familiar with the customers, products and values in order to promote the worth of the library. And we should let the users know that librarians are instrumental in offering them quick and easy access to resources.

Libraries not only need their staff to be smart and have expert knowledge, but also to be helpful, willing to serve, outgoing, lively, brave, persistent, flexible and capable of delivering services in a courteous and friendly manner. Three of the characteristics Coffman (2003) used to describe the virtual reference librarian are also useful here. The first one is 'enthusiasm'. It is believed that a person who is excited about what they are doing and interested in the project will have the resources needed to learn what they do not know, and be able to deal more effectively with the inevitable frustrations this new venue presents. The second one is 'quick on their feet'. That is, to have a thorough familiarity with sources and to get the answer out fast. The third one is 'good customer service skills'. Staff should be able to show the patrons they are approachable and genuinely interested in helping the patrons find the information they need.

Professional librarians should also be knowledgeable with updated technological skills, effective and proactive in marketing. They should be global in perspective, expert in public relations, and fully involved in 'selling' our very valuable products to our reader communities. In short, they should be *passionate* about what they do. In the multicultural environment of the academic libraries in Hong Kong, users from different countries often have different expectations on the level of services and attention given. Staff members particularly need higher levels of patience to serve users who are from a different culture.

When libraries are recruiting new staff, higher priority should be placed on the attributes mentioned above. For the existing staff members, even those who have joined the library for a number of years, the same personal and professional requirements should be expected. Yet if some of them do not possess such attributes, it is the library's responsibility to educate them and to help promote and develop the required qualities.

9. Educating Staff for Better Customer Service

In the old days, users initiated a visit to libraries and consulted librarians when they had information needs. Library staff members used to wait for users to come to the service counters; library services reached only those who came to the library for help. The corresponding traditional staff attitude was always service-oriented but not always very proactive. Now with the increasing virtual use of libraries, staff members need to be aware that this traditional service delivery is outmoded. To serve the new generation of users in the new information world, they should provide a new model of customer service.

As Coffman (2003, p. 60) has depicted, "Customer service is the one area that we have control over. We can't control how Google improves its search engine, but we can control the personal touch that comes with working one-on-one with another person. This is the only area of reference where we can make ourselves indispensable. Resources will continually become easier to obtain, but having a conversation with another person who cares about your needs will never be available from a search engine."

It can never be stressed enough how crucial the staff element is in marketing, and how much the reputation and brand of any library service relies on its own staff. It is indeed important for the library to make certain that staff members are ready and willing to provide patrons with great customer service. To achieve this, library management should orient staff to the necessary personal and professional attributes mentioned above as well as educate staff to alter their service delivery approach.

What is even more important is that the whole team of staff needs to identify with the mission, goals and plans set forth by the management as well as the library's marketing strategy. The library should teach staff to be responsive to user suggestions and to learn from user surveys and service outcomes. The new approach needed is no longer simply *service*-oriented but *needs*-oriented —towards the needs of users, that is, user-focused, emphasizing interaction with users. Library management should cultivate such a consumer culture.

Not all staff members are aware of the need to adopt a new approach to service delivery. Even those who are aware may not make any changes without a push. This new environment, which combines the formal and the informal approach, might confuse them. After all, a library has always been in effect a bureaucracy with 'strict' rules which library staff are asked to administer. Library management thus has the role to enhance staff members' awareness in this aspect and foster a fundamental transformation in their service attitudes.

10. Supporting and Training

To meet the new demands of users, newer and more innovative information skills are required. Since only continuous staff learning can enhance sensitivity and proactive approaches to new challenges, tailor-made refresher training and developmental courses must be provided on a regular basis. Apart from professional attitude and technical skills, support should be given to develop practical experiences for staff in marketing.

As learning takes place in the situation, libraries should serve as a community of practice where staff learning can take place. Staff participation in library publicity projects like workshops or conferences is the most practical way of providing staff with a social learning environment to motivate and stimulate them to learn.

Both the ULS and the RRSL actively encourage professional exchange between internal staff and librarians from the Mainland and overseas libraries. This is also an effective way of enabling staff to participate in actual marketing. The two libraries also encourage team learning by setting up Faculty Liaison Teams in which professional librarians are given a lot of chances to communicate with teaching faculty. Some librarians also engage support staff in subject liaison activities, which encourage more interaction between staff and users. The Management Group Meeting is one of the training opportunities for the ULS staff to participate in senior management. This arrangement allows professional librarians to have a better understanding of the organization policy, which ultimately will develop a shared vision.

11. Conclusion

Libraries are facing unprecedented change. To be able to adapt continuously to the changing environment and attract new generations of readers, library staff members do not only need to offer a wider range of facilities and provide collaborative teaching and learning spaces, but also need to engineer a fundamental change in their approach to service delivery.

With effective and proactive marketing strategies, library readers will be able to appreciate the librarians and their services. They will more fully understand what is different about the library—what the *brand* of the library is. Yet it is the people who make libraries different from the search engines and any other information providers. Users come to the library not just because of the comfortable environment but they can also find someone who is ready to help them eagerly. Therefore libraries need to recruit the right staff with the right attributes—open minded, brave, outgoing and lively—and retrain current staff in order to enhance a culture that emphasizes helpfulness, participation and outreach, and passion for learning.

Both the ULS and the RRSL librarians have tried to make themselves more visible to users and provide 'marketing-led' library services. They also actively support lifelong learning among staff as well as promoting and encouraging interaction between staff and users. It is believed that in focusing library people on ever-evolving interaction with, and surveys of, readers, in constantly re-engineering the branded product and its physical location, and learning from service outcomes, any library will secure its place as a dynamic learning engine for both its readers and its staff.

References

1   Albanese, AR 2003. 'Deserted no more', *LibraryJournal.com,* April 15. Retrieved March 26, 2006, from http://www.libraryjournal.com/article/ CA289156.html.

2   Carlson, S 2001. 'The deserted library: As students work online, reading rooms empty out—leading some campuses to add Starbucks', *The Chronicle of Higher Education,* vol. 48, no. 12, pp. A35-8.

3   Carlson, S 2005. 'The Net generation goes to college: tech-savvy "Millennials" have lots of gadgets, like to multitask, and expect to control what, when, and how they learn. Should colleges cater to them?', *The Chronicle of Higher Education*, vol. 52, no. 7, pp. A34-7.

4   Coffman, S 2003. *Going live: starting and running a virtual reference service,* American Library Association, Chicago.

5   de Saez, EE 2002. *Marketing concepts for libraries and information services,* 2nd edn, Facet, London.

6   Demas, S 2005. 'From the ashes of Alexandria: what's happening in the college library', in *Library as place: rethinking roles, rethinking space,* Council on Library and Information Resources, Washington, D.C., pp. 25- 40.

7   Dove, A 2006. 'Library design as marketing: the Swedish experience', *Update,* vol. 5, no. 3, March, pp. 28-31.

8   Fister, B 2004. *The point-and-click generation goes to the library: how academic libraries adapt to changing expectations.* June 3. Retrieved March 26, 2006, from http://homepages. gac.edu/~fister/Linfield.html.

9   Friendlander, A 2002. Dimensions and use of the scholarly information environment: introduction to a data set assembled by the Digital Library Federation and Outsell, Inc. Digital Library Federation and Council on Library and Information Resources, Washington, D.C.

10 Huczek, M & Socha, I 2002. 'The role of inside marketing in the quality improvement of library work', EBIB, no. 3. Retrieved May 10, 2006, from http://ebib.oss.wroc.pl/english/ grant/huczeksocha.php.

11 Jackson, PA 2005. *Academic libraries in the Net generation: Embracing technology to infuse information literacy throughout the curriculum.* Retrieved April 15, 2006, from https://www-rohan.sdsu.edu/~pjackson/ netgen.ppt.

12 Jones, S 2002. *The Internet goes to college: How students are living in the future with today's technology,* Pew Internet & American Life Project, Washington, D.C. Retrieved March 28, 2006, from www.pewinternet.org/ pdfs/PIP_College_Report.pdf.

13 Kavulya, JM 2004. 'Marketing of library services: a case study of selected university libraries in Kenya', *Library Management*, vol. 25, no. 3, pp. 118-126.

14 Lenhart, A, Simon, M & Graziano, M 2001. *The Internet and education: findings of the Pew Internet and American Life Project*, Pew Internet & American Life Project, Washington, D.C. Retrieved June 12, 2006, from http://www.pewinternet.org/pdfs/PIP_Schools_Report.pdf.

15 'Libraries in the digital age' 2005. *NLM Newsline,* vol. 60, Spring Special.

16 Lippincott, JK 2005, 'Net generation students and libraries', *EDUCAUSE Review*, vol. 40, no. 2, March / April, pp.56-66. Retrieved March 27, 2006, from http://www.educause.edu/ir/ library/pdf/erm0523.pdf.

17 Lippincott, S & Kyrillidou, M 2004. 'How ARL University communities access information: highlights from LIBQUAL+', *ARL Bimonthly Report*, no. 236, October. Retrieved April 16, 2006, from http://www.arl.org/newsltr/236/lqaccess.html.

18 *OCLC White Paper on the information habits of college students: How academic librarians can influence students' web-based information choices* 2002, OCLC, Dublin. Retrieved March 30, 2006, from http://www5.oclc.org/downloads/community/informationhabits.pdf.

19 Sass, RK 2002. 'Marketing the worth of your library', *LibraryJournal.com,* June 15. Retrieved May 24, 2006, from http://libraryjournal.com/article/CA220888.html.

20 Sweeney, RT 2005. 'Reinventing library buildings and services for the Millennial generation', *Library Administration and Management*, vol. 19, no. 4, Fall, pp. 165-175.

Part II

How to Organize and Promote Library Services

Different Strokes for Different Folks: Strategies in Promoting Library Services to International Customers—A Case Study

Grace Saw and Fei Yu
The University of Queensland

Abstract

In just under a decade, the University of Queensland moved from having virtually no international students to over 6,000 international students from 125 countries now studying at the University. This growth is the result of strategic and systematic marketing by the University on its reputation as one of the leading teaching and research-intensive universities in Australia and internationally.

One of the key reasons for this success has been the invaluable access that international students have to meet their information needs provided by the first class services, resources and facilities at the innovative and award-winning University of Queensland Library. This paper looks at how the Library provides and promotes its products and services to the University's international students and the integral role it plays in the internationalisation activities within the University. The University of Queensland Library offers special products, services and staff support to the international students and these are regularly measured in biennial user surveys for continuous improvement and verified in testimonial outcomes. Library staff represent and participate in the University's international committees, liaise with key international associations and present at International Education conferences. Strategies used to create awareness and promote the above products and services include publications, presentations, websites, displays and exhibitions, tours and talks, liaison activities with academics, and building relationships with units within the University.

The Library has also been successful in marketing its professional expertise to its international colleagues in the region. These include advice and consultancy, visits and tours, work experience and internship training programs.
The Library offers a unique professional internship training program covering
all manner of topics of interest and importance to library professionals in the
region. This internship training program has now attracted professional participants from Myanmar, Thailand, Vietnam, Fiji, Malaysia and Saudi Arabia
with its innovative and practical approaches to current and challenging issues
that face library management personnel in the 21st century.

1. Introduction

The University of Queensland Library provides services and support to over
5000 staff members and over 37,000 students including more than 6,000 international students from 121 countries. It is also a member of several international organisations, such as Universitas 21, IFLA (International Federation of
Library Association) and IATUL (International Association of Technological
University Libraries), which it has close professional relationship. Recognising that it has a clientele and working partners with vast differences in social,
economical and cultural background, the UQ Library strives to adopt different promotional strategies to market the Library services and support. This
paper looks at those strategies used in promoting library services and support
to international customers: UQ international students and international library
profession colleagues.

2. Background

2.1. University of Queensland

The University of Queensland is one of the eight key universities in Australia and is recognised internationally as a premier research institution. It is the
largest and the oldest university in Queensland. The University has received
numerous awards for its outstanding teaching and research. In 1998 the University of Queensland was listed the University of the Year by the *Good Universities Guide to Australian Universities*. The University's graduates employment rate is 87% (national average is 81%). Graduate salary is $46,556
($40,000 national median). The University's income in 2004 is $157 million,
$73 million from competitive grants.

2.2. International students at the University of Queensland

At the University of Queensland, an "international student" is defined as "a student who is neither an Australian citizen nor a New Zealand citizen nor the holder of permanent resident status" (University of Queensland Management Information Glossary). In just under a decade, the University of Queensland moved from having virtually no international students to over 6,000 international students from 125 countries now studying at the University. This growth is the result of strategic and systematic marketing by the University on its reputation as one of the leading teaching and research-intensive universities in Australia and internationally.

International EFTSL

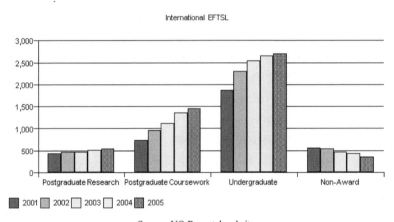

Source: UQ Reportal website

One of the key reasons for this success has been the invaluable access that international students have to meet their information needs provided by the first class services, resources and facilities at the innovative and award-winning University of Queensland Library.

2.3. The University of Queensland Library

The University of Queensland Library has 13 branches located on three university campuses and 3 major teaching hospitals. It has a budget of AU$30 million and 250 dedicated staff. The Library has one of the largest collections among academic libraries in Australia and by far the largest in Queensland. The Library collection comprises:

- over 2 million volumes

- 11,241 print journals and 33,590 electronic journals
- 867 networked databases
- 360,566 electronic books
- 30,583 videos

The Library has won the Australian Teaching Awards – Institutional category twice for its excellent contribution to the University teaching activities. UQ Library is the only library in the country to have won this Teaching Award.

3. Analysis of the Needs of International Students

As part of its ongoing commitment to the provision of excellent services, the University of Queensland Library conducts biennial Rodski client surveys (Saw 2004). The outcome of the most recent Rodski survey shows that for international students have very similar needs to those of local students, and that like their local counterparts they would like to have more:

1. computer workstations;
2. computer facilities and electronic equipment; and
3. photocopying and printing facilities.

International students, however, do have two unique requirements which are at the top of their list: they would like to see longer opening hours and to have more study spaces in the library. This is perhaps an indication of international students' reliance on the Library as a study space either because they used the library as their study space when they were at home, or because they do not have a quiet and comfortable home environment to study like many locals do (Saw 2004).

Recently the Library has also conducted four focus groups on three University campuses seeking feedback from international students on the Library's international students webpage. Forty-five students participated, 73% of whom were postgraduate students and 27% undergraduate students. Overall comments from international students indicated that they thought they were no different from other students starting at UQ and they had the same needs as local students (Gauld & Bordchardt 2006). The fact that international students are enrolled in UQ courses indicates they have sufficient English skills to enable them to study in an English language environment. However at the beginning period, they would still need language assistance in their study, as a few students pointed out that they really appreciate that we have online dictionaries available. Also one other special need raised by international students was they would like to keep in touch with their home country and their family and friends.

Comments reflected that the Library has excellent information resources, and the university has provided sufficient support, however, many international students are not aware of some library services, and have problems using the library resources as well as the university support services. They all know one library resource to be very useful: the online newspapers from their countries.

From Rodski survey, focus groups and comments we receive at branch service points on various occasions, we felt that if international students need any special services and support, they should focus on training, explaining and informing the Library existing services and support rather than providing extra information sources. International students need to be informed and trained in a special way that they can easily understand, because things that local students take for granted may be considered very different and difficult by international students. The Library staff, on the other hand, need to be aware that international students come from different social, economic and cultural backgrounds. Many of them are away from their family and friends, away from their familiar environment. All of these factors warrant extra effort in training, explaining and informing international students about the Library services and support.

Based on these findings the UQ Library management refocuses its services and support to international students on providing guides and training to raise their awareness of the Library resources and to help them use those excellent resources to their full capacity.

4. Promoting UQ Library Services and Support to International Students

The University of Queensland Library offers services and staff support to international students to help them understand the UQ Library system and how to make better use of the Library resources for their study. The promotion strategies for those services and support include:

- Publications and presentations at various conferences and fora to promote the Library resources and raise the Library profile to the international community.

- Displays and exhibitions in the Library to raise cultural awareness among the general UQ community as well as international students.

- Tours and talks to international students to show the Library services and support and how to use them; and also promote library publications Subject Guides and How to Guides.

- Designated International Students Liaison Officers on three campus library branches to help international students, apart from their subject liaison librarian.

- Multilingual library staff list for international students if they need help with language problems.

- Specialised software Microsoft Global IME on library computers to enable international students to read and write in languages other than English (when they email to their family and friends at home).

- 39 electronic international newspapers, 26 print international newspapers and 14 print Australian newspapers to keep them up to date with what is happening.

- A specialised webpage for international students as a gateway to information sources as well as a marketing tool for the services and support provided by the Library and the University to international students.

- Liaison activities with academics as a means to identify international students' study needs and how to best support them in their study.

- Building relationship with various UQ units which are involved with international student service to familiarise them with the Library services and support so that they can pass the information on to international students.

4.1. Publications and presentations

The University of Queensland Library produces several publications to introduce services and support offered in the UQ Library. These publications follow
the principle that they use simple words and sentences, are easy to carry and
eye-catching. The publications are distributed at the University student support service section, all academic faculties and schools as well as all branch
library service points. They are also on display or supplied in the information
bag at various university functions such as orientation week activities.

Presentation of the Library services and support to international students
is another promotion tool used frequently in the University of Queensland

Library. From the University Librarian and executive managers to liaison librarians who work at the front line, everyone from the Library is encouraged to bring the attention of the international students to the library resources and to explain in simple and easy to understand terms how to use the resources. Presentation is also given to university staff who have close contact with international students so that they are able to give correct information to those students. The format of presentation can be formal and informal. PowerPoint presentation, seminar and discussion are the most commonly used formats, however, "presentation" can also happen when we have morning tea or afternoon tea with academics or general staff; and when informally chatting to students.

UQ Library management also views that attending and presenting at various especially international conferences is the best way to promote UQ Library services not only to our colleagues nationally and internationally but also to academic and general communities. The following is the list of papers presented at conferences since 2002.

- The Cybrary and the consortium: mutual benefits
  (paper presented at First Shanghai International Library Forum, July 2002).

- The Learning Resource Catalogue Workshop in Birmingham UK, September 2002.

- Report on the Successful AusLit: Australian literature gateway implementation of the FRBR and INDECS event models and implications for other FRBR implementations (paper presented at 68th IFLA General Conference and Council in August 2002, Glasgow UK).

- The Cybrary: an entrepreneurial approach to collaborative partnerships for information support for borderless e-education
  (paper presented at EDU-COM November 2002, Thailand).

- Australian Education International Industry Seminar March 2003.

- Funding down under: entrepreneurial approaches to generating income at the University Queensland Cybrary (paper presented at Combined annual conference of the American Library Association (ALA) and the Canadian Library Association (CLA) June 2003).

- Sustaining user-centred website development in an online environment: approaches taken by AVEL sustainability knowledge network
  (paper presented at DigiLib Conference at Helsinki Finland, October 2003).
- Reading Rodski – user surveys revisited
  (paper presented at 25th IATUL international conference at Krakow, Poland, June 2004).

4.2. Displays and exhibitions

Exhibitions of various themes have been used for awareness purposes for the UQ community as well as for international students. Over the past five years, the UQ Library has put on display photographs, picture, posters and memorabilia from personal collections. The displays include the introduction of different cultures, customs and religions. For example, in 2004 there was a Chinese National Day display with many photographs loaned from the Chinese Embassy. The aboriginal culture was also on display to help international students understand Australian culture and history. The Library also actively participates in the University annual event, the Diversity Week, where activities are organised to raise awareness of cultural and equity issues.

Displays of UQ Library brochures and posters are at all branch library service points and the university student support centre, faculties and school offices. International students can easily obtain information about library services from anywhere on campus.

4.3. Tours and talks

The University of Queensland Library conducts many tours each year to our international visitors. The tours include presentation of the UQ Library overview, services points such as the information desk, loans desk, and AskIT desk. Study space with computer facilities, printing and photocopying facilities and the cafeteria which is attached to the Library are also shown to the visitors. There are usually one of the executive managers and a few designated librarians to receive the guests and to tour and hold presentations. Visitor information packets and professionally made UQ Library promotional videos were specially prepared for the visitors to take home. From 2002, the Library received about 1141 visitors from 37 countries across five continent, many of them from China, Japan and Korea. The following figures show each year from 2002 to May 2006 the number of tours and visitors and number of visitors from China, Japan and Korea.

Number of Tours & Visitors

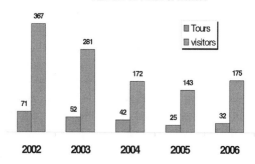

Number of Visitors from China Japan & Korea

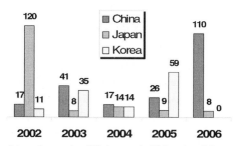

Source: UQ Library data on International Visitors to the University of Queensland Library

We also provide orientation and induction workshops for international students at the beginning of the semester. At the workshops the students are shown how to navigate the library website to find information on opening hours, library printing and computing facilities, borrowing and using online resources. The class is conducted in an informal and interactive way to create a relaxed and friendly environment for international students, so that they would not feel too intimidated and too daunted to ask any questions.

International Students Presentations

	2003		2004		2005	
	Sessions	Attendees	Sessions	Attendees	Sessions	Attendees
Introductory Academic Program (AusAid)	10	181	11	145	7	110
Academic Preparation Program (non-AusAid)	8	137	8	296	8	234

4.4. International students liaison officers and liaison librarians

In the UQ Library there are three international student liaison officers on the university main campus and one on each of the two other campuses. Their names and contact details are listed on the website. These librarians are also involved in trainings offered at the beginning of semester so international students get to know them from the start.

"Subject" liaison librarians are also very useful in helping international students. Once international students start at the University, they tend to use more subject liaison librarians because the help they need is mainly related to their study and research, especially those postgraduate international students. Because international students may have problems remembering English names and faces, the pictures of liaison librarians are posted on the library webpage to help them easily locate their liaison librarians.

4.5. Multilingual library staff list on the library webpage

The UQ Library has a group of staff who are fluent with 24 non-English languages. They either are from different ethnic backgrounds whose mother tongues are foreign languages or just have talent with languages. This list of multilingual staff was designed for the purpose of providing extra support if needed by international students. It is found that international students would still need language assistance especially at the beginning even though many of them have passed English tests before they came to Australia and therefore they should have a sufficient level of language skills to enable them to cope with study and research. It is also observed that when they discover a librarian who can speak their language, they are very happy to approach him/her for help.

4.6. Microsoft Global IME on library computers

The Microsoft Global IME is available on all library computers. It allows international students to read and write in their own languages to communicate with their families and friends and to keep in touch with what's happening at home. Being able to read and write in their own language would make the transition period from their home country to Australia easier for international students. This excellent resource is promoted at all trainings, tours, talks and service points in the Library. It is very popular among international students.

4.7. Electronic newspapers website

In the UQ Library there are 91 electronic international newspapers and 26 print international newspapers from 39 countries, including 6 newspapers from China. There are also 34 major Australian newspapers available online. Many of them have archived collection available from some of the UQ Library databases. The electronic newspaper website serves the purpose of a gateway not only for the general UQ community but also for international students in particular. The website promotes the Library resources that international students can utilise to keep in touch with their home country. Also easy online access to Australian newspapers is helping them to understand better Australian social, economical and political issues, which will help them to be integrated into Australian society. A book mark was made and distributed widely in the university to promote the website to international students.

4.8. International students website

The University of Queensland Library has a dedicated website for service information for international students. The website is not the duplication of what's available on other library and university websites but it aims at one-stop shop to provide links to important information sources for international students. Those links include: library information such as opening hours, location of branches, special software available on library machines for students to read and write in non-English languages, and newspapers from other countries. There is also information about university activities, accommodations and support for international students.

4.9. Liaison activities with academics

In the UQ Library each librarian liaises with one or several academic units. They work closely with their academic staff providing innovative and dynamic support for their teaching and research. This relationship also serves as a channel to gather information on international students' needs and requirements, their problems and concerns in study. At the same time, the liaison librarian brings awareness to academics of library support and services available in the Library to international students so that those academic staff who are in close contact with international students can provide correct information to them when necessary.

For example, liaison librarians are often invited to attend schools' postgraduate induction programs, giving brief introductions about the library services. Among the postgraduate students, many are from overseas without any previous experience in Australia. Liaison librarians spend more time explaining to those students not only about how to use the library resources but also about the special services and support we have for international students. Many things, which local students take for granted, are new to international students and are not easily understood. By working closely with academics liaison librarian can better understand international students' special needs and specific problems regarding finding and using information.

4.10. Building relationships with units within the university

The University of Queensland has international student support units and units that deal with offshore teaching and learning matters. The UQ library has representatives in each of these units to build close working relationships. Some special presentations and short workshops are conducted to introduce services and support provided by the Library as well as library resources in general, so that those staff who are dealing with international students are aware of not just general library services and resources but also special services for international students.

5. Services to International Colleagues

So far we looked at how the UQ Library promotes its services and support to international students studying at UQ. The Library also offers a unique professional internship training program covering all topics of interest and importance with its innovative and practical approaches to current and challenging issues that face library management personnel in the 21st century. The program includes advice and consultancy, visits and tours, work experience and internship training programs.

The Library has been successful in marketing this unique program to its international colleagues in the region (Saw 2004). It has now attracted professional participants from Myanmar, Thailand, Vietnam, Fiji, Malaysia and Saudi Arabia.

Special brochures, presentations at international professional conferences and various other marketing strategies are used to promote the service. It is believed by UQ Library Management that providing this service gives UQ Library staff an opportunity to liaise with and learn from our international colleagues.

6. Conclusion

Globalization and internationalization are salient features of our time. This article illustrates the numerous strategies employed by the Library to market and promote its variety of services to the University's international community as part of the crucial role it plays in providing academic support to 15 percent of the University's student cohort.

Experience informs us that one size does not fill all and while international students have some different requirements and needs compared to domestic students, still others within this group will have expectations and skills that require different service approaches from the Library. By offering relevant and immediate library services, we are better able to serve the international students by building their confidence and competence which in turn assist their academic success and lead to better retention of those international students enrolled at the University of Queensland.

References

1 Saw, G 2004. 'Managing international education: the Cybrary's perspective', paper presented to 18th IDP Australian International Education Conference, Sydney, 4-8 October 2004.

2 Gauld, M & Bordchardt, K 2006. *Perceptions of the University of Queensland Library's web pages for international students: Report on focus group findings*, University of Queensland Library, Brisbane.

Dealing with Evidence Based Management: Roles and Dimensions of Library Services Promotion

Leonor Gaspar Pinto
Library and Archives Department, Lisbon Municipality, Portugal

Paula Ochôa
Information Consultant, Portugal

Abstract

The aim of this paper is to present evidence-based management initiatives carried out by the Department of Libraries and Archives of Lisbon Municipality in the context of Lisbon Municipal Libraries Network Performance Assessment Program (BLX-PA Program) (2003-2006). This Program's central goal was the implementation of an Integrated Performance Evaluation System that would assist managers and staff in their decision-making process, monitor resource allocations, improve libraries' efficiency and effectiveness and, therefore, provide evidences of Lisbon municipal libraries' social value.

Three methodologies support this system: (1) Development of library performance indicators; (2) Service quality and user satisfaction evaluation; (3) Organizational self-assessment. This paper describes these methodologies and examines their potential role in the promotion of library services to find out what indicators and benchmarks are required to deal with evidence-based management dimensions and whether there are any lessons that can be drawn for public libraries with multicultural clients.

This line of research is focused on reflection in action, centred on skills management as a strategy for continuous improvement. It is another role for the promotion of LIS professionals and services.

1. Introduction

Few studies of public libraries with multicultural clients needs are made in Portugal. A comparison with other European countries allows us to identify factors that influence clients' participation in library services and to realise how Portuguese traditional structures and concepts of library promotion poorly address their motivations, needs and cultural trajectories.

Reflecting on the concept of lifelong learning, Calixto (2005) assesses its implications for public libraries and school libraries, requiring them to move towards a client-centred provision of services and a trans-disciplinary approach, characterised by interaction between users and brokers of knowledge.

In a broader perspective, the evolution of quality methods in public libraries is being thought of as a management strategy to expand the kinds and types of services provided and to diversify the criteria by which they are judged and promoted. This is the result of a new societal transition to a more knowledge-intensive concept and of various efforts to increase stakeholders' interest in public libraries' results and outcomes. Cultural perceptions of public librarians were one of the most interesting aspects in the construction of a new vision, new roles and dimensions to promote LIS services. In the context of these changes, this paper addresses four specific issues:

- The creation of an integrated performance evaluation system
- Development of library performance indicators
- Services quality and user satisfaction evaluation
- Organizational self-assessment

The analysis draws upon recent initiatives and recent developments carried out by the Department of Libraries and Archives of Lisbon Municipality (2003-2006). For analytic purposes, it was useful to use an external consultant to bring an external view into the case study[1].

The key objectives that drive this study are, therefore, to describe and analyze best practices in reflection in action, centred on skills management as a strategy for continuous improvement, along with the conditions that appeared to increase the importance of evidence-based management as a powerful tool in decision support.

2. The Organizational Dynamics

Twenty libraries—one central library, sixteen branch libraries, two mobile li-

braries and one public garden service point—form Lisbon Municipal Libraries Network[2]. Since the creation of the first municipal library in 1887 till now,
Lisbon Municipal Libraries (BLX) have generated several innovations[3] at process, product-service and technological levels. An overview of the last seven-
teen years, allows us to identify six major innovation cycles[4]:

- **Remodelling the Municipal Libraries Network** (1991–2002)
  according to UNESCO's concept of public library and to a policy
  of providing the public with specialised information services[5].

- **(Re)designing the Municipal Libraries Network** (2002-   )
  according to a new, more effective and more efficient concept of
  public libraries network.

- **Automated Cataloguing** (1989–2002)
  this cycle started with the introduction of the first microcomputers
  in the Central Library and the beginning of automated cataloguing
  using software free of charge—PORBASE[6]. In 1993, a network
  catalogue solution was implemented using a new version of POR-
  BASE and a Novell network.

- **Networked Library Management Integrated System**
  the implementation, in October 2003, of a networked Library
  Management Integrated System (HORIZON) opened the doors
  to a huge change in libraries' processes, services and products, as
  well as in all back-office structures.

- **Collecting and Reporting Performance Information**
  the creation in 1992 of a system for collecting and reporting information based on the main findings of an academic study on performance measurement of Portuguese public libraries[7]. This system,
  supported by Excel spread sheets, shaped most of the municipal
  libraries' performance collecting and reporting routines for more
  than ten years.

- **Building a Culture of Assessment**
  in 2003, the Director of the Department of Archives and Libraries
  of Lisbon Municipality, in the context of a wider quality strategy,
  set the goal of building an organisational culture of assessment,
  as a mechanism for continuous improvement and enhancement of
  libraries' social value. To achieve this goal, the Department of Ar-

chives and Libraries outlined a key strategy: the implementation of an *Integrated Performance Evaluation System* that would provide performance evidences and guide the promotion of Lisbon municipal library services.

3. Reflecting in Action: Cultural Understandings

Like countries, each organisation has its own and particular organisational culture. For more than thirty years, this theme has been central to organisational behaviour studies and Social Psychology, and among all definitions one can find in the literature, Schein's (1985) definition of organisational culture is, perhaps, the most frequently adopted. For this author, organizational culture is a set of fundamental values, behaviour rules, artefacts and behaviour patterns that shape the way people interact in the organisation and commit themselves to work and to the organisation. Organisational culture is quite similar to an iceberg (Chiavenato, 2004): in the top, above water level, there are the visible and superficial cultural aspects that can be observed—the type of building, spaces, furniture and equipment, the work methods and procedures, organisational strategies and goals, performance measures, etc.; below, there are all invisible and deep aspects, which are much more difficult to observe or perceive—people's perceptions and attitudes, values and expectations, emotional relationships, group feelings and rules, etc. The deeper we go into the "cultural iceberg", the more difficult it is to change an organisational culture.

One way an organization makes itself known is by incorporating its organizational reflections in its ongoing discourse (Czarniawska, 1997). In more general terms, cultural self-expression includes all the references to collective identity (Jenkins, 1996) and it's a source of identifying evidences that can be used to impress others in order to awaken their sympathy by stimulating their awareness, attracting their attention and interest and encouraging their involvement and support (Hatch; Schultz, 1997). Strategic projection is therefore a component of organizational identity dynamics. This concern for the impressions libraries make on others brings us to the importance of libraries' public image: "An image is something we get primarily through coincidental, infrequent, superficial and/or mediated information, through mass media, public appearances, from second-hand sources, etc. not through our own direct, lasting experiences and perceptions of the core object." (Alvesson, 1990, p. 377).

As an answer to the increasing pressure on Portuguese public services towards accountability and performance evaluation, in the last trimester of

2003, the Department of Archives and Libraries initiated a program aimed at the development of an assessment culture in Lisbon Municipal Libraries Network—the BLX Performance Assessment Program (BLX-PA Program). As defined by A. Lakos (1998), a "Culture of Assessment is the attitudinal and institutional changes that have to occur in order for library staff to be able to work in an environment where decisions are based on facts, research and analysis, and services are planned and delivered in order to maximise positive outcomes and impacts for library clients. Culture of assessment is an integral part of the process of change and the creation of a customer-centred culture" (p. 5).

4. Implementing the BLX Integrated Performance Evaluation System

BLX-PA Program's main focus was the implementation of an *Integrated Performance Evaluation System* that would assist managers and staff in their decision-making process, monitor resource allocations, improve libraries' efficiency and effectiveness and, therefore, provide evidences of BLX social value.

BLX-PA Program is carried out by a project team of 2 librarians (project leaders) and 34 facilitators (16 library coordinators and 18 local collaborators). Acting as change agents (Freire, 2000), *BLX-PA's* project leaders have been playing two important functions: creating the vision for the project, in articulation with the Department of Archives and Libraries' goals and objectives; and motivating team members in order to make them willing to overcome obstacles and create an open and participative work environment. We consider the process of creating and transferring the vision a key success factor. In fact, as Tjosvold (1992) puts it, "Successful teams are committed to a *vision* of innovation and experiment, feel *united* and cohesive behind this vision, and believe that the organization itself wants continuous improvement and will respond openly to the team's recommendations." (p. 85).

The approach followed by the Library and Archives Department was structured around three methodologies: (1) *Development of library performance indicators*; (2) *Service quality and user satisfaction evaluation*; (3) *Organizational self-assessment*. Figure 1 shows how these methodologies relate to each other and support the integrated performance evaluation system in the emergent organisational culture of assessment.

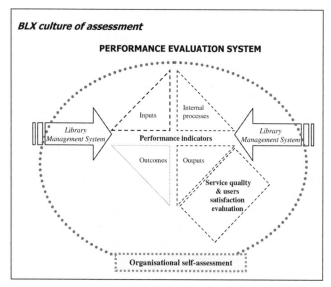

Figure 1. BLX Integrated Performance Evaluation System

4.1. Performance indicators

Based on a diagnosis of the Department of Libraries and Archives and libraries' performance information needs and on international standards[8], a set performance measures were tested and validated by libraries. During this phase
(end of 2003 to 2004), Excel spreadsheets were prepared in order accommodate the initial 126 measures and to allow libraries' local data inputs as well
as central inputs and collective data analysis and reports. Based on a partnership between the Department of Libraries and Archives and the Portuguese
firm that represents Horizon library system in Portugal (Novabase), a statistical module that automatically generates a significant part of theses performance measures was developed. As a result, some of these measures were dis-
continued since they could be extracted from the statistical module whenever
needed. Presently, we are collecting 65 performance measures: 8 are gathered
daily, 34 monthly, 20 every three months and 3 annually. In 23% of the cases,
performance data is gathered by sampling methods.

In the beginning of 2005, using Microsoft Excel, 50 performance indicators were tested and discussed with libraries' coordinators and staff. As a
result, in 2006, we are managing performance evidences resulting from 41
performance indicators grouped under three broad categories (performance
areas): General, Resources-Infrastructures and Public Services (see Table 1).

Assessment Categories	ID	Performance indicators
General	iG1	Population to be served per active library
Resources / Infrastructures	iR-B1	Libraries inactivity rate
	iR-C1	Computers directly available to users per 1000 population
	iR-C3	Types of computers as a percentage of total computers directly available to users
	iR-L1	Seats per 1000 population
	iR-Cl2	Collection turnover rate
	iR-Cl8	Withdrawn documents as a percentage of total collection
	iR-Cb1	Staff per 1000 population
	iR-Cb2	User services staff as a percentage of total staff
	iR-Cb3	Staff attending training sessions as a percentage of total staff
	iR-Cb4	Average time spent on training per member of staff
	iR-Cb5	Staff with information-documentation qualifications as a percentage of total staff
User services	iS-G2	Visits per 1000 population
	iS-D1	Libraries total functioning hours
	iS-D2	Percentage of time libraries were unexpectedly closed
	iS-D3	Libraries availability
	iS-I1	Computers use rate
	iS-I2	Availability of computers directly available to users
	iS-I3	Seat occupancy rate
	iS-I4	Computers directly available to users per 1000 population
	iS-F1	In-library use per 1000 population
	iS-F2	In-library use per library visit
	iS-F4	Percentage of unused documents
	iS-E1	Collection turnover
	iS-E2	Loans per 1000 population
	iS-E3	Loans per registered user
	iS-E4	Loans per staff member
	iS-E5	Documents on loan as a percentage of the collection
	iS-E3	Loans per registered user
	iS-A1a	User interactions per user service staff member
	iS-A1b	User interactions per library functioning hour
	iS-A1c	Distant user interactions as a percentage of total

Assessment Categories	ID	Performance indicators
	iS-Ac1	Users of library promotion activities per 1000 population
	iS-Ac1	Users of library promotion activities as a percentage of total library visits
	iS-P1	Searches per user service staff member
	iS-P2	Searches per library functioning hour
User services	iS-C1	Copies per library visit
	iS-U2	User registration rate
	iS-U3	Active users as a percentage registered users
	iS-U4	Electronic services users as a percentage of library visits
	iS-U5	External active users as a percentage total active users

Table 1. BLX performance indicators

These indicators provide important evidences of BLX performance supporting the Department of Library and Archives' communication strategy towards its clients and stakeholders, namely towards municipal top level management. It should be noted that Lisbon municipal libraries previous experiences on performance measurement (the *Collecting and reporting performance information* innovation cycle that was mentioned above) helped us identifying significant cultural barriers that had to be overcome to create an organisational assessment culture. Figure 2 shows those major cultural barriers, as well as some related factors that were expected to help overcoming those barriers.[9]

Cultural barriers	Success factors
Library staff skills are much more aligned to (technical) librarianship than to marketing and business	Development of library staff performance assessment skills
Perception of performance evaluation as a threat	Create a vision capable of capitalizing on performance evaluation value and potential
Unawareness of the need to demonstrate libraries' and library professionals' outcomes and social value	Focus the library profession on customers' needs and libraries accountability, outputs and outcomes (impact)
Gaps between strategic, coordinating and operational levels	Involve libraries coordinators and teams during design, test, implementation and evaluation phases

Figure 2. Major cultural barriers

4.2. Service quality and user satisfaction evaluation

In the process of establishing a performance evaluation system for Lisbon Municipal Libraries, BLX's users could not have been forgotten. So, in September 2004 the Department of Libraries and Archives launch a research project aimed at the evaluation of BLX service quality and user satisfaction. This project was carried out by two ISCTE Business School researchers, assisted by one *BLX-PA Program* librarian[10]. The study was performed in two phases: in the first one (September 2004-June 2005), targeted at adult users, 13 libraries participated in the study; in the second one (July 2005-March 2006), aimed specifically at users with 0 to 14 years old, 10 libraries participated.

Every organization's service as a quality dimension (Hernon and Altman, 1998). Service and quality are, therefore, inseparable concepts. Each client who interacts with a library forms an opinion about the quality of the service provided. This *service experience* is a very important element in the *perception of service delivery*. In that sense, we can say clients' view of quality is synonymous of service quality.

Among several possible definitions of quality, BLX study considers *perceived quality* as the *discrepancy between service users' perceptions and expectations* (Berry and Parasuraman, 1990). In other words, there is service quality whenever user perceptions of a given service exceed his or her expectations. In order to analyse BLX's service quality and user satisfaction, the research team used Zeithmal, Parasuraman and Berry's *Gap Model* (1990) to characterize the gaps that could arise between Lisbon municipal libraries and their multicultural and diverse clients. BLX model of analysis that was constructed for the first phase was structured around six discrepancies, five internal and one external to the organization (Neves *et al.*, 2005).

1. Clients' expectations and management's perceptions of these expectations
2. Management's perceptions of clients' expectations and service quality specifications and standards
3. Service quality specifications and standards and actual service delivery
4. Performance perceptions of user services staff and clients perceptions
5. Actual service delivery and what is communicated to customers about it
6. Clients' service expectations and the perceived quality of service delivery

During a week, data were collected using three types of questionnaires (aimed at managers, user services staff and library clients). A total of 1.486 questionnaires were collected; 94% of these were filled by library clients.

The results of this study were very important to keep BLX's libraries attuned to the expectations of their multicultural clients, enlightening areas of organizational performance improvement and of potential service promotion. All evidences gathered were discussed within libraries' team and at the Department of Libraries and Archives management level. Several organizational improvement actions were taken as result of the service quality and user satisfaction study.

A similar methodology was used in the second phase study aimed at children and young clients' perceptions and expectations of service quality and satisfaction.

4.3. Organizational self-assessment

Conducting a self-assessment exercise is a way of showing an organization is willing to embrace a change process. By incorporating its organizational reflections in its ongoing discourse and practices, an organization makes itself known and demonstrates it is trying to build a culture of assessment.

Though this methodology was considered as an essential element in BLX performance evaluation system and a major component of the emergent assessment culture, it has decided that it would be implemented after the quality and user satisfaction study was completed. The self-assessment initiative is expected to begin in the last trimester of 2006. A pilot project integrated in this initiative as already started at BLX Acquisitions, Cataloguing and Indexing Central Services.

As pointed out by some Portuguese experiences in self-assessment of Public Administration services, the critical success factors of such initiatives are: Leadership involvement, Vision, Motivation / Information, Training and Process implementation (Andrade, 2004). During the preparation phase of BLX self-assessment initiative, particular attention will be paid to these factors.

5. Conclusions and Further Work

This paper has suggested that there are a number of key challenges for public libraries, staff and clients involved in the delivery of new services, and an emerging model of Assessment is presented as a way of addressing these challenges. The model considers a number of factors that interact one another and enables reflection, evaluation and promotion of libraries services and organizational image.

BLX-PA Program impacts are most evident in the role of services promotion. Our library system has become a more distinct entity within Portuguese public libraries. Others may see a possibility to redefine their quality policies and opt for new strategies to promote their services if they find that dealing with evidence-based management will make it easier for them to gain access to privileges/prestige. At the same time, it has been an instrument of management, embracing new values and multiple areas of performance.

At the micro-level, the value of this program remains strong. This can be observed in the evidences collected.

Building a culture of assessment in Lisbon Municipal Libraries Network needs an Integrated Performance Evaluation System, but, above all, it would need a change in people's beliefs, attitudes and skills. In that sense, BLX-PA Program was restructured in September 2005 to accommodate another main (interrelated) focus: the development of a Knowledge Management Initiative to support the emerging culture of assessment. Focusing on the knowledge side of performance assessment made us pay closer attention to organisational and individual learning. In fact, we realised the creation and development of a repository of structured internal knowledge was an important step, but it did not guarantee information would become knowledge.

Building on the evidences from this case, there are a number of research avenues which should be explored to gain further insights into the influence of this case in other public libraries. Like any innovation, building a culture of assessment is an uncertain, knowledge intensive, controversial, interdisciplinary and inter-functional process (Kanter quoted by Ochoa, 1993), but can be copied by other libraries or can be adapted to other organizational cultures. Research that examines the influence of such factors on academic performance may contribute to the body of literature exploring success factors in dealing with evidence-based librarianship. Several researchers have highlighted the importance of accurate performance and knowledge assessment for maturing and progressing as a best practice (Lakos, 1999; Lloria and Moreno-Luzón, 2005; Tidd, Bessant and Pavitt, 2001). Associated to this, there is a need to develop a better understanding of the factors which may influence stakeholders' impressions. The process is complex, requiring as it does both validation and strategy renewal as the BLX-PA Program benefits may be perceived differently by the stakeholders involved. Future developments in Lisbon Municipal Libraries Network the organization are, therefore, likely to be determined by what public authorities and citizens define as an image of quality and what kind of interests they will form in the future.

Notes

1   This joint venture was the follow-up of a partnership organized under the auspices of the Department of Libraries and Archives of Lisbon Municipality and the Information Service Unit of the Portuguese Ministry of Education a decade ago, which had developed different levels of learning in evaluation and performance skills.

2   More information on Lisbon Municipal Libraries Network can be found at http://blx.cm-lisboa.pt/blx.

3   *Innovation* can be defined as the process of creating and introducing something new in the organisation or in the market (Freire, 2000).

4   In general, any innovation project goes through a six phase cycle: opportunity detection, idea generation, development of selected ideas, prototype testing, new service, product or process introduction and its diffusion (Freire, 2000).

5   This cycle was strongly determined by the library vision and strategy defined by Lisbon Local Authority during socialist and communist coalition municipal governments (1989-2001).

6   Until the 1980s, Portugal had no tradition in library automation. Cataloguing rules based on ISBD appeared only at the end of the 70s and loans, serials or acquisitions were managed manually. In the mid eighties, the National Library launch a project aimed at the construction of a National Bibliographic Database. UNESCO's Mini-micro CDS/ISIS was used to develop a bibliographic database following UNIMARC standard, which was named PORBASE. In 1987, after negotiating with UNESCO the free of charge distribution of the Portuguese version of Mini-micro CDS/ISIS, the National Library distributed more then 200 copies of PORBASE to libraries (António and Ferreira, 1996).

7   Pinto, L. G. (1992) - *A medição da performance de bibliotecas públicas portuguesas*. Study submitted in partial fulfilment for the degree of MSc. in Information Management (University of Sheffield, UK).

8   ISO 11620:1998; ISO 2789:2003; ISO 11620.1998/Amd. 1:2003; ISO/TR 20983.2003.

9   In what concerns libraries teams' deficient performance assessment skills, it should be noted this is not a specific characteristic of BLX staff. In fact, a recent study on self-image and external image of Portuguese information professionals' skills, carried out by the *Observatory on the Information-Documentation Profession* (OP I-D), shows "Diagnosis and evaluation skills" are among those skills information professionals consider to be the least important to their present and future performance (Pinto and Ochôa, 2006). As Lakos and Phipps (2004) point out, "Assessment has not been

taught or appreciated by the profession. It involves "visioning" by the organization, which requires knowing what customers value and focusing on continuous improvement. The evolution of library activities into functional "silos" such as circulation, cataloguing, acquisition, and reference service has imposed an organizational structure that assigns to the administrative periphery the activities concerned with planning, data gathering, assessment and evaluation. In the same way, it has assigned its customers to the periphery." (p. 351)

10 José Neves, Maria Helena Vinagre and Leonor Gaspar Pinto.

References

1   Alvesson, M. (1990). "Organization: from substance to image", Organisation Studies, 11, pp. 373-394.

2   António, J. R., Ferreira, M. J. (1996). 10 years of Mini-micro CDS/ISIS in Portugal: a success history. In Pan-European CDS/ISIS meeting, 2, Londres - Papers. [Consult. 18-03-2006]. Available at http://www.axp.mdx. ac.uk/~alan2/pan96.htm.

3   Calixto, J. A. (2005). As Bibliotecas Públicas Portuguesas: transformações, oportunidades e desafios. Páginas a&b. (16), pp. 61-88.

4   Chiavenato, I. (2004). Comportamento organizacional: a dinâmica do sucesso das organizações. São Paulo: Thompson.

5   Czarniawska, B. (1997). Narrating the organization: dramas of institutional identity. Chicago: University of Chicago Press.

6   Freire, A. (2000). Inovação: novos produtos, services e negócios para Portugal. Lisboa: Verbo.

7   Hernon, P., Altman, E. (1998). Assessing service quality: satisfying the expectations of library customers. Chicago: American Library Association.

8   ISO 2789. 2003. International library statistics. 3rd ed.

9   ISO 11620. 1998. Library performance indicators.

10 ISO 11620.1998/Amd. 1:2003. Library performance indicators: amendment 1: additional performance indicators for libraries.

11 ISO/TR 20983. 2003. Performance indicators for electronic library services.

12 Lakos, A. (1998). Library management information systems in the client server environment: a proposed new model. In Northumbria International Conference on Performance Measurement, 2, Northumberland, 1997 – Proceedings. Newcastle : Information North, 1998. pp. 277-286.

13 Lloria, M. B., Moreno-Luzón, M. D. (2005). Construction and validation

of measurement scales for enablers of knowledge creation. Management Research. Vol. 3 n. 3. pp. 225-238.

14 Neves, J., Vinagre, H. (2004). Bibliotecas Municpais de Lisboa: qualidade de serviço e satisfação dos utilizadores: relatório. [Lisboa]: GEST-in.

15 Neves, J. [et al.] (2005). Avaliação da qualidade de serviço e satisfação dos utilizadores das bibliotecas municipais de Lisboa. In Congresso Nacional de Administração Pública, 3, Lisboa, 2005 – O novo ciclo de desenvolvimento da Administração Pública: [Documento electrónico]: abertura, eficiência, independência. 1 disco óptico (CD-ROM).

16 Pinto, L. G. (1992). A medição da performance de bibliotecas públicas portuguesas. Study submitted in partial fulfilment for the degree of MSc. in Information Management (University of Sheffield, UK).

17 Pinto, L. G., Ochôa, P., coord. (2006). A imagem das competências dos profissionais de informação-documentação: relatório. [S.l]: Observatório da Profissão de Informação-Documentação.

18 Ochôa, P. (1993). Estudo do impacte dos projectos comunitários para bibliotecas no Instituto da Biblioteca nacional e do Livro (1989-1993). Study submitted in partial fulfilment for the degree of MSc. in Information Management (University of Sheffield, UK).

19 Schein, E. (1985). Organizational culture and leadership. San Francisco: Jossey-Bass.

20 Tidd, J., Bessant, J., Pavitt, K. (2001). Managing innovation: integrating technological, market and organizational change. 2nd ed. Chichester: Wiley.

21 Zeithaml, V.A., Parasuraman, A., Berry, L. L. (1990). Delivering quality service: balancing customer perceptions and expectations. New York: The Free Press.

22 Zeithaml, V., Parasuraman, A., Berry, L. (1993). The nature of determinants of customer expectations of service quality. Journal of the academy of marketing science. 21 (1). pp. 1-12.

The Impact of Health Informatization on the Organization and Administration of Medical Libraries in China

Li Zhang, Chunhua Yang, and Guizhi Wang
Medical Library of Chinese PLA

Abstract

In recent years, China has made great achievements in health informatization, especially after implementing the "National health informatization developing plan (2003-2010)". With the application of information technologies and networks, the way medical libraries used to operate and service has changed, and the directors of medical libraries encounter great challenges in library organization and administration. The authors analyse the managerial problems that have emerged and the trends of organization and administration for medical libraries, including forming an efficient and flexible management concept accordant with informatization; implementing organizational change; in view of the requirements informatization makes on personnel structure and quality, forming a strategic human resources development plan; and developing an organizational culture that emphasizes teamwork, self-management, learning and innovation.

With the development of information technology and society, China urgently needs to intensify its informatization to accelerate development and improve decision-making. As an essential element in this process, medical libraries face not only opportunity, but also challenges. How to meet health informatization and explore new patterns of organization and administration are important issues for medical libraries.

1. The Status of China's Health Informatization

In recent years, the Chinese government has placed more and more emphasis on health informatization. The Ministry of Public Health has put forward the "National Health Informatization Development Plan Compendium (2003-

2010)" and formulated a series of policies. So far, great achievements have been made in health informatization, including implementation of the national health information network program, construction of the informatization infrastructure, speeding up of computer-based operation for government, information network construction, application of information systems in hospitals, construction of information systems for community health, health supervision, disease control, women's and children's health care, long-distance treatment, and long-distance medical education[1]. However, as a whole, China's health informatization is still in an early stage, and many problems, such as imbalance in development, standard disunion, and nonstandard administration, are yet to be solved. There is still a long way to get to the goal.

2. The Challenges Medical Libraries Are Faced With

Health informatization is an engineered system. As an organic part of this system, how medical libraries face its development and play their important role in information services is an urgent problem to be resolved. Meanwhile, with the development of the economy and technology, traditional management ideas and patterns are increasingly unsuitable to the present status, and China is experiencing a reform of management. Since informatization and management reform are interactive and mutually promotive[2], the organization and administration of medical libraries are bound to face challenges during informatization.

2.1. Management ideas to be improved

The majority of medical libraries only pay attention to the digital resources, but not to organization and administration. Although hardware and network construction is taking place in some medical libraries, the application and administration are ignored. According to the survey in Jiangsu Province and Chongqing city[3,4], the information systems constructed by health institutions are mainly single-tasked transaction systems, while the development of integrated management information systems and decision-making support systems is slow, and even nonexistent, in medical libraries. All these are due to a lack of advanced management ideas in a digital environment, and poor understanding of the importance of informatization. This is not only a technical issue, but a shift in the content and mode of users' demands, and a shift of libraries' operation and work efficiency. Against this background, developing strategies and objectives of medical libraries and the essential process of management should be adjusted, and advanced management ideas should be established to meet the goals of informatization.

2.2. Organization structure is not adapted to the shift of service mode and work flow

As medical libraries are mainly a subsidiary section of hospitals or health departments, the organization structure is traditional and gradational. With the development of information technology and the shift of readers' demands, the organization structure of medical libraries needs to be improved.

Health informatization requires prompt and comprehensive access to information and comprehensive knowledge service from medical libraries. Readers are no longer content with going to libraries to get print or digital resources, but expect to get information anytime and anywhere, and get illustrations or relevancy analysis of the complicated content and the internal relations[5]. The traditional organization structure of medical libraries is gradational and rigid. Since there is not enough communication between managers and staff, it is hard to develop comprehension and collaboration. In this structure, functional departments are strictly divided, and their communication and cooperation are not easy to achieve. As a whole, the blocked information flow and the organization's sluggish response cannot reach the libraries' goal of satisfying readers in all aspects.

2.3. Informatization brings challenges and demands to human resources management

Medical libraries are turning from personnel file management to human resources management, but it is mainly according to the current needs of the work or position, without a long-term holistic plan. Meanwhile, health informatization has new requirements concerning personnel structure and qualification, with more emphasis on personal career development and the essential position of people.

2.4. Culture to be reformed

Medical libraries are affected by traditional values for libraries, and therefore lack attraction and cohesion. This culture can not keep up with the development of health informatization. According to a relevant survey, compared with hospitals and research organizations, the atmosphere in libraries is not very good: many people work there because of the easy environment, without adequate morale and professional confidence. Research also suggests that most library staff members are not satisfied with the work status and do not recognize the value of the library's vocation[6]. Moreover, the staff is not aware of the essential role libraries play in informatization.

The organization system is limited by job and rank, and there is a lack of motivation and flexibility. As to the administrative rules, they are not sufficiently systematized and standardized; therefore, it is hard to form a positive culture that emphasizes initiative and collaboration.

3. The Development Strategy for Organization and Administration in Medical Libraries

3.1. To form effective and flexible management ideas for informatization

The managers of medical libraries should understand how information technology and facility affect operation and administration, and thereby get a better understanding of the practical function of information systems, so that they can utilize information technology to improve their management efficiency and level of decision-making. Information and knowledge are important strategic resources. In the process of health informatization, as professional information resource management centers, medical libraries should realize their essential position and analyze readers' different demands, extend their service concept, innovate types of service, and improve performance and value by meeting readers' demands completely.

3.2. To construct an adaptable organization structure

As health informatization progresses, the organization structure must be reformed. The relation between informatization and organization is complicated due to many influencing factors, such as outside environment, operation process, power distribution, organizational culture, etc. We should construct a new, adaptable organization structure according to the changing situation. In general, a new service concept and model require such an organization structure with good communication, cooperation, and fast response.

The movement toward efficient organization combined with application of a network makes information more transparent, and communication more convenient, which is helpful to work implementation and control. Matrix organization and net-like organization are breaking through the rigid structure, and power is distributed flexibly, thus helping to make the employee more active and creative in providing more individual services for readers. For more advanced requirements, diversified knowledge and information resources, both inside or outside the organization—like knowledge of different subjects and the experience of more experts—could be used synthetically, forming a virtual organization, to provide readers with information services with high value added. For example, in the PLA Medical Library, there are many research subjects and service programs staffed with persons from different departments with various backgrounds, and senior experts and professors outside the library. This improves the scientific research level and service competence.

3.3. To draw up a strategic development plan of human resources

Human resources are the most important resources of the modern organization, and human resources management is the most important management activity. As informatization development makes new demands on the medical library staff structure and qualifications, holistic human resources management and plans will change accordingly. The shift of service model evoked by informatization requires that medical librarians should have computer application capability and information processing ability. Consciousness of collaboration and innovation, along with study competence and an exploratory spirit, have become the basic requirements for librarians.

The staff should be composed of mainly persons with medical and information background, or those having majored in computer, management, systems engineering, and other relevant subjects. With the increasing need for "just in time" and valued information for medical researchers, clinicians and health officers, medical libraries should provide face to face services. Currently, medical libraries are in the important period of informatization and management reform; the managers should analyse seriously current and future job descriptions and personnel demands in combination with assessment of staff and career development, and draw up an innovative human resources development plan.

3.4. To form an organization culture that emphasizes study, innovation, teamwork and self-management

The shift of service model, management concept, and organization structure in medical libraries that has been induced by health informatization will consequently require a suitable organization culture. During the transition to a knowledge economy and knowledge-based society, it is essential but very difficult to reform libraries' traditional value systems. This could be achieved by deepening staff's comprehension of the libraries' future development potential. Medical libraries should enhance librarians' professional confidence and vocational recognition, and improve their general morale and work enthusiasm. Medical libraries should construct scientific rule and regulation systems, including a hiring protocol, performance management, and a rewards and punishment system, and encourage self-management based on respect and trust, creating a positive atmosphere that is open, fair and competitive. The organization structure should foster communication and cooperation. Information management should be transformed to knowledge management to facilitate the spread and exchange of factual knowledge and intuitive knowledge. An organizational structure should be formed that stresses innovation, knowledge renewal and self-improvement.

References

1   Ministry of Health Peoples Republic of China. National Health Informatization Developing Plan Compendium (2003-2010).

2   Wang ZT. Corporation informatization and management reform. Beijing: China People University Press, 2003.

3   Yin F, Zhou YP. The status of Jiangsu Province health informatization and demands analysis. Jiangsu prevention medicine 2003(2):75-77.

4   Sun AL, Wang SX, Zhao Y, Wang XK, Mu WL. Chongqin city health institution informatization status investigation. Chongqin medicine 2004(4):497-498.

5   http://www.chinainfo.gov.cn.

6   He ZY. The study of libraries' human resources development under network environment. Beijing: Beijing Library Press, 2004.

How to Promote Library Services: Academic Libraries in India

Preeti Mahajan and Rupak Chakravarty

Abstract

Do things differently and do different things. This paper has been written with the belief that the foremost thing to be done to promote library services is to strengthen the quality of the existing library services itself. If the existing services are not up to the mark, no promotion activity whatsoever can do magic for the library. Let the caliber of library services speak for itself. Once we are satisfied with what we have and that we are offering it to the user community in the best possible manner, we can go ahead with new ideas, innovations and tools for library promotional activities.

The library promotion activities may vary from institution to institution, so the identification of the user group whom we are serving is a must. Promotional activities must take care of new user groups and ways and means to convert non-users into potential users.

Readers must be provided new and innovative product/resources and services. Rational adoption of IT is needed for all this. This paper presents the tools and methods of re-engineering and customization of all the existing services and judicious incorporation of new products/resources and services while harnessing the power of IT enabled services.

We discuss issues like personality grooming of professionals, user-professionals interaction, library branding, library services branding, best practices. Value added modern tools and services must be offered to academia. This may include setting up of Institutional Repository, Open Course Ware, alerting services, blog service, chat service, document delivery services and the like. IFLA's MatPromo project is a very useful tool for library promotion.

Organization of talks, seminars, conferences, library foundation day, library week, exhibitions and readers' active participation in them will also help in library promotion.

1. Academic Libraries in the Indian Higher Education System

The Information Communication Technology (ICT) revolution has given the world an opportunity to simplify our jobs, our lives and what not. Libraries throughout the world utilize ICT for simplifying their in-house tasks as well as for services and communication of information. Libraries in India have also implemented ICT tools for simplifying and augmenting their efficiency. But unlike the developed countries like US, UK and Canada, the marketing and promotion of products and services in Indian libraries has not received much attention and appreciation. Although there are some libraries that have started Marketing, yet the whole marketing and promotion process is not very well organized and planned.

The academic libraries are considered to be the nerve centres of academic institutions that support teaching, research, and other academic programmes of a country. The situation in academic libraries in India is the same as that of academic libraries the world over. These support the curriculum and research needs of the students, faculty and staff of the universities in the best possible manner. However, these are facing the problems of limited infrastructure including human resources. Hence, they will have to opt for marketing and promotion (M&P) processes, as it will solve many of their problems. The 'Promotion' concept will help the academic libraries in India to offer library services at the right time, at the right place, to the right person in the right way. However, the academic libraries in India have not yet adopted the promotional methods very strongly nor have they visualized promotion as a component of marketing. UGC-INFONET consortium of INFLIBNET and INDEST-AICTE consortium covering Indian universities and technical institutions have provided many scholarly e-journals, now it is up to the libraries as to how well they can manage their usage, promotion and marketing that has not yet been started. It is in this context that the present paper is highly relevant.

2. M&P in the University Libraries of India: Need and Significance

In India, the university libraries use different degrees and levels of M&P process. The rating may be done as follows:

Average: In this case, one can find M&P activities slowly picking up, but a coordinated and systematic effort is still absent. The library may be lacking in M&P plans, futuristic approach and a well-defined vision. They may be practicing M&P but within a very narrow scope.

Poor: In such cases, the academic libraries have no M&P activities and plans. They will have to work out the formulation of excellent M&P strategies, exploit all means and methods and opt for a futuristic and continuous approach, i.e., always look for new services that can be offered to the users and formulate M&P strategies for them.

2.1. Need for adoption of M&P in university libraries

Lack of a well-organized promotional campaign will have the following consequences for the academic libraries in India:

- Many library services will remain unused or underused. The library will lose the opportunity to attract potential users and the existing users may stop using the library services. The library may witness "death of a service" due to no takers of existing services.

- There would be low satisfaction level amongst the library clientele.

- The wrong message will be conveyed to the user and the higher authorities thereby tarnishing the image of the library that may lead to the budget cut.

- The overall result would be negligence and ignorance of the library by the authorities.

2.2. Significance of promotion for academic libraries

The promotion of library services in academic libraries is important, as:

- It convinces and motivates the users to use a library service or to buy its product.

- It leads to the optimum usage of the library services and products, thus strongly supporting the vision of the library.

- It leads to sales, thus enhancing financial strength for the library.

- It provides more visibility and value in the university setup.

- It serves as a prominent tool for "Library Advocacy", thus earning the due importance and considerations from the higher authorities.

- It leads to comprehensive user satisfaction by fulfilling their demands and expectations in the best possible manner.
- It facilitates current users to avail library services more, thereby converting the potential users into the actual users.

3. Promoting the Library Services

Promotion is all about informing your users what you are doing and what you can do. It is the 4th "P" of the marketing mix and the other three being 'product', 'place' and 'price'. The marketing process has many steps like marketing audit, market research, plan of action, setting up of goals and objectives, developing strategies and implementing them. Promotion doesn't happen until these steps are completed. Understanding the strengths and weaknesses of the library and knowing its users are assets in successful promotional strategies. Promotion is more successful if the selected product, the target market, and the marketing plan goals are based on research. Market research helps the libraries in knowing the users' information requirements. This plays a key role in selecting the right promotional tool. However, the methods of promotion vary from one user group to another and depend upon the type of library services to be promoted.

Promotion involves description of the services requiring publicity, description of the audience to which publicity is targeted, details of the campaign, methods to be employed including type of publicity to be used and methods of distribution, execution of campaign, analysis of campaign performance, etc. Although promotion is one of the core components of the marketing process yet the libraries can not jump directly on a promotion campaign without considering the previous steps.

3.1. Aim of promotion of library services for a university library

The promotion of the university library services aims at

- Sales, that is profit oriented.
- Quality service leading to user satisfaction and library advocacy.
- Profit through user satisfaction and Library advocacy.

The resultant factor will be sustainability and excellence. In an academic library, the aim should not only be to earn money but to work in a direction so as to materialize the vision of the library. Keeping in view the five laws of library science as propounded by Dr. S.R. Ranganathan, the academic library must do its best to optimize the library services for the complete satisfaction of the users.

4. Prerequisites/Pre-promotional Planning

Since Indian academic libraries have to initiate the process of promotion, they will have to do all the necessary homework so that they don't face any problem later on. Some of the basic considerations they must keep in mind are:

- Multidimensional and comprehensive research must be undertaken before starting the promotion of any library service.

- Services in bad shape can't be promoted as it will lead to losing the readers' loyalty towards the service and would become very difficult to regain the users' attention or likeness towards that service. It's better if services are first made effective and then only they are considered for promotion.

- Library services once promoted can't be stopped. If any library service is identified for promotion, it cannot be stopped, as it will give a bad image to the library.

- Library must create and develop a conducive environment for service promotion and ultimate delivery of services.

5. Promotional Barriers for University Libraries of India

The first and foremost barrier for promotion of library services in academic libraries in India is the lack of initiative, undefined responsibility and unaccountability. The traditional library setup in academic libraries in India does not provide much scope for undertaking promotion initiatives. The academic libraries here have to concentrate on finding ways and means of making the library fit and capable of a promotional campaign. The whole academic library setup needs to be reexamined. The human resource of the Indian academic library is mostly working in the age-old traditional library setup doing only traditional activities of classification, cataloguing and circulation, thus leaving very limited scope for taking new initiatives and innovations. The staff is not encouraged to think beyond their traditional work routine. Moreover, the strength of staff is not adequate to carry out the promotional activities in a planned manner. A number of professionals lack marketing and promotional skills. Moreover, the fear of taking up a new task and the fear of failure also proves to be an obstacle. In addition, the academic libraries in India also fail to allocate budget, however small, for M&P.

6. Solutions

The professionals working in the academic libraries in India should be familiar with the advantages of M&P. They will have to understand that promotion of library services will not only enable them to survive but to excel as well. It can also boost their decreasing financial status and increase their visibility in the university setup. To start a promotion campaign, the university libraries in India will have to create and develop an M&P team, impart training and skills, repurpose HR instead of outsourcing, and develop cost-effective methods for M&P.

6.1. Assessment of users' needs

Before we go for promotion of library services in an academic library in India, it is very important and essential to assess what type of users we have. What do they want? What do we have? How we are utilizing it? How satisfied are the users? What more can be done and how? To answer these questions, it is better to proceed systematically. The first step in this direction is:

6.1.1. Areas for study

- To find out the existing users and the potential users of the library services.
- Categorization of users into different target groups and creating user database so as to develop a multi-dimensional promotional program. This will help in developing diverse promotional methods for different cross-sections of the user community and introducing new services for each of them according to their needs.
- Information needs of the library users ,i.e., their expectations, liking/ disliking, preferences, etc.
- Information seeking behaviour of the users will facilitate the library to streamline the services so as to make them more user-driven. It will also help the library to rectify or modify a faulty or ineffective method adopted by any user group to locate the information.
- Users' opinion should be taken regarding the paid vs. free services. Before its actual launch, we can assess the users' attitude regarding the cost criteria. This will not only allow the library to estimate and fix a price tag for a service but will also prepare the users' mindset towards the paid services.
- User density, i.e., season, months, timings, etc. when a particular

service is required more. This will enable the library to analyze the timings when a particular library service attracts maximum users.

- Usage statistics of online library resources available on library website.

There are many methods which can be adopted for such studies including survey method, questionnaires, interviews, Internet polls, creating online groups of library users, chat, library blogs, feedback forms, suggestion boxes and contact mechanisms.

6.1.2. Actions to be taken

Based upon the in-depth user survey, several follow-ups are required by the library to move ahead. This includes developing plans to reshape library services according to the priorities and demands of the user, developing promotional strategies according to their behaviour, strategies to convert potential users into "real-users", user education, etc.

6.2. Assessing library infrastructure

Once we have undertaken the user survey and made plans for future action, it is time to analyze the library infrastructure. This assessment should match our users' requirements in the ideal conditions. In case it is not so, the library will have to think about the ways and means to arrange for the missing resources because without adequate infrastructure, they will not be able to optimize their services and promoting the same would be meaningless. Once the library knows what they have, and once they fine-tune their resources in line with what is expected by the user groups, libraries can find out the methods to provide the services smoothly and also enhance their service capabilities.

The infrastructure will include the components required by traditional library services, modern IT-enabled library services as well as the future requirements of the library. To start with, it's better to analyze the infrastructure needed per service, i.e., take one service at a time and find out what's needed to make that service its best. The study of the existing gap between the demand and availability will suggest the actions to be taken to make the service as valuable as per the users' expectations. Such a method adopted for one service may be extended to all other library services and the efforts should be made to bridge the gap between the "need" and the "availability".

The library requires proper infrastructure for Document Delivery Services, Inter-Library Loan, Database access, facility for access to e-journals, Web-OPAC, Digital Repository for article search and download, etc. The infrastructure should be such that the professionals offering the services must find it convenient to offer and the user must be satisfied with it.

6.3. Assessing human resources

The university library will also have to study the available human resources before promoting a service. In Indian university libraries, the shortage of library professionals and para-professionals is not very rare. To run the library services smoothly, libraries hire staff for a fixed tenure. Hence, the academic libraries will have to see how best they can utilize their total human capital for a marketing and promotion campaign. In the Indian university setup, cooperation and coordination with the staff working in the departmental libraries and affiliated colleges will make the task easier. The procedure adopted for this can be put into simple steps:

- Assessment of total strength available
- Assessment of staff available for M&P
- Feasibility study for repurposing of staff
- Imparting necessary training for handling the promotional campaign

Consulting the University Business Schools that run MBA programs will be very helpful, as the focused, brief and customized training sessions can be organized for the M&P team. Certification will be an added advantage as more and more participants will be encouraged to attend the program and will also help in achieving Professional Development Goals of the library staff. Such schools can also undertake the evaluation and categorization of library staff for undertaking the M&P projects, as assigning the right person on the right job plays a crucial role in the success of the marketing efforts. Categorization may reveal who can take the challenge, who has the innovative ideas, levels of management, assigning roles and responsibilities, etc. All these initiatives will not only ensure a successful marketing and promotion case but will also offer additional benefits like improved visibility of the library in the parent organization, self catalyzed library advocacy campaign, etc. The inclusion of departmental libraries and affiliated colleges will facilitate a wide, comprehensive and effective promotional campaign.

6.4. Optimization of library services

After going through the stages discussed above, the academic library is now in a position to move ahead. Now the library has the answer to what it has, what its users' want and how best it can be offered to the users. The question now is how to accomplish these goals in the best possible manner. The library will have to think about certain issues at this stage, such as: Are the users satisfied with what it is offering? Are they satisfied with the way it is being offered? Is there something more that can be done in this regard? What new things can be added? The professionals will have to understand the basic philosophy and vision of the service. Unless the library service is at its best, promotion can't increase the demand for the service. It's the service quality that will ultimately enhance the service usage. The objective of the service should be crystal clear to the person involved. This will help in understanding the user need and time delays can be avoided. Promotion will be best carried out if the library has:

- Predefined service policy
- Service provided according to the different categories of user groups
- Well defined scope
- Simplified procedure for users' convenience
- Suitable promotion policy

User-driven services will become the strongest tool of promotion of library services. Efforts must be made for value addition to the services so that the users avail the service again and again. The library must sort out the USP—Unique Selling Proposition—of every service, which can be the carrier for promotion of that particular service. The USP can be utilized for Branding of the library service, as the library service is known by its USP. The strength and weakness of a particular service may be assessed through SWOT analysis. The USP of a service makes it different from others. It gives users the reasons as to why they should use the service. Hence, the USP of the service promotes the service itself. The library website and the library guide must contain all the above information, especially the service policy and other useful details. This will minimize the wastage of time and the user will be prepared to use the service without any confusion and inconvenience.

6.5. Developing a targeted and feasible promotion plan

Academic libraries in India should follow the "Integrated Marketing Communication" (IMC) approach for promotion of their services. IMC is a management concept that is designed to make all aspects of marketing communication such as advertising, sales, promotion, public relations, and direct marketing work together as a unified force, rather than permitting each to work in isolation. It captures and uses an extensive amount of customer information in setting and tracking marketing strategy. Academic libraries in India, by following the IMC approach, can achieve a great success in their marketing and promotion efforts. A marketing communication plan has the following elements:

6.5.1. The context

What is the context of the communication activity? This briefly outlines the challenges, barriers, opportunities, relevant research, and other key factors useful for promotion.

6.5.2. Goals

The library must determine and define goals of the promotional campaign. Questions that are to be answered include why do you want to do media or advocacy outreach? This may include converting potential library users into actual users or generating enough revenue in a particular year, etc.

6.5.3. Objectives

One goal may have several objectives that may be specific and quantifiable. The library has to determine the objectives derived out of the broader goals. Objectives answer questions like "What will be accomplished?"—e.g., Website visitors will double during the coming year.

6.5.4. Positioning statement

The positioning statement answers the question "How do you want the library to be perceived"? It focuses on the image of the library to be built up amongst the target audience. The positioning statement must be drafted and visualized very carefully because the library image relies on it.

6.5.5. Shaping the key message

The key message contains the most important message the library wishes to deliver. Crafting of the message should be done in such a way so as to reach all or most of the audience selected. The key message(s) can be shaped up as :

> your library → your lifelong partner
> Get involved—get a library card
> @ my library
> research@library
> knowledge@desktop

6.5.6. Designing and outlining strategies and tactics

Drafting of strategies and tactics to be deployed in promoting the various library services is the most crucial and comprehensive step. While formulating strategies in an academic library environment in India, the following points must be kept under consideration:

- Same strategies may not work for different categories of target audience.
- Same strategies may not work for different library services.
- Same strategies may not work for different types of document formats like print and electronic.
- Promotional strategies must be carried out depending upon the best time suitable for the strategy when it can find maximum audience.
- The ultimate focus should be to maximize the outreach to the users.

6.6. Methods and tools for the promotional campaign

The following methods can be used for the promotion of academic library services in India where the concept of marketing and promotion is new and the libraries find it difficult to utilize a huge fund for promotional activities:

6.6.1. Public relations

Public relations and publicity are not synonymous. Publicity is the spreading of information to gain public awareness of a product, service, etc., whereas the public relations includes the activities that ensure a strong public image for the organisation. Often, it is conducted through the media, i.e., newspapers, television, etc. Public relations concentrates more on selling the library products as a whole, developing an identity or an image, and disseminating a clear message to the users about the library's mission and goals. As PR forms one of the core components of marketing, the academic libraries in India should consider it as a significant tool for promoting their library services. In the university setup of India, the libraries can work in coordination with the Public Relation Officer (PRO) of the university who delivers all news related to any event that has happened or will take place in the library and also about any new resource acquired by the library. The libraries may have a separate PR department and budget exclusively allocated for this purpose.

6.6.2. Media relations

According to ALA in its "A communication handbook for libraries" media publicity can increase public awareness of the library services, create or enhance the image of the library, work for library advocacy, clarify misunderstandings and ultimately help in networking with local, national and international libraries and organisations. However, it also mentions that media relations may sometimes include negative coverage as well and cannot be compensated for poor quality of library service. According to the Association of Research libraries, "the benefits of good press can be extraordinarily rewarding". It helps in recognition of hard work of the employees and can support fund raising. However, it depends on the way you communicate with the media. Alison Buckholtz has mentioned that for media relations, first one needs to understand its impact on the library, convert the controversies into positive criticism, keep the interview under control, be precise and lucid, and maintain media relations even when there is no breaking news.

6.6.3. Advertising

Advertising is important for promotion of library service. Traditional print advertising includes brochures, pamphlets, newspaper advertisements, etc. However it requires a lot of funds. The more the funds, the more elaborate and widespread is the advertising campaign undertaken by the library. If separate allocations are not possible for advertising, the library has to try innovative means and methods for presenting the products and services to the library users. A lot of expenditure can be saved by localizing the advertising campaign within the library, but the impact will be less as the outreach will be limited to those who are physically present in the library.

On the other hand, if it is determined to undertake marketing and promotion in a big way and one wants to attract the specialized group of users (like professionals of some local companies, etc.) it would have to make its campaign reach out to them. This can be done especially in those university libraries that are running industry-oriented courses like Pharmaceutics, Engineering, Chemical Engineering, Biotechnology, Biochemistry and the like. The academic library in such cases acquires many scholarly e-journals, databases and other academic resources pertaining to these fields and the library along with departments can frame an advertising campaign to maximize the returns by offering its use to outsiders. For such a purpose, Internet advertising can be used that is a more efficient, effective, and extensive means of communication in a cost-effective manner. In fact, the advantages of Internet advertising far exceed those of traditional print publications through costs, availability, wider consumer markets, and the potential for increased profit margins. The best way for this is to use the library website, which can be accessed "24/7/365", thus leading to greater outreach that will ultimately help libraries achieve their promotional goals. The complete details including the service policy and the terms and conditions of the services, etc. must be posted on the library website with frequent updates. The website may hold graphics and multimedia-rich advertising content that is likely to have greater and long-lasting impact on library website visitors.

Advertising can be done through newspapers as well because the newspapers have huge readership. The university library can get the news published regarding any new resources acquired, any achievement made, any new project undertaken like a digitization project, addition of a new floor or space for reading, a conference, workshop, any new initiatives etc. This way the newspapers get the content for publication and the libraries get the promotion of their services. So "what they need is what we have, and what we have is what they need". This means non-paid advertising and publicity of the library and its services.

In a traditional form of advertising, huge expenditure is to be borne by the library on promotion, printing fees, and storage facilities including distribution cost, labour cost, transportation cost, postage charges, etc. If television, cable, radio and other mass media options are used, then the cost increases many times. The advantages of Internet advertising include its reduced costs, the '24/7/365' availability, the expanded consumer market, and the overall profit margin per consumer.

6.6.4. Imaging, branding, positioning

6.6.4.1. Image

Maintaining a positive image is critical for the library especially to market its products. Branding is associating the library with a name, logo, or slogan. Positioning involves establishing the image of the library as it functions within the community. Library users' perceptions and feelings about libraries affect everything we do to market our services. What do the library users think of when they hear the word library? Is it a positive image? Marketing research identifies the users' perceptions and outlines promotion and promotes a positive image of the library.

6.6.4.2. Library Branding

Library Branding is a combination of elements: the library name, the name of a library service or product (e.g. Ask a Librarian), symbols, logos, consistent design of publications, etc. Logos or symbols, etc. are easily recognizable. These elements give a product or service its own personality and establish an association in the mind of the user. The branding of the library services should be based upon the USP of the service. This will help libraries to reach a concrete idea that can be implemented in branding. Apart from the library services the library itself must be branded, as it will make the library familiar and popular among the audience. One such example is the American Library Association's marketing campaign that uses a branding element—the "@YourLibrary" slogan.

6.6.4.3. Slogans

A slogan should be easy to remember, express your mission, and identify you strongly with concepts and ideas of value to your users. A slogan should be something everyone can easily understand. Slogans should be short, eye catching and meaningful.

6.6.4.4. Positioning

Branding, slogans, and promoting an image are ways to establish the library's position within the community. What is the library's "position"—how are you seen? Is the library considered an active and necessary part of the academic community? How is the library viewed in comparison to other agencies or institutions? The public relations department of the library or the university works on positioning libraries in the community. Libraries must offer their professional expertise and knowledge of the information world.

6.6.4.5. Visioning

In India, most of the university libraries don't have a well drafted and well-placed vision and mission statement. They will have to ask, What is the library's vision for the future? Has it been addressed in library planning and in the marketing plan? Communication of the vision of the library to the user, providing them with an image of the library as a changing organization is very important.

6.6.4.6. Prioritize

Libraries have limited budgets as well as staff with free time. These will have to decide just how much marketing, research, promoting, and positioning you can do—and still get the day-to-day work accomplished. Attitudes can't be changed in a hurry. But the important consideration is that promotion of one service in the right way and at the right time can improve the users' perceptions about the library as a whole.

6.6.5. Using Internet exhaustively as a promotional tool

The library intranet site should constantly be updated to tell the users what exactly the library has at any given moment. It should be interactive so that the users can directly communicate with the staff. For this purpose, the Directory of the staff members is to be posted on the site along with their photographs and email addresses so that the users can communicate with them. The site should have the logo of the library, a section on 'what's new on our web' (having links to important internet sites of e-journals, e-publishers, etc. that are useful for the users) and a section dealing with new announcements about the library products and services. From the marketing point of view, it will demonstrate the relevance of the library in the information age. While marketing of the e-resources is possible, their promotion is also very easy, as most of the reputed publishers like Thomson Gale, Elsevier, Springer, Taylor and Francis, etc., have ready-to-use resources for user education/guides, tutorials, graphics and labels, promotional literature, multimedia files, on-site user training programmes, training materials etc. on their websites.

The only thing is to place such links at appropriate places in the library website. Arranging user-training sessions for teachers and students will also be beneficial for the promotion of services as well as usage promotion for the betterment of the academics. Moreover, the library portal can play a vital role in self-promotion of a library and its services. The portal with scholarly-rich content will attract more and more users and the academics will be greatly benefited by it. Academic libraries can also use IFLA's MatPromo database meant exclusively for promotion of library services.

This image database of library promotion tools collects images of objects currently used by all types of libraries to promote their services and to raise their profile: posters, leaflets, badges, calendars, stationery and all kinds of objects from all over the world. Graphic description, kind of object and the role it plays in the promotional task are described for each image.

The MatPromo database has the features like Simple Search, Advanced Search, Database Usage Statistics, etc. The documents can be searched by the fields like Title, Campaign, Slogans, Subject, role, date, institution, Scope, Place, Abstract Description, Graphic Description, Type of document, Physical description, Spread, File. A keyword search is also possible with the facility of sorting the results by date or title. Under advanced search, complex boolean searching is also possible. Filtering by scope like first national, then international, local, national, provincial, and regional is also possible. The resources offered are very useful for the libraries that want ideas in the marketing and promotional fields. A very significant feature of the MatPromo database is the "contribute" part, where one can upload their file or creative work directly to the database.

6.6.6. Library e-Newsletter

It is an inexpensive and simple means of making regular and targeted contact with the clients and others. Libraries can disseminate helpful information and keep their name in front of clients, without the expense and bother of postage and printing. Newsletters help build the web site's popularity and effectiveness. A library newsletter is a very effective and successful tool for communicating the promotional message. It's also very meaningful and relevant, as you are not forcing or pushing it but the potential client actually requests the information by subscribing to it. When someone chooses to receive information from you, they are automatically more receptive to your message. The e-mail newsletter allows the libraries to keep in touch with existing users and build relationships with potential clients.

Library Newsletters can

- Drive traffic to your site, which means more visitors to the library website.
- Reinforce areas of expertise or interest.
- Check the number of new subscribers you get when you run an ad or get a mention of the newsletter in an article, which can provide the library with important quantitative measures of the effectiveness of other marketing.
- Have all the benefits of "push" technology.
- Facilitates "permission-based" marketing or "opt-in" marketing.
- E-mail newsletters are more timely and cost less or nothing.
- Provide an opportunity for user-education and empowerment of existing users.
- It can increase your client's confidence level of the library's ability and strengths.

For an academic library, the library newsletter provides a free tool for dissemination of its message that helps in achieving marketing and promotional goals. For this purpose, it should properly be placed at the homepage of the library website.

6.6.7. Blogs

Promoting your library services, resources and programmes online can be a lot easier with the help of a blog. The libraries, for promotion of their services and products, are using blogs that are normally free of cost. Academic libraries can set up an RSS feed for the library blog and alert the users regarding any new event and programme. The libraries should encourage visitors to sign up for the e-mail subscription that provides an opportunity for the visitors to visit the website repeatedly. For this purpose, the library blog must be creative and appealing to the visitors. Special alerts about new resources acquired according to various disciplines and special services must be highlighted on the blog. Comments and suggestions to get feedback can be invited for the improvement of the services.

6.6.8. Discussion groups

Apart from newsletters and blogs, discussion groups are proving to be a very effective means of communication that libraries can exploit for marketing and promotion as well. Google Groups is one such service (free) which helps groups of people communicate effectively using email and the Web. The new version of Google Groups lets you easily create your own announcement lists, mailing lists, newsletters and public discussions in just minutes. The new Google Groups also make it easier to read and participate in discussions. In fact Google itself is running a newsletter called "Google Librarian Newsletter" which can be accessed at the "Google Librarian Center".

References

1   Berry, Aimee. Promoting Special Library Services Online. http://www. libsci.sc.edu/bob/class/ clis724/SpecialLibrariesHandbook/promoting.htm.

2   The Campaign for America's Libraries @ your library: Toolkit for Academic and Research Libraries "Messages, ideas, and strategies for promoting the value of our libraries and librarians in the 21st century: ACRL, 2003. http:// www.ala.org/ala/pio/campaign/academicresearch/ academicresearch.htm.

3   A communication handbook for libraries: ALA, Chicago, 2004. http:// www.ala.org/ala/pio/   mediarelationsa/availablepiomat/commhandbook. htm.

4   Darlene, Fichter. Why and how to use blogs to promote your library's services. http://www. infotoday.com/mls/nov03/fichter.shtml.

5   Extreme Makeover: OCLC NextSpace news letter. www.oclc.org/ nextspace/001.

6   *Glossary of Marketing Definitions.* http://www.ifla.org/VII/s34/pubs/glossary. htm.

7   http://groups.google.com/intl/en/googlegroups/about.html.

8   http://www.google.com/librariancenter/.

9   http://www.ala.org/ala/issues/issuesadvocacy.htm.

10 http://www.chrisolson.com/marketingtreasures/mtcontent/MTPDFs/ MTVol15PDFs/Vol15N1Jan06.pdf.

11 http://www.llrx.com/extras/ir31.htm.

12 Kassel, Amelia. Practical tips to help you prove your value : Marketing library services. http://www.infotoday.com/mls/may02/kassel.htm.

13 Marketing the library web-based training for public libraries. www.olc. org/marketing.

14 Nicholas, Julie. Marketing and promotion of library services: Library and information services in astronomy. http://www.eso.org/gen-fac/libraries/ lisa3/reprints/nicholasj.html.

15 Sass, Rivkah K. Marketing the worth of your library. http://www. libraryjournal.com/article/ CA220888.html.

Library Usage and Readership Enhancement: Best Practices to Promote Library Services of CORD, NIRD

Tella Rama Devi

National Institute of Rural Development, Rajendranagar, Hyderabad, India

Abstract

The National Institute of Rural Development (NIRD) is an apex research, training and consultancy organisation in the rural development sector. With the developments in the field of Information and Communication Technologies, the Centre on Rural Documentation (CORD) has gained further significance and metamorphosed into a specialized resource centre to fulfill its obligation as a one-stop location for information on rural development in India. This paper attempts to share the experiences and benefits of adopting such best practices.

The center conducted a learning programme in 1991, 1992 and 1998 on LURE. This programme provided a forum for the users of information and the library personnel to come together, to understand each other's way of dealing with information and how the information barriers can be overcome and what best practices are to be adopted to increase the utilization of the resources of the Library. The sessions offered a set of simple but effective steps to increase the library use with suggestions. These recommendations were taken seriously, as they were particularly innovative in the overall development of the library utilization as well as promotion of services. After LURE-II in 1993, there was marked improvement in the appreciation of library services. Non-book material like CD-ROMs, videos, and electronic journals have slowly started to show their presence. In the mid-90s the Internet opened gates to information sources worldwide, and made possible access to information from a remote location. As a result it has become more important to look into the problems of transforming a traditional library into an information clearinghouse. The LURE III programme was made into a National Workshop inviting papers from all over India on various themes such as library utilisation; techniques of readership enhancement; conducting user studies; evaluation of library services; Internet and changing role of the librarian etc. (NIRD, 1998).

Adoption of best practices resulted in the following:

1. Transformed from traditional library to high-tech library

2. Designed and developed the digital resource base, i.e Computerised Library and Information Clearinghouse (CLIC, available on www. nird.org.in). It is an in-house unit for selection, acquisition, processing and retrieving of data/information in an electronic version in a specific field of activity relating to the mission of NIRD.

3. Bibliographies/abstracts and other relevant material browsed from library database. CDs, Internet etc. relating to the training programmes (180 programmes in a year) are being provided by the library to the faculty to improve the quality of training material. This service was well received and appreciated by the faculty.

4. Open discussion and personal interaction facilitated to establish good rapport between library staff and users

5. Identified as one-stop location and recognized as one of the best libraries in the field of rural development in South Asia

6. Library staff are nominated as a member in the review committee on training programmes

7. The library is recognized as a faculty and encouraged to conduct research and training programmes (3 programmes in a year) in information science

8. Improved the quality of information products like CORD Alerts, CORD Index and Abstract based on the evaluation studies conducted periodically

9. Marketing the services through institutional membership

To handle the above tasks, the librarian has to be proficient in devising ways of social marketing, conceiving and designing appropriate information products and luring the readers to the library in order to enhance the readership. He has to truly act as a facilitator and a total quality-conscious person, keeping in view the user needs to continuously better the best practices. The best practices are those which will reduce the library anxiety and invite readers to come to the library and use the services optimally.

1. Introduction

The changes that are coming in the organization and administration of libraries and the pressures affecting the role of a librarian to fulfill the demands of users and the top management are reflected in the literature of the last decade. (Sabaratnam 1995, Vavrek 1998, Wormel 1997) An important issue in fulfilling the needs of researchers is how human behaviour influences the ways to seek information and how the supply of information suits the needs and requirements of users. User behaviour studies of social scientists as to how they seek, retrieve, read and select materials suggest how these attributes can be used to enhance the search and deliver facilities of the existing library and its resources. These may also provide clues to what changes or modifications are to be brought about in the supply side of information provision.

The channels of information are many and varied. The library is also seen as one of the channels that is intended to control the information flow and minimize the impact of information explosion and maximize its utility. For this purpose, the library procedures should be made simple, and the library environment conducive and the library staff should be outgoing and co-operative. The importance of the library as a resource centre and the endeavour of the management to exploit the resources gathered painstakingly over the years with a lot of investment need not be overemphasized. However, it has been the experience of many a library, especially those attached to organisations, that the use of their resources appears to be little compared to the efforts put in building up the resources. As such there appears to be a constant need to initiate outreach programmes in order to enhance the usage of the library to the maximum extent.

The library is looked upon as a centre for learning. In view of the knowledge explosion, it may not be possible for the individual to know what has been published in his field of specialization. The library has to strive to repackage the material that is received in the library in the form of reviews, digests, abstracts and databases to enhance library utilization and improve readership. Also, in view of the rapid developments in information technologies, the role of a librarian is not like what it used to be a few decades ago. Satellite communication systems, networking, Internet and intellectual property rights have all made the library environment more complex. Further, the budgetary constraints, inadequate infrastructure, and falling standards in human resources are all compelling the librarian to change his attitude from a mere custodian of information to that of a facilitator. As the library is a service institution, there should be close interaction between the information providers, processors and users to enhance the effectiveness of any resource centre (Raju, 2000).

The National Institute of Rural Development (NIRD) is an apex research, training and consultancy organisation in the rural development sector. With the developments in the field of Information and Communication Technologies, the Centre on Rural Documentation (CORD) has gained further significance and metamorphosed into a specialized resource centre to fulfill its obligation as a one-stop location for information on rural development in India. The paper attempted to share the experiences and benefits by adopting such best practices.

The center conducted a learning programme in 1991, 1992 and 1998 on LURE. This programme provided a forum for the users of information and the library personnel to come together, to understand each other's way of dealing with information and how the information barriers can be overcome and what best practices are to be adopted to increase the utilization of the resources of the Library. The sessions offered a set of simple but effective steps to increase the library use with suggestions. These recommendations were taken seriously, as they were particularly innovative in the overall development of the library utilization as well as promotion of services. After LURE-II in 1993, there was marked improvement in the appreciation of library services. Non-book material like CD-ROMs, videos, and electronic journals have slowly started to show their presence. In the mid-90s the Internet opened gates to information sources worldwide, and made possible access to information from a remote location. As a result it has become more important to look into the problems of transforming a traditional library into an information clearinghouse. The LURE III programme was made into a National Workshop inviting papers from all over India on various themes such as library utilisation; techniques of readership enhancement; conducting user studies; evaluation of library services; Internet and changing role of the librarian etc. (NIRD, 1998).

2. LURE - I

In the first workshop on LURE in 1991 several issues were brought up such as the following.

2.1. Issues for consideration

As the reader is reluctant to come to the library, it may be necessary that the library has to go to the reader. Naturally, that situation will determine the kind of services that are planned or envisaged to enhance the usage of the library. The issues that influence the usage hinge upon how the information needs are gauged and the methods that are adopted to identify those needs. Some of the other major issues identified are:

- Focus of the parent organizations
- Information collection, collation and dissemination
- Information search strategies followed
- Information barriers

2.2. Focus of parent organisation

In a special library, the focus of the parent organization should become the concern of the librarian. He should make special attempts to keep track of the activities of the faculty or the staff of the organization and accordingly plan the procurement of material and design appropriate information products.

2.3. Information collection, collation and dissemination

Acquisition has a bearing on the satisfaction of any expressed need. Balanced acquisition, keeping in view the needs of the staff would enhance its utilization. Though the Internet may come to the rescue of the librarian, where the "buy by wire" would enable him to expedite the procurement process, access to the Internet was yet a big problem and not that widespread at that time. Also, the traditional classification and cataloguing procedures were yet to be modernized by using the computer techniques. To educate the readers, personal guidance along with instructional manuals were found to be more helpful. This display of literature in attractive ways at different points in the library would provide more browsing opportunities to the readers.

2.4. Information search

As the library is recognized as one of the major options for a search for information, readers come to the library because they would like to supplement their existing information. Then it is up to the library to convert these potential users to regular users. The information search mechanisms available and strategies to be adopted should not create 'library anxiety' and should become user-friendly. Added to this, the library should assure the readers that it has other sources of information for exploitation, by resorting to interlibrary cooperation or networking.

2.5. Information barriers

Finally, to add to the travails of the reader, there are several information barriers to cope with. They are of different kinds: physical (non-conducive atmosphere or limited space or inadequate lighting etc.), administrative (library procedures, organisational constraints), economic barriers (like lack of funds), structural barriers (like the arrangement of books in a given library or its disorganised material), behavioural patterns (unhelpful attitude of library staff, or not so helpful behaviour of users) are some of the known barriers which could be overcome with a little more attention and patience and patronage of those concerned. When the library's motto is service, the staff of the library should be sufficiently educated and motivated to develop personal rapport with the users. It is also essential to know thoroughly what they have got in library stock to explain to readers.

The workshop offered a set of simple but effective steps to increase the library use with suggestions like involvement of users in procurement of literature, client based services, etc. The other major recommendations include: (a) The book selection and deacquisition are both important and modalities like participatory practices have to be followed; (b) User education and user services have to be frequently conducted by the library to improve the interaction between users and the library personnel; (c) A brochure on the library highlighting the library collection, cataloging and classification system followed and the services offered would be more useful; (d) Immediate computerization of all activities of library; (e) Creation of new services like abstracting, reference and making digests on specific topics etc., (f) Augmentation of facilities for document supply and other physical facilities like proper sign boards, stools to reach higher shelves, etc., and (g) Strengthening of the resource sharing at the local level.

These recommendations were taken seriously as they were particularly important in the overall development of the library utilization. Fortunately, most of the suggestions would be implemented with a telling effect on the positive response of the readers.

3. LURE - II

For any library's development and for better utilisation of its resources automation of the library operations is the key. The automation of library using LIBSYS software developed by an Indian firm, was taken up in 1992 and the total collection of over 50,000 books and an equal number of journal articles that were being indexed from 1970 onwards was made available as a database. At that time NIRD became one of the first few special libraries that was fully automated in Hyderabad.

After a gap of nearly two years, CORD thought of again reviewing the library utilization with the completion of library automation. Accordingly, in 1993 a second programme on LURE was conducted. This time with a difference. The impetus came from the management of parent organization. There was a constant refrain from the management that with automation is there any improvement in the utilization of library resources? How many faculty are visiting the library? What is the ratio between faculty and participants of various training programmes that visit the library? What special arrangements were made to familiarize the participants with the new automation etc., These were a few of the questions that were bothering the management. Also, with computerization of library procedures, a new barrier is likely to be perceived by the users. Such 'Automation anxiety' may have to be taken into consideration in designing training programmes on library initiation. Accordingly, the participants were chosen from not only the users of the library but also the participants of the then running courses, besides other librarians of neighboring institutions.

The programme was conducted in 3 sessions. In these sessions several papers based on cases illustrating the circulation facility, visitors register, pattern of usage of library on different dates and use of various information products of CORD were presented. These studies provided a picture of the pattern of library usage after the automation which appeared to be promising and provided the guidance as to how to increase awareness and access to information. Several suggestions emerged based on the discussions and some of which are as follows:

- Information products
  - o The coverage of indexing and abstracting services done through CORD Index and CORD Abstracts is found to be satisfactory. However, emphasis may have to be given to the immediate interest of the faculty members depending on their research and training programmes.
  - o The journals that are covered in CORD Alerts may have to be displayed at a designed place for their immediate location and identification of articles given in the service.
- Maintenance
  - o Upkeep and maintenance of various sections will provide the necessary incentive for the users to browse.
  - o Library staff should be trained and motivated to assist the readers.

- User studies
  - Though the faculty members are patronising the library, there is a scope for improvement.
  - Visitors to the Library are not always recording their visits in the prescribed register and so it did not reflect the total visits made by the academic staff in comparison with nonacademic staff. A strict vigil on the visitors register may have to be maintained to satisfy the management.

The other major recommendations include (a) promotion of library with a professional image is essential; (b) Library staff should be trained in inter-personnel communication skills; (c) There is a need to display current journals in more attractive and useful manner like displaying latest issues at a prominent place, rearranging of primary journals in alphabetical sequence, etc., (d) NIRD publications should be displayed prominently for outside visitors. (e) A marketing approach to its library and information products is essential. For this purpose Library counters and surrounding areas should be used for display of not only for acquired publications but also NIRD publications. (f) There are about 3000 participants in a year coming to NIRD to participate in the training programmes, who should be given orientation tour to the library for better appreciation of the resources. Also, a session on information resources, and information management relevant to the theme of any course wherever possible should be arranged apart from display of the publications pertaining to the training programme. (g) A faculty directory, user manual, training of staff on information technology etc., are other suggestions that emerged from the programme.

After LURE-II in 1993 there was marked improvement in the appreciation of library services, the physical facilities and the environment in the library. Non-book material like CD-ROMS, videos, electronic journal have slowly started to show their presence. In the mid 90s internet opened gates to the Information sources world wide, and made possible access to information from a remote location. As a result it has become more important to look into the problems of transforming a traditional library into an information clearinghouse.

4. LURE - III

Against this backdrop a third LURE programme was conducted in the year 1998 after a gap of 5 years. This learning programme was made into a National Workshop inviting papers from all over India on various themes such as library utilisation; techniques of readership enhancement; evaluation of library services; internet and changing role of the librarian etc. (NIRD, 1998).

Participants from several parts of the country made their presentations based on their own back-home experience in user education and identification of user needs. This workshop revealed various kinds of experiments that are on-going in several parts of the country by innovative librarians and demystifying the Internet for the librarian and the user. Information search in the Internet era has totally changed the way the readers look for information. Searching the Internet should become a matter of routine in any special library, to make the expression "Internet is Librarianship" truly applicable. Some of the other major recommendations of the workshop were:

- Continuous study of user needs
- Development of communication skills of the library personnel
- Role of parent organization in recognising the contribution of their libraries and supporting their activity.
- Design and update of user manual in the fast changing information technology environment.
- Change of attitude of librarians to the market driven economy and interact with the users more closely and make users appreciate the library services.
- A thematic approach to all the library services, i.e., the information products of the library like CORD INDEX, CORD ABSTRACTS should follow the themes identified for the research and training of the institute.
- The Selective Dissemination of Information (SDI) service can perhaps be concentrated on a faculty or a discipline at a time. Once a faculty is studied for a period of 6 months or so as a focussed group the impact on the group and its activities can perhaps be quantitatively measured.

5. Project CLIC

As a follow-up to the learning programme, CORD had initiated a project called "Computerized Library and Information Clearinghouse" (CLIC) in June 1998. Earlier CORD was declared as a clearinghouse of information for Rural Development sector. As a result a continuous database build-up was taken up keeping in view various information needs of not only the faculty of NIRD but also the development community consisting of policy makers, planners, researchers, trainers and various other functionaries at different levels operating throughout the country. Data collection and dissemination being the major activity under the project, it was decided to first collect the data on institutions, individuals and programmes of rural development that are operating at various levels. Further, to strengthen the database, Internet resources were also to be exploited. As many of the institutions in India are beginning to have their web sites, if we are able to identify the URLs of the institutions, much of the information about the institutions, their research and training programmes, publications, achievements and profiles of individuals working in these institutions could be obtained and a virtual library could be created. (Raju, 2002). Thus searching internet resources would be very crucial for database build-up.

Thus a new era emerged where information driven activities gained importance which will hopefully energize the users as well as information specialists to come together and work for the better utilization of information following the best practices in information dissemination.

6. Results

The adoption of best practices resulted in the following:

- Transformed from traditional library to high-tech library
- Designed and developed the digital resource base, i.e., Computerised Library and Information Clearinghouse (CLIC, available on www. nird.org.in). It is an inhouse unit for selection, acquisition, processing and retrieving of data/information in an electronic version in a specific field of activity relating to the mission of NIRD.
- Bibliographies/abstracts and other relevant material browsed from library database. CDs, Internet, etc. relating to the training programmes (180 programmes in a year) are being provided by the library to the faculty to improve the quality of training material. This service was well received and appreciated by the faculty
- Open Discussion and Personal Interaction facilitated to establish good rapport between library staff and users
- Identified as one stop location and recognized as one of the best libraries in the field of rural development in South Asia
- Library staff are nominated as a member in the review committee on Training programmes

- The library is recognized as a faculty and encouraged to conduct research and training programmes (3 programmes in a year) in Information Science
- Improved the quality of Information products like CORD Alerts, CORD Index and Abstract based on the evaluation studies conducted periodically
- Marketing the services through Institutional membership

6.1. Best practices

To handle the above tasks, the librarian has to be proficient in devising ways of social marketing, conceiving and designing appropriate information products and luring the readers to the library in order to enhance the readership. He has to truly act as a facilitator and a total quality conscious person, keeping in view the user needs to continuously better the best practices. The best practices are those which will reduce the library anxiety and invite readers to come and use the library services optimally.

In the dissemination of information, display makes a very important contribution in improving awareness and access to the material and it will also add to the beautification to the library. Similarly display of current journals in a more attractive manner in a prominent place will enhance their utilisation. A marketing approach to the library and library products is essential. The library counter area and surrounding areas should be used for attractive display. Also, a users' manual should be prepared delineating different areas of the library, which material is where and how the information technology environment is made user-friendly and what kind of thematic approaches to the library services were followed, what a user can derive out of automation together with highlights of library practices, etc.The support of the parent organisation and the user community in recognising the contribution of the libraries goes a long way in sustaining the best practices and makes the library a place to visit for a pleasant reading experience.

7. Conclusion

The best practices that are to be adopted in any library are basically to take into consideration the user needs. As the needs vary from time to time based on the activities that are taken up by the users, a periodical assessment of user needs is essential. Also, it would be essential to keep good relations with support departments such as administration, the computer centre, information and communication and media services to project the library activities properly as well as to support its services internally (Barlow et al., 2000).

The best practices are those which will reduce the library anxiety and invite readers to come to the library. The impact of information technology, networking with the local libraries, information brokerage, communication and feedback are all to be taken into consideration for creating intellectual infrastructure. Also, as the great libraries of the future are not those with great collections but those with great staff, knowledge must be rediscovered in the library before it is used (Lowry, 1991). The trained and dedicated librarian would act as an intermediary in this rediscovery process.

For this purpose, the librarian has to be proficient in devising ways of social marketing, conceiving and designing appropriate information products and luring the readers to the library in order to enhance the readership. He has to truly act as a facilitator and a total quality conscious person, keeping in view the user needs to continuously better the best practices.

References

1   Barlow, J. Frame and Hayes-Farmer, N. (2000). Disseminating good practice: The role of internal learning and teaching conference. Innovation in Education and Training International, 37 (4).

2   Lowry, C.B. (1991). Information Technologies and Transformation of Libraries and Librarianship: A changing world. New York, Howarth.

3   Raju, K.A. (1991). Issue paper for the Workshop on LURE, Hyderabad, September 30, 1991, National Institute of Rural Development.

4   Raju, K.A. (2000). A different mind-set in needed for modern day librarians. Paper presented at the 'workshop on Application of Information Technologies in Libraries' held at Agricultural University, Hyderabad, 7 March, 2002.

5   Sebaratnam, J.S. (1995). Transforming libraries to support change and growth: Meeting the challenges of the 21st Century in Networking as the future of libraries: Managing intellectual record, an International Conference, 19-21, April, 1995, London, University of Bath.

6   Vavrek, Bernard (1995). Rural information needs and the role of public library. Library Trends, 44 (1), 21-48.

7   Wormell, Irene (1997). The new information professional in library and information science: Parameters and perspectives.

From Australia to China Online: Delivery of Online Library Services to Off-Shore Students in China

Sharon Karasmanis
La Trobe University Library, Victoria, Australia

Abstract

The La Trobe University Library provides library services to 28,550 academic staff, undergraduate and postgraduate students located in campuses and research centres in Melbourne and regional Victoria; as well as remote off-campus students throughout Australia; and off-shore students predominantly in South-East Asia. The University provides online library support to all patrons to support teaching, learning and research. In 2005, the University enrolled 1,125 students in off-shore programs where the teaching was carried out in the students' home country. Although the University provides face-to-face teaching in block mode, the Library provides all services to off-shore students online.

This paper describes the range of services available to off-shore students, with emphasis on students in Kunming in China, and Ho Chi Minh City and Hanoi in Vietnam. The range of online services includes training, catalogue and database searching, document delivery, reference service and online help. The comprehensive training options include a text based web tutorial for database searching, an online audio/video tutorial for document delivery, a website tailored for off-shore students, and online help via email. An analysis of online help requests received in 2005-2006 is presented.

The problems of delivering library services remotely are discussed: particularly the complexities of online access, bandwidth problems, and student awareness and interpretation of available services. Current and long-term solutions are discussed, as well as proposals for future streamlining and enhancement of service delivery for all off-shore students.

1. Introduction

La Trobe University was established in 1967 and currently provides higher education to 27,194 students across the main campus at Bundoora; the City Campus in Melbourne; regional campuses at Bendigo, Albury/Wodonga, Shepparton, Beechworth, Mt Buller and Mildura; major off site research centres; hospital clinical schools and health centres, and remote off campus and off-shore students.

The mission of the University is pursued within the context of a number of defining features. Two of the relevant features are:

- Provide teaching, scholarship, research and professional practice in specified traditional/basic and vocational/professional fields of study.

- Maintain a strong international profile encompassing opportunities for local students and staff and the export of higher education and training services.

La Trobe University operates within a framework, and under the guidelines of the Australian Government and the Australian Vice Chancellors Committee, in the provision of off-shore programs. Requirements that are relevant to the provision of Library services as outlined in the La Trobe University External Programs manual are to:

- Comply with the AVCC Code of Practice and Guidelines for Australian Universities. Included in the guidelines is reference to services and facilities for off-shore students, including library resources at a level equivalent to the learning environment in the host country (AVCC 2005, p. 14).

- Comply with the Australian Universities Quality Agency guidelines, including integration of library services into the overall management of off-shore activities.

- Comply with Australian Quality Framework Guidelines.

- Comply with the Council of Australian University Libraries (CAUL, 2005) Principles for Library Services to Off-shore Students. This document sets out principles and guidelines for provision of core library services, including authentication for remote access to information resources.

One of the definitions outlined and emphasised in the La Trobe University External Programs Manual is Comparable Quality (2004, p. 4). La Trobe University uses this term as a way of linking the standards and provision of external and on campus programs and support services. This term enables regional, cultural and environmental differences - which will have influence on programs and program delivery, and the educational experience of students - to be recognised. In consideration of the relevant guidelines, the Library aims to provide comparable services for all off-shore students.

The total enrolments for international students in 2005 numbered 4,731 —of this number 3,606 study on campus, and 1,125 students were enrolled in off-shore programs, where teaching is delivered online, or in block mode on-site in the students' home country. Undergraduate and postgraduate courses encompass both coursework and research. Off-shore teaching is carried out in China, Vietnam, Cambodia, Mongolia, Singapore, Hong Kong, Japan, Bhutan, Thailand and France.

This paper will focus on delivery of online library services to China, Vietnam and Cambodia. These students comprise one third of the total students enrolled in off-shore programs. The School of Educational Studies at the Bundoora campus teaches and supervises Doctor of Education, Master of Applied Linguistics, and Master of Applied Linguistics by Research students. The courses are conducted in Kunming PR China, in partnership with Yunnan Normal University, and Ho Chi Minh City and Hanoi in Vietnam, in partnership with Vietnam National University. Further information is available from the School of Educational Studies' web page: http://www.latrobe.edu.au/educationalstudies/offshore-programs.htm.

The off-shore undergraduate program in Cambodia is conducted by the School of Human Biosciences, Department of Podiatry, as a Bachelor of Prosthetics and Orthotics. The teaching is conducted in partnership with the Cambodian School of Prosthetics and Orthotics.

2. History

The University first commenced teaching off-shore programs in Vietnam in 1996, in China in 2000, and more recently in Cambodia in 2005.

Initially, the Library's primary support role was document delivery and reference services. Document Delivery Services supplied photocopies of journal articles or book chapters from the Library's collections, and also provided documents through interlibrary services, and posted to the student. Book loans were not available to off-shore students. As the online environment expanded and more students gained local access to personal computers, the Library was able to capitalise on the emerging technology to enhance services for students. The next improvement in document delivery services was an online form, available from the Library home page, easy and convenient to use, however students were still limited by postal delivery. The last three years have seen expansion of the Library's full text electronic journal collection. This enabled document delivery staff to trial transmission of electronic delivery of documents to students as PDF email attachments.

In 2004, the Library introduced technology to manage the document delivery function via a web-based customer interface. Students can search, order and track requests, and download articles from a document store.

Postgraduate research students require comprehensive library services — online database access, assistance with literature searching, subject specialist support, copying service from the Library's collections, and copy via interlibrary document delivery. To give an indication of the volume of requesting activity, the number of requests received from off-shore students in 2005 was 2,068, comprising copies from the local collections and interlibrary copies.

3. Available Services

- **Information for Off-shore Students** web page provides a step-by-step guide to the Library's services: http://www.lib.latrobe.edu.au/document-delivery/offshore-help.php.

- **Online tutorials** provide guidance with database searching: http://www.lib.latrobe.edu.au/libskills/.

- **Online Databases** are available via authentication for students to search off-shore: http://www.lib.latrobe.edu.au/databases/index.php Databases provide citations, abstracts and some full-text journal articles for immediate download.

- **Reference Support** including help with literature searches is available from subject specialist librarians.

- **Document Delivery Services** provide online delivery of journal articles, book chapters, conference papers and reports, from the La Trobe University Library collections. No limits are imposed on the number of articles the students are able to request: http://www.lib.latrobe.edu.au/document-delivery/.

- **Interlibrary Document Delivery** provides online delivery of journal articles, chapters, conference papers, reports and theses not available within the La Trobe collections. Documents are sourced from within

Australia and overseas for eligible postgraduate students. There is a limit of 100 requests per year for Masters and PhD students, and no charge for this service.

- **Online audio/video tutorial** guides the students through the document delivery system. Instructions for downloading the viewing software are available on the web page: http://www.lib.latrobe.edu.au/document-delivery/user-guides.php.

- **Document Delivery User Guide** can be downloaded from the above link.

- **Online help** is available from the Document Delivery web page including:

  o Document Viewing Instructions

  o Frequently Asked Questions

  o Online Help Form—assistance is also available by email, and questions are answered as soon as possible, but within 24 hours on business days.

4. Marketing the Services

How are the students made aware of what services are available, and how do they organise access when their only link to the Library is by email? It can be quite challenging for students to understand and interpret online Library services, whether the student is on campus, off campus or off-shore. Viggiano (2004, p. 38) notes that on campus students engage in the library experience as if they were distance learners, and the line between distance and not distance students becomes very blurred. However, unlike on campus students, the only contact between off-shore students and the Library is by email.

This presents both opportunities and challenges for the Library, to adapt traditional services into the online environment, tailor existing online products to meet specific needs, and ensure that remote off-shore students receive comparable services to support their learning needs. Operating a customer-oriented library service for off-shore students requires a clear understanding of the challenges faced by users when accessing online information resources and services. Debowski (2000, p. 177) discusses the need to focus more effectively on training users in information retrieval, increasing electronic support, and raising the profile of electronic resources through creative marketing approaches. Librarians need to be attuned to the information needs and usage patterns of the 'Hidden User'.

When determining and marketing services, the Library needs to be aware of geographic factors and lifestyles of the students (Fisk 2004, p. 84). Many students travel long distances to teaching centres, work and family commitments are constant pressures for students, and access to high-speed Internet connections can be challenging.

To reach out to students, the Library has adopted a creative multi-pronged approach with a combination of tailored web page information, online tutorials, and email assistance from subject specialist librarians and document delivery staff.

5. Marketing Tools

The primary marketing tool is the Library home page. Debowski (2000, p. 176) talks about the new class of library user—the *Hidden User*—and the important issue of library services becoming *increasingly marginalised and hidden*. The utmost consideration has been applied in development of the Library home page, in particular the Document Delivery web page. Students link to Document Delivery from the Library home page, the link sits above the *fold* (Welch 2005, p. 226) making it visible on a typical monitor screen without the need to scroll. It is critical that clients are able to locate and access this web page 24 hours a day, and that the online assistance, when required, is simple, intuitive and customer-friendly. As well as displaying information resources to students, the Library home page is used as an important communication tool to advise students of new information resources, and any pertinent administrative changes.

Figure 1. La Trobe University Library

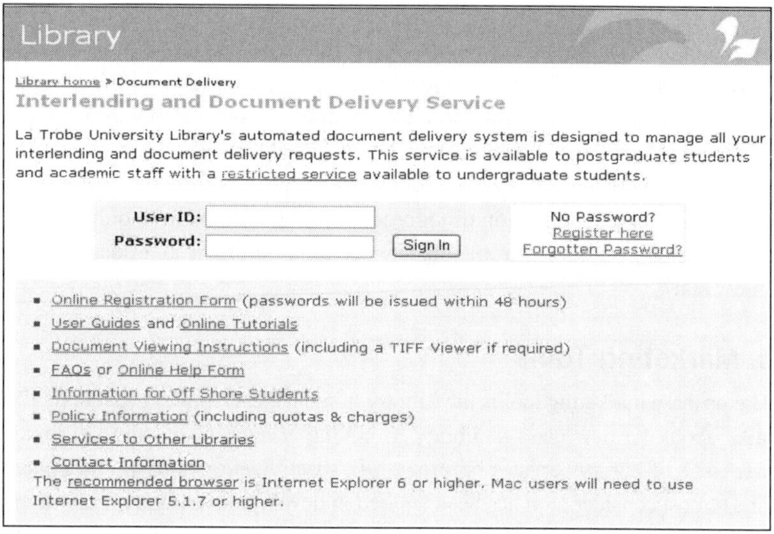

Figure 2. Interlending and Document Delivery Service

Information for Off-Shore students is a separate web page, tailored specifically to introduce students to the necessary online Library services. This systematic approach guides the students through the entire process of searching for information on a topic, requesting a literature search, identifying relevant resources, requesting materials, and downloading requested documents.

The teaching staff form a vital link in connecting students with Library services. The students are shown how to register online for document delivery services, thereby providing the first contact with the Library.

A welcome email to the student from the Library confirms the user identification number and password, a link to the Document Delivery Service, a link to the Information for Offshore Students web page, and other relevant information about online library services. (See Appendix 1 – Offshore Registration Confirmation).

A separate email to the student explains the database login process. (See Appendix II – Access to La Trobe Databases)

Library

Library home > Document Delivery > Information for Off Shore Students
Information for Off Shore Students

If you live outside Australia and you are studying, researching or being taught by La Trobe University staff, or by staff employed by, or employed in consultation with La Trobe University, you are eligible for *Off Shore Student Services*.

1. Register with Interlending and Document Delivery Service

- this can be done online and you will receive an email to confirm your registration;
- this email will provide you with information about accessing the Library's online databases
- and will also provide you with your User ID and Password to request journal articles, chapters etc via Interlending and Document Delivery Services.

2. To find information on your topic

- search the Library's online Databases
- tutorials to help with database searching are available, such as Library Skills Online
- you can also request help searching the databases.

3. To request journal articles, chapters etc

- login with your UserID and Password to the Interlending and Document Delivery Service

- a user guide and online tutorial are availabe to help you
- **Undergraduate students** – only eligible for copies from La Trobe University Library collections
- **Postgraduate students** – eligible for copies from La Trobe University Library collections and copies from external libraries as well.

4. Other services available include:

- guides to subject resources
- general online help with computer and technical problems, using the catalogue and other searching and information management tools
- assistance with literature searches by subject librarians at Bundoora and Bendigo.

Please note that book loans, including loans from other libraries, are not available to off shore students.

Figure 3. Information for Off-shore Students

6. Use of Online Library Services

6.1. Kunming, China

Kunming, capital of Yunnan Province, is located in southern China, 1092 kilometres west of Guangzhou, China's third largest city. With a population of 3.89 million people, the city is the political, economic and cultural centre of Yunnan, and the provincial centre for transport, science and technology. Although there are eight universities in Kunming, La Trobe University off-shore students are not eligible to access local academic libraries (Gao, 2006) and rely totally on online library support. The students in Kunming comprise masters by coursework and research, and PhD by research in the School of Educational Studies. The requests for documents cover all areas of education and applied linguistics—journal articles, book chapters, conference papers, reports, theses and ERIC (Education Resources Information Center) documents.

6.2. Ho Chi Minh City and Hanoi, Vietnam

Hanoi, the capital of Vietnam, in the north of the country is 1150 kilometres from Ho Chi Minh City in the south of Vietnam. The students travel long distances to attend classes in Vietnam from the far north, to Pleiku in the central highlands, the coastal area of Haiphong and from the south near the Cambodian border. The students in Vietnam do not have access to local library sources and rely totally on online library support. These students also study the same courses as the students in Kunming, and require the same mix of materials.

6.3. Cambodia

This group of undergraduate students enrolled in March 2006 in the Bachelor of Prosthetics and Orthotics course. The primary learning mode of this course is web-based with some face-to-face teaching, in partnership with the Cambodian School of Prosthetics and Orthotics. Students live in Phnom Penh for the duration of the course, but come from rural areas of Sri Lanka, Pakistan, Laos and Cambodia. These students have very limited access to local academic libraries and rely on online library support.

7. How Does the Library Client Access the Services?

7.1. Databases

Remote database access is available via a login using the student number and Library PIN (Personal Identification Number). The student is given guidance to the relevant databases by the teaching staff, and help with searching is available using text based online tutorials. Assistance with literature searching is available from subject specialist librarians.

7.2. Document delivery services

Document Delivery Services are accessible via a user identification (student number) and password, emailed to the student on registration for Library services.

7.3. Assistance

An online help form, or email is available for assistance with any aspect of database searching, document delivery access and services, and technical support.

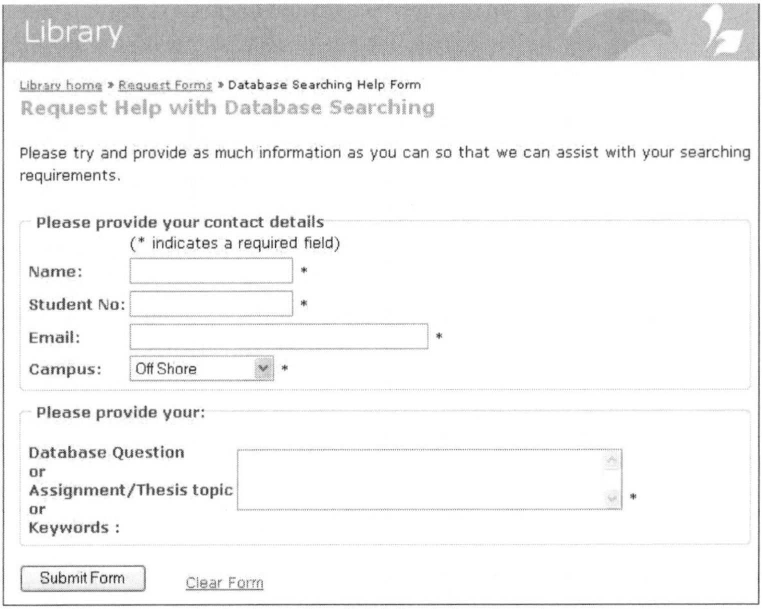

Figure 4. Request Help with Database Searching

8. Analysis of Online Help

One of the most effective tools in developing marketing applications is the analysis of feedback from the services offered; either from formal surveys or online requests for assistance, and targeting solutions to effectively address the problems. All requests for help from off-shore students are received as a direct email or an email generated from the Online Help form. A sample of 250 emails during the period 2005-2006 were collated and analysed, with four areas of need identified:

8.1. General enquiries

- General questions regarding the services available, progress reports for outstanding materials, management of document formats, damaged documents, passwords and university enrolment queries.

- Requests for information about, and access to the Library's databases including requests for PINs.

- Interpretation and understanding of the range of services available.

8.2. Document delivery system enquiries

- Questions related to the process of requesting documents, and understanding the management of the user account within the Document Delivery System. This web-based portal using the OCLC PICA VDX software provides management of the life cycle of a request—from end user requesting to desktop delivery. The system manages all requests regardless of the location of the materials - requests are supplied from the local collections or from an external library supplier. Whilst the system was able to improve document delivery services to the Library's clients, students both on and off campus faced operational challenges. One of the features of the system is the ability to search multiple catalogues for book or journal titles and create requests from the record retrieved. This feature can create confusion for students as the catalogue search feature simulates a database search. With consistent support from document delivery staff, offshore students are systematically guided through the most efficient methods of managing requests within the system.

8.3. Reference enquiries

- Requests for literature searches, citation assistance, access to theses, and assistance with database searching. Other problems related to formulating search strategies, retrieval process, evaluation and interpretation of search results and understanding the difference between full text databases, and databases that only held abstracts. Boyd-Byrnes (2005, p. 219) identifies several areas of difficulty that students experience through recent interviews and case studies, and discusses possible solutions. Some of the challenges include technological glitches, procedural problems, conceptual or cognitive issues and personal obstacles.

- Requests for information regarding individual monographs, contents pages and requests for chapters to be scanned, this relates to the catalogue search feature of the document delivery system as described on the previous page.

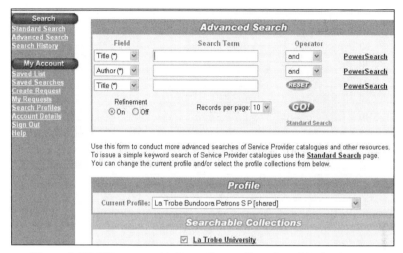

Figure 5. VDX Document Delivery System Search and Order Screen

8.4. Technical enquiries

- Approximately 40% of technical enquiries related to document download. Documents are delivered in either TIFF or PDF format. Although PDF files are easier to download and view, TIFF documents require a specific viewer. Instructions to download the viewing software are provided on the web page: http://www.lib.latrobe.edu. au/document-delivery/view-documents.php.

- Login problems included registration expiry and password problems.

- Email access relating to these problems was addressed by encouraging the use of more robust web-based email accounts.

- Databases access and authentication, including PIN numbers. Some of these problems resulted from the delay between the student's enrolment and subsequent authentication from the University student database.

- In some remote areas, bandwidth can be a problem, as it limits access to online databases, and it can be time consuming to download and view documents.

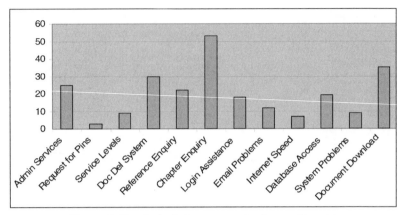

Figure 6. Graph depicting type and volume of inquiries

9. Solutions

Analysis of the email requests for assistance provided an opportunity to target problem areas and implement solutions to enhance the service. The above chart highlights areas of most need. As well as forward planning to enhance the services offered, it is necessary to confront each issue individually and provide simple and efficient solutions, which fall within the capacity of the Library to implement and are easy for the student to utilise. Problems are discussed in order of highest need.

9.1. Chapter enquiry

Students use the Document Delivery system to search the catalogues and create requests for monographs. In response to these requests, staff scan contents pages, and the student selects a chapter for electronic delivery. This is inefficient for staff, and creates unnecessary delays for the student. A systematic and structured database search would retrieve a more efficient search result. Gao (2006) conducted surveys with off-shore students in Kunming in 2005 and notes the traditional Chinese teaching style where textbooks were heavily used as the main source of teaching and as a learning tool. Off-shore students may not be alone in this approach. However, on shore students have the benefit of on site training and assistance, whereas the off-shore student relies on the teaching staff and online library support. Whilst teaching staff encourage students to use the databases for information retrieval, there are other opportunities to market the database services more prominently to off-shore students. Solutions now implemented include:

- An email sent to the student explaining how to access the databases.
- Information on the web page rearranged to position database searching more prominently, and titled *To find information on your topic.*
- A link from this web page to the online tutorial for database searching.
- Database searching and document delivery services now appear as separate entities on the web page and in a logical order.
- *Online Help* is clearly identified, and follow up support for assistance is provided as quickly as possible.

9.2. Document download

This issue presents difficulties for some students, regardless of geographic boundaries—on campus, off campus or off-shore. Whilst students on and off campus can contact the Library for assistance, it is more difficult to provide assistance by email. Solutions implemented to assist with document download include:

- Email assistance given a high priority by Library staff.
- An audio/video online tutorial provided.
- A user guide in PDF format available to download.
- Alternative delivery of documents provided if required.
- Targeted PDF delivery for offshore students.

9.3. Document delivery system

Enquiries about access and functionality of the system require immediate attention. Solutions implemented to assist with online training include:

- Email assistance given a high priority by Library staff.
- An audio/video online tutorial and user guide.

9.4. Reference enquiry

Enquiries are received by document delivery staff, and then referred to subject specialist librarians for investigation. Solutions implemented include:

- An online form titled *Help with Database Searching.*
- Links to Subject Specialist Librarians from the Off-shore web page.
- Links to Subject Resources from the Off-shore web page.

Other issues identified in the analysis are investigated with high priority by staff in the document delivery area. Solutions implemented include:

- Communication with teaching staff.
- Frequently Asked Questions link on the Document Delivery web page.
- An Online Help form and email contact.
- Policy Information provided.
- Information for Off-shore Students link.

10. Human Face of the Library

One of the challenges facing off-shore students is the absence of the Reference Desk, or the Human Face of the Library. Students on and off campus have a range of contact options when requiring assistance, whilst off-shore students must rely on email for communication and assistance. It is important that all users of the Library perceive a personal service connection with the Library. In the absence of a face-to-face reference interview, staff need to rely on written communication from the off-shore student, to negotiate the reference question. Without non-verbal clues such as facial expressions, body language and tone of voice, it may need several exchanges of emails to determine the exact nature of the enquiry (Gandhi, 2003 p. 143). Furthermore the emails need to be welcoming and warm to encourage confidence in the student in an effort to simulate the reference interview. Debowski (2000, p. 279) notes the need to maintain a sense of 'person' in the information service. Radcliffe (1995, p. 497) notes interpersonal connections between the clients and service providers are critical to the long-term relationship between these parties. As well as the Online Help form offered by Document Delivery Services, the Library provides reference assistance to all clients via the Ask Us, Tell Us service, available on the Library home page.

11. Challenges and Opportunities!

Off-shore students experience many of the same problems as students studying on campus. The changing environment between the library and the library client, and the associated complexities of online access, interaction, and service delivery all add to challenges for the Library and the student. The identification of the audience and purpose, and the assumptions of the students' level of technical and or academic knowledge, is another important factor when marketing online library services (Lee and Burrell 2004, p. 21). Debowski (2000, p. 179) discusses the ongoing issue of the difficulty that libraries face in assisting users to become information literate. Schmidt (Schmidt, 2000) notes that students often bookmark specific pages on the web page rather than entering via the home page, therefore communication opportunities may be missed. The pace of technological development in libraries has enabled sophisticated online systems to develop in pursuit of more flexible methods of information delivery. The challenge for librarians is to create a happy medium where all students can benefit from these emerging systems with confidence. The main challenges to be addressed are:

- Continuous improvement in delivery of online training.
- Development of diagnostic services to evaluate searching skills.
- Development of user skills and competencies with online reference support.
- Delivery of a tailored online information literacy program.
- Streamline document delivery requesting for students. Students will be able to create requests for articles directly from a database search result. This feature will be available later in 2006.
- Continue to provide timely and efficient support by email.

12. Conclusion

The sophistication of online library resources is matched by the challenges for the students to master these applications. Although dedicated staff commit to continuous improvement in library services, on and off campus students are still required to have an advanced level of efficiency in using online resources. From a personal home computer, an Internet café, workplace or university, students have a range of challenges. These include navigation of the library web site, including interpretation of Library services and privileges. Understanding which databases are relevant, and searching efficiently and effectively within the databases and subject resources. One of the most difficult concepts for students to address is the formulation of search queries. Although the Library provides online tutorials, without face-to-face instruction, assistance with database searching will always be necessary. Students are required to understand the authentication, navigation and access to full text journals, including the differences between full text and abstract only databases. The Document Delivery Service requires understanding, using the search and order process versus creating requests—tracking, downloading viewing software, and accessing and viewing documents.

It has been challenging and satisfying promoting online Library services to remote off-shore students. The students are diligent, patient and enthusiastic whilst learning about access to online information resources. All efforts have been made to ensure the web page is welcoming, information is displayed in a logical order, and online help is positioned to ensure ease of communication with the Library. The growth of off campus and off-shore students has compelled the Library to change the way services are provided, and the way in which these services are marketed to students. Off-shore students have unique needs, and the development of online Library services for these students has assisted on campus students as well. By seizing the opportunities and challenges in online delivery of services to remote students, the Library has been able to more clearly define and improve services for all students.

Acknowledgements

The author would like to thank staff from the Library for their assistance: staff in the Document Delivery section for their support, patience, and their cheerful and tireless support of off-shore students, and Jan Finnin for assistance with construction of the web pages. The author would like to acknowledge useful discussion with Dr Lloyd Holliday and Dr Howard Nicholas from the School of Educational Studies at La Trobe University, Wesley Pryor from the National Centre for Prosthetics and Orthotics at La Trobe University, and Lily Gao, PhD candidate, Charles Sturt University, N.S.W.

References

1   Boyd-Byrnes, Mary Kate & Rosenthal, Marilyn 2005. 'Remote access revisited: disintermediation and its discontents', *The Journal of academic librarianship*, vol.31, no.3, pp. 216-224. (Accessed: 2006, 28 May)

2   Debowski, Shelda 2000. 'The Hidden user: providing an effective service to users of electronic information sources', *OCLC Systems & Services,* vol.16, no.4, pp. 175-180. (Accessed: 2005, 15 December)

3   Feeney, Mary 2004. 'Centralizing information about library services and resources: delivering the library to users at any distance', *Internet reference services quarterly*, vol. 9, no.1/2, pp. 129-146. (Accessed: 2006, 7 May)

4   Fisk, James 2004, 'Got distance services? Marketing remote library services to distance learners' *Internet reference services quarterly,* vol. 9, no.1/2, pp. 77-91. (Accessed: 2006, 14 May)

5   Gandhi, Smiti 2003. 'Academic librarians and distance education: challenges and opportunities' *Reference & user services quarterly,* vol. 43, no.2, pp. 138-154. (Accessed: 2006, 14 April)

6   Gao, Lily X.L. 2006. 'Access and using Australian University Libraries' online resources and services – an offshore experience' paper presented at *VALA 2006: connecting with users,* 13th Biennial Conference. (Accessed: 2006, 14 April) http://www.valaconf.org/vala2006/ papers2006/52_Gao_Final.pdf.

7   La Trobe University 2004, *External Programs Manual – Associates Version 2.* Bundoora, Victoria.

8   Lee, Scott & Burrell, C. 2004. 'Introduction to streaming video for novices', *Library Hi Tech News,* vol. 21, no.2, pp. 20-24. (Accessed: 2005, 9 December)

9   Radcliffe, C.J. 1995. 'Interpersonal communication with library patrons' *RQ,* Vol. 34, no.4, pp. 497-506. (Accessed: 2006, 3 June)

10 Schmidt, Janine 2000. 'Unlocking the library: marketing library services: a case study approach' *AVCC Staff Development and Training Programme. University librarians in the 21st century: threats? Challenges? Opportunities?* Melbourne. Available: http://www.library.uq.edu.au. (Accessed: 2006, 31 May)

11 Viggiano, Rachel G. 2004. 'Online tutorials as instruction for distance students', *Internet Reference Services Quarterly,* vol. 9, no.1/2, pp. 37-54. (Accessed: 2006, 6 January)

12 Welch, Jeanie M. 2005. 'The Electronic welcome mat: the academic library web site as a marketing and public relations tool' *The Journal of academic librarianship,* vol. 31, no.3, pp. 225-228. (Accessed: 2006, 28 May)

Web Sites

1   AUQA – Australian Universities Quality Agency http://www.auqa.edu.au/ (Accessed 2006, 31st May)

2   AVCC Australian Vice-Chancellors Committee: the Council of Australia's university presidents 2005, *Provision of Education to International Students: Code of Practice and Guidelines for Australian Universities* (Accessed: 2006, 31 May) Available: http://www.avcc.edu.au/documents/ publications/CodeOfPracticeAndGuidelines2005.pdf

3   Council of Australian University Librarians 2004, CAUL Principles for Library Services to Offshore Students 2004 (Accessed: 2006, 14 May) Available: http://www.avcc.edu.au/ documents/publications/CodeOfPract iceAndGuidelines2005.pdf

4   La Trobe University, viewed 14 April, 2006 http://www.latrobe.edu.au/ about/mission. html

5   La Trobe University, viewed 16 April, 2006 http://www.latrobe.edu.au/ stats/pages/ statistics.html

6   Travel China Guide, viewed 7th May 2006 http://www.travelchinaguide. com/cityguides/ kunming.htm

Appendixes

Subject:	Access to La Trobe Databases

Dear Lily

I have created a pin for you to access the online databases. http://www.lib.latrobe.edu.au/

From the Library home page, click on *Databases* and select which database you require.
e.g. Linguistics and Language Behaviour Abstracts. Select *Other Borrower* and enter the following information:

Family Name: Chan

Student Number: 15276928

Pin Number: 1234

Help is available: http://www.lib.latrobe.edu.au/document-delivery/offshore-help.php
|
If you forget your Library pin, please email us to reset your pin.

Interlending and Document Delivery Services
Borchardt Library
La Trobe University
Bundoora 3086
Australia
Phone: 613 9479 2927
Fax: 613 9471 0993
Email: docds@latrobe.edu.au

Appendix I. Access to La Trobe Databases

Subject:	Document Delivery Registration

Dear Lily

Thankyou for your registration details.

User ID: 15276928

Password (case sensitive):   Chan

You may link to Interlending & Document Delivery from the Library home page via:
http://www.lib.latrobe.edu.au/document-delivery/
An Online Tutorial and User Guide for Offshore Students are available on the website for your assistance.

You may request as many documents as you need from the La Trobe University Library Collections, and 100 documents per year from other libraries. **This is a free service.**

Please also see our web page **Information for Offshore Students**
http://www.lib.latrobe.edu.au/document-delivery/offshore-help.php

Interlending and Document Delivery Services
Borchardt Library
La Trobe University
Bundoora 3086
Australia
Phone: 613 9479 2927
Fax: 613 9471 0993
Email: docds@latrobe.edu.au

Appendix II. Document Delivery Registration

Part III

Marketing Library Services
to the General Public

Globalization and Library Management: Practical Ideas for Effective Strategic Methods

Antonia Arahova and Sarantos Kapidakis

National Library of Greece – Ionio University

Abstract

Our paper includes a proposed model related to statistics according to the Greek reality. We demonstrate evaluation practices and mainly best-practice and "best-vision" strategy encouraging the improvement in the provision of library services not only in Greece but in a generally implemented framework. Greece is making a great effort to achieve a continuous improvement of the libraries' services as globalization is a reality and multilingual people from many different countries are staying in Greece and they demand high level electronic services. The paper aims to demystify marketing for librarians in our new multi-cultural world. Practical solutions are provided on how to implement a marketing strategy, with particular emphasis on the value of using electronic information resources.

1. Introduction

In an age where we need to compete among the myriad of Internet content providers and fight for the limited attention span of our library patrons, marketing and promotion of our services are paramount to our best well-being. Because of their heterogeneous clientele, age, nationality and language, libraries owe to themselves and to the public to satisfy the customers' needs. So, with the active collaboration with The Greek Ministry of Education and especially with The Greek Ministry of Interior Affairs, we gathered statistics, and attention is given to the following parameters:

- Promotion of Services
- Understanding Customers' Needs

- Community
- Profile Marketing Plan
- Marketing Audit
- Management Strategies

Realistic and measurable targets set should be subjected to an ongoing evaluation process as part of the marketing plan, and used to adjust or revise the marketing activities. Evaluations can be in the form of official measurement systems including financial accounting, computerized usage tracking, user satisfaction surveys, or the less structured methods of verbal or written feedback from users. As librarians we should be actively marketing and promoting our library services. We live in a global world that is changing rapidly and we are obliged to respect the particularities of our patrons, their needs adjusting in a right way our practices.

2. Globalization

Globalization in the twenty-first century is no longer just about translation and localization. Effective globalization requires an awareness of technologies and how they are adapted around the world. It also calls for the ability to differentiate products from competition that can originate anywhere in the world, from Austria to Zimbabwe. Even as new technologies provide emerging opportunities for companies looking to go global, they also disrupt our ability to conduct business in accustomed channels. Globalization is a term used to describe the changes in societies and the world economy that are the result of dramatically increased trade and cultural exchange.

Globalization is indeed a great and inevitable event if it is done on a fair and equal basis only. The Earth is an amazing place because of its diversity— culture, history, arts etc. Globalization is bringing changes we see around the world in economics, politics and government. It has an impact everywhere. To begin with, it is a question of transforming use value to exchange value —which is to turn what is not a commodity into one. National libraries have a tremendous use value. It is almost invaluable. But the exchange value is low. However, compared to many other areas—I am thinking of the schools, nursing and health care and communications sectors—libraries have a strong position among the citizens as a non-commercial activity. Their policy of aiming to collect all national printed publications remains intact, but they have had great difficulty in extending deposit to other forms of publication, including material available only online. Today international access is improving yearly as the catalogues of more and more significant libraries become accessible online and libraries come to take more seriously their obligation to supply books in their ownership to other libraries.

All libraries are affected by Information Technology. At the same time it both poses threats, particularly that of being bypassed in favour of direct access, and offers opportunities. The ultimate threat is non-existence, which some think is a real prospect: public libraries because there are other priorities for funding and other opportunities for enlightenment and entertainment; academic libraries because students and researchers will soon be getting everything online. Some do believe in their transfiguration into new types of organization. Others see the likelihood of gradual change, with some new activities added and some old ones fading away. The ultimate opportunity is transformation (rather than transfiguration) into information stores and providers, reaching a larger number and wider range of users in a wider variety of ways and playing an interactive part as information exchanges. Whether threats or opportunities dominate will depend on government policies and (not always the same) practices, on people—both librarians and their consumers—and on chance events.

The fact that globalization's features are usually exaggerated and often explicable does not change the criticism, which is often accompanied by an expressed desire to see the libraries improved. Opportunities for national libraries certainly exist, and they are being taken by many but they tend to constitute even greater opportunities for others. The only more or less unique opportunities they have are those based on exploitation of their collections. How far they go beyond building, maintaining and preserving collections to exploiting them will be a big issue. Doubtless the better national libraries will continue to explore possibilities. And there are opportunities that academic and public libraries have, in serving a prescribed body of users with personal services, that are not open to national libraries.

3. The Greek Reality

The population of Greece is quite homogeneous, with an estimated 98 percent of Greek descent. The largest minority groups are Albanians, Armenians, Bulgarians; Gypsies, Slavs, Pomaks (ethnic Slavs from Bulgaria), Turks, and Vlachs (a Romanian group). The Muslim population, estimated at about 120,000, is concentrated in Thrace (Greece's easternmost land region) and the Dodecanese Islands off the southwestern coast of Turkey, because the Treaty of Lausanne (1923) repatriated all Turks from Greece except for those in Thrace and the Dodecanese Islands. In the early 1990s, the Albanian population fluctuated and caused international tension as illegal refugees entered Greece to escape Albania's unstable conditions.

3.1. Action plan of the Greek Ministry of Interior Affairs

3.1.1. Demographics and segmentation

Part of the environmental analysis is to determine target markets, the specific user groups. For Greek area, locate demographic information for at least the sex, age, language, religion, nationality, family size, educational level, income, and occupation statistics relevant to your community. Find out if any of this data has been gathered for library users specifically.

3.1.2. Context: Environmental or situation analysis

While assessing internal capabilities, also assess the environment, or situation, that affects how the Greek libraries functions. Consider what's happening in the community, region, state, or world-wide that will affect demand for library services. Look at community demographics and the local economy and political situation. Assess the following:

- Structure of libraries in Greece, system affiliations, networks.
- Technology, issues of access, expectations for Internet services and access.
- Economic situation, changes in primary industries of the area.
- Politics, the realities of support and funding for services.
- Demographics and population, growth or decline, distribution within age groups.
- Lifestyles and activities demographics in the area.
- Media, national campaigns or local news that affect how users think of the library.
- Education opportunities, types of schools, alternative libraries, home schooling.

3.1.3. Promoting the message

The same methods used in marketing are used in libraries' public relations to let people know who and what you are and to build relationships with the media covering and the minorities groups. Examples include press releases, newsletters, brochures, annual reports, or well-designed publications.

Plans include:

- Establishing favorable press relations to get news out about the library on a regular basis.

- Creating publicity for specific services and resources and to create and maintain awareness of library capabilities in the community.

- Representing the library and participating in community planning and organizations, to establish the library as a player in community development.

- Establishing regular communications channels to promote an understanding of your organization internally and externally.

- Maintaining awareness of laws and regulations that affect libraries and lobbying to ensure legislation that helps libraries provide effective services.

- Watching for community and national trends and issues that impact the library's image, and informing library administrators.

Not everyone loves libraries! Not everyone uses libraries or finds them worthy of funding. Sometimes successful public relations involve overcoming negative attitudes.

Public libraries "provide services and programs that support literate, productive, and informed communities" in these ways:

- Libraries are great places for children, even though they are not Greeks.

- Libraries bridge the "information divide."

- Libraries protect our right to know.

- Libraries connect people with ideas, information and each other.

- Libraries are for everyone, regardless religion and nationality.

- Libraries are a shared community resource.

- Libraries support lifelong learning.

- Libraries support a productive workforce.

- Libraries are community information centers.

- Libraries foster community identity.

- Libraries are a source of community pride.

- Libraries are a "port of entry" to learn more about their new community.

- Libraries support a community of readers.

- Libraries provide global reach and local touch

The enormous potential for international co-operation in the exchange and utilization of information which today's technology offers, and tomorrow's technology promises, presents a unique opportunity to library and information professionals. The growing demand for bibliographic exchange, multicultural Internet resources, research unhampered by geographic or linguistic limitations, and cross-cultural networking, both in the sense of online technology and offline partnerships, is a challenge to libraries which should be welcomed and which must be addressed.

The Global Information Infrastructure which is developing and which will surely be in place early in the 21st century, will require information professionals with a sense of obligation, both to their national needs and to the larger goals of the international community, to digitize, navigate, distribute and preserve all the world's knowledge for all the world's people.

3.1.4. Basic philosophy

Marketing library service is not just a question of money, but of the attitudes of the staff and the entire nation. Goods are used, but service is experienced. The public image of service is born primarily out of the experiences of the people who receive the service. This image crystallizes gradually. Approaching marketing from a philosophical standpoint can help any nation achieve the objectives for which it was established. In library and information services, marketing can help us clarify the following aspects of our work:

- A focus on the users' goals and on helping users articulate these at every level.

- A focus on providing an environment in which all users can study and work.

- The belief that each user has unique needs, requirements, and expectations when he or she visits the library.

- A commitment to helping the user develop skills to acquire information from various sources.

We who work in the library are the most important marketing resource. The deciding factors for success are our attitude and our commitment to our users, clients, customers, patrons, or employers. Implementing a marketing approach requires that top management establish the marketing concept and that the frontline departments share responsibility for the customer with the rest of the organization. The marketing concept must guide all functions and departments of the library and must be understood and accepted by every-one—from the chief librarian to the circulation clerk. This process must also establish carefully designed measures of customer satisfaction. We must remember that marketing library services is not a separate function—it belongs to everyone: It is a way of working and a way of living.

There is an extreme interdependence between marketing and the trinity of library and information services (acquisition and organization and delivery). The service trinity includes the following key relationships:

- A library's service strategy must be clearly communicated to its customers, every nationality, language and religion one has.

- The service strategy must be communicated to all employees, from circulation clerks to top management.

- To maintain consistency in services, the strategy must include systems to run the day-to-day operations of the library.

- Organizational systems must support the service staff, and their impact on customers must be understood.

3.2. Consortia of Hellenic libraries

The "necessary merit" of the Digital libraries. The level of development of new information technologies determines the co-operational relations between libraries. A brief, comparative retrospection on the evolution of new information technologies, the collaborative relations of Greek libraries and the main role that libraries are playing each period, verifies the above predicate. Emphasis is laid on (yet under formation) collections of electronic journals of Greek libraries, prevalent tendencies, economic, technical and institutional variables. These variables objectively establish libraries collaboration as the "necessary good" of the digital libraries. A framework of positions and rules is also described for a feasible and reasonable policy on the coordinated development of the national collection of electronic journals.

Programs—Libraries consortia in Greece:

- ARTEMIS—interuniversity digital library for electronic documentation of modern Greek grey literature

- Greek Academic Library Network
- Total Quality Unit for Academic Libraries
- SKEPSIS: Digital Library of academic material
- School Libraries—Project presentation
- http://www.ekt.gr/school-library/project.htm

Greek libraries have experienced a tremendous evolution towards modernization during the last few years. The lack of tradition in libraries and the existence of an educational system based on the single textbook did not favor until recently the development of libraries in Greece. However, the European Community action aimed at enabling European libraries to play an important role in the information market, and the Community Support Framework, through which libraries could be funded at the national level, allowed for a dynamic set of actions for Greek libraries. All types of libraries, academic, public and school are moving ahead—500 school libraries were established in secondary schools alone. In the academic libraries, the horizontal action can be proud of the creation of a consortium called HEAL LINK that shares journal subscriptions and will also operate a Union Catalog of bibliographic records. Library-related organizations such as the National Documentation Center and the National Book Center, offer additional support in this movement of progress.

Greek libraries implement the innovation and technological changes which happen in libraries worldwide. It was a question, if these technological changes are followed by the organizational ones and which are the responses of the staff. Overall, Greek libraries are keeping their focus to improve diversity, and results in terms of demographics and pay show improvement. It is likely medical library management will need to focus on recruitment of minorities as a long-term solution.

3.3. The Greek schools' network

The Greek Schools' Network (GSN—www.sch.gr) is the educational intranet of the Ministry of Education and Religious Affairs (www.ypepth.gr), which interlinks all schools and provides basic and advanced telematics' services. Thus, it contributes to the creation of a new generation of educational communities, which takes advantage of the new Informatics' and Communication Technologies in the educational procedure.

The implementation of the Greek Schools' Network is funded by the Framework Programme for the Information Society (www.infosoc.gr), in close cooperation between the Ministry of Education as well as 12 Research Centers and Highest Education Institutes, specialized in network and Internet technologies.

3.3.1. Educational exploitation of the Greek schools network

The current design and implementation of the Greek Schools Network focuses in providing useful services to all members and to the minorities of the basic and middle education community, fulfilling among others the following goals:

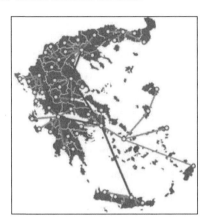

- Access to telecommunication and informatics services

- Access to digitized educational material

- Distance learning, e-learning

- Encourage collaboration

- Information and opinion exchange

- Conduct of thematic discussions, seminars, lectures, etc.

- Access to digital library services

- Communication and cooperation of all educational degrees

- Communication with European educational networks

- Facilitate complementary educational programs

- Provide education to individuals with special needs or disabilities

- Inform, educate, entertain

3.3.2. Network architecture

The network is hierarchically structured into three layers. In order to maintain the educational orientation of the network, its users are certified individuals, educational or administrative entities of the National Education. In particular, the users are divided in the following categories:

- Schools: At least one user account have been provided to all middle grade education schools and 92% of first degree education schools.

- Administrative units: At least one user account has been provided to more than 2.282 administrative units of National Education.
- Educational staff: The Greek Schools Network offers fully personalized access to all educational staff, with the dial-up service being broadly used under certain terms.
- Students: Network access is provided to students through the school laboratories. In addition, pilot personalized access is offered to second grade students of Achaia and Corinthian Prefectures.
- Administrative staff: as with educational staff.

3.3.3. Available services

The Greek Schools Network offers a broad package of services to its units and users. The most important of these are:

- Automated registration procedure for educational staff and students Users Administration Service
- Remote network access (dialup)
- E-mail lists
- Web Portal offering news services and personalized access to tele-communication and informatics services
- Controlled access to the World Wide Web, prohibiting access to web sites with harmful content for underage
- Wizards for automatic webpage creation
- Asynchronous distance learning, for hosting and distributing digitized lessons
- Teleconference
- Video On Demand delivering streaming educational multimedia material
- Live Internet transmission (webcasting)
- News and Discussions
- Electronic Magazine Personal Calendar, Personal Address Book, Notes and "To Do", accessible through the World Wide Web
- Directory Service
- Voice over IP

- Online statistics
- Help-Desk, for immediate solution of technical problems.

3.3.4. Networking progress

Currently, all educational and administrative units of the second educational degree are part of the Greek Schools Network, as well as (approximately) 96% of the first degree educational units (estimated time of completion: end of 2006). The Greek Schools Network is also exploited to interconnect other important units, such as Public Libraries, Second Opportunity Schools, the General State Archives, etc.

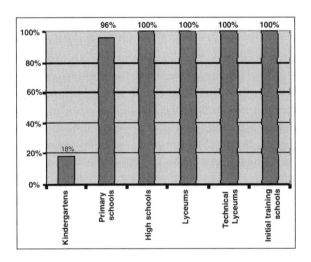

4. Attitudes—Questions

Greek libraries have undergone extensive changes, particularly since the 1970s when automated systems were first being introduced and utilized. Those were the days when the public came to the library for information, information that could not be found anywhere else. There was no Internet, nor were cable companies offering two hundred channels to surf out everything from how to make the perfect golf swing, to indepth analysis of health and financial matters. It is pointed out, globalization meant that globalization was increasingly hard to maintain [because] the nation state was undermined by the international flow of information around and across the globe . . . with information playing an integral part. Conceivably, libraries are currently global information sites, with librarians funneling through and disseminating information for their clients.

Libraries will be expected to operate like businesses, with budget concerns, and a greater dependence upon technology to be the panacea for all the problems that come with financial cutbacks and loss of staff (Harris 1997,7). Therefore, it is realistic to say that since the transnational corporations are now the key players in the powerful sphere of global economics, and information plays an integral role in its societal manifestations (Webster 1995,162), then the kinds of information available, and how it is distributed, would be critical areas of concern for a "global", citizen of my nation and of the world, librarian.

In the middle of this paradigm shift, stands the librarian, a constantly reskilled, information connoisseur who performs a multitude of tasks through the organizational practice of team management, always with an eye to the business world to see how to reengineer libraries in fundamental and structural ways (Shapiro 1994,285). Currently, the organizational patterns of individual libraries have been broken down, developing large departments within libraries, which are often somehow merged with the computer services branch. Shapiro and Long suggest "that libraries can no longer afford a small cadre of technological wizards to manage technology. Rather, technology must be integrated throughout the library" (Shapiro 1994,289). Library systems in general, are becoming decentralized, creating huge networks of interconnected links, or the global 'virtual library'. This concept of flexibility has "everything to do with maintaining highly centralized control through decentralized tactics" (MacDonald 1991,193).

4.1. Internal impact

- Attitudes
  - o From "how do I relate to the nation? (dualism)
  - o To "how do I relate to the world? (pluralism)

4.2. External impact

- Economics
  - o NC businesses sell goods abroad = job gain
  - o NC jobs transferred overseas = job loss
- Demographics
  - o We go there, get married, have kids...
  - o They come here, get married, have kids

4.3 Questions

Q1. If the library becomes mainly a marketing tool, will every city and every citizen need one in the new modern global era?

Education is a commercial enterprise in many parts of the world, and universities compete for the best faculty and the best students. Good library services may help to attract both researchers and students. Economy and competition may very well determine the future of library services. Commercial libraries, or information management service-companies, may provide library services to all on demand. Thanks to the internet we can choose to be our own travel agents.

Q2. Why not be our own librarians?

The digital library is available 24/7, and provides information from anywhere to anywhere. With cordless broadband technology it may be used almost everywhere. Used sensibly it provides society with a perfect tool for distance learning, as well as life-long learning. It may contain all textbooks needed in a university, in addition to all necessary research material. Even primary-source material is being scanned, and thus made accessible to the world—at a price. Proper training in information literacy will become even more vital. Mandatory general courses will be given—supplemented with specialised and tailored courses on demand. Librarians or subject specialists with teaching skills will train faculty and students according to their needs. Basically the library should be a self-service operation. Patrons should be taught all necessary skills needed to use the collections in full.

Q3. How will the library global world be in 2016?

In 2016 we will need less people with traditional library skills. At the same time we shall need more people with skills in teaching, marketing, IT, and digital publishing. In Japan increasing numbers of young people are reading books on their cell-phones. In a small country like Greece, national subscriptions to information databases could be considered an option. The nationally stated goal of life-long learning, and the rapid spread of broadband-technology both pull in this direction. This would remove large numbers of digital publications and databases from the exclusive collections of the university libraries, and put them into the public domain. Management of these accounts would be done centrally, saving significant labour costs. From a national economic point of view, this might be a sensible solution.

4.4. Respecting the diversity

Their cultures:

- Our users come from different cultures that are also based on a set of assumptions.
- While there may be individual differences, the culture or community they come from shares a common set of experiences and values that shape their perceptions of the library.

The community libraries:

- Front lines
  - o Preparing students who have lost their manufacturing jobs to labor
  - o Educating new immigrant populations from Armenia, Bulgaria, China, Poland, Pakistan, Turkey and elsewhere

Global curriculum:

- Political science, sociology, communication, criminal justice, economics, geography
- English as a second language
- International business
- Industrial science
- Marketing and retail
- Medical laboratory technology
- Horticulture technology
- Almost every subject can and should have a global perspective.

Our audience—our tools:

- Supporting staff
- Supporting students
- Supporting the community
- Instruction Outreach
- Collection development

Issues:

  - o International and/or Greek students tend to underutilize library services

- o Unfamiliar with the organization and mission of libraries in the Greece
- o May not have access to professional reference and information services
- o Access to books and other forms of information may be limited
- o May have never used a library database

Both populations:

- May have used computers on a limited basis
- May feel intimidated by technology
- May be afraid to ask for help
- May not understand how to seek, obtain, or evaluate information (a.k.a. information literacy)

Issues:

- Use of language

Issues:

- Nonverbal Communication
  - o Greek students use direct eye contact to indicate attention and respect
  - o students from other cultures look away or down as a sign of respect
- Space
  - o Middle Eastern students tend to get physically close, while Japanese students keep a fair distance

Opportunities:

- First steps
  - o Talk to groups of students to listen to their concerns and what they want and need from the library
  - o Talk to your colleagues and student workers in the library about the importance of being sensitive to different cultures

Suggestions and recommendations for library instruction:

- Be culturally sensitive

- o Many may have never had library instruction
- o Can't make assumptions about what they do and don't know
- o Many are not used to instruction that is interactive, group or discussion-oriented

- • Be language- and communication-sensitive
  - o Don't be afraid to repeat things
  - o Avoid library jargon
  - o Demonstrate things visually, as well as verbally and do it slowly

Suggestions and recommendations for library instruction:

- • Offer one-on-one instruction whenever possible
- • Offer online instruction (coming soon!)
- • Recruit and hire students to act as "peer" consultants
- • Conduct open houses and orientations especially for international, or returning adult students
- • Design a series of handouts that can be distributed through the international center or other campus support units

5. What Is the Government's Will for the Future?

The YPEPTH has established a new strategic framework for the school library service: outlining the Government's long-term strategic vision for the role of libraries. The new strategy will enable libraries to build on existing strengths and ensure they position themselves at the heart of the education. School libraries, a place where pupils of different nationalities are gathering, are a valuable infrastructure, which have the potential to help pupils and students. By clarifying key priorities they provide a focus for future work across the provision of the proper library services through the country's school libraries in order to meet the needs of the educational community, adapted to best suit local circumstance. The Greek Government's drive for better education for our young, and its determination to make lifelong learning a possibility for all our citizens, puts a heavy demand on the libraries in order to become access points to a nation-wide treasure-house of digital content as well as creators of unique digital content themselves. The Special Secretary of Libraries & Archives with goodwill and determination is paving the way for cross-domain co-operation in its areas of concern, so the time is right for a bold initiative to forge new links between school libraries and the educational sector, school libraries and technology.

6. Conclusions

Libraries have an organizational culture based on a set of assumptions we have either invented, discovered or developed to cope with external adaptation and internal integration. We deliver services based on these culturally and intellectually-based assumptions. The library of 2016 might be open 24 hours a day—based on self-service. The very scale of the Internet and its information resources will demand the existence of people able to advise users, educate them in information issues, and point them in the right direction. Students attend a university to learn, not only a special subject, but also the art of pursuing knowledge in general. The librarians and subject specialists of the university library can help them do just that. Greek libraries should not become museums of old dusty volumes. They should be beacons of knowledge on campus. Places where mind meets mind and new thoughts are shared. They should be repositories of all the help students, teachers and researchers might need regarding information issues. The future is coming rapidly – and if we still want to keep our slice of it, we have to determine who and what we are. Globalization is not a threat, is a challenge and we have to do a good dealing with it.

References

1   Cornish, G.P. 1992. The Changing Role of the National Library in the New Information Environment. *Alexandria*, 4(2), 125-141.

2   Harris, Roma M. and Victoria Marshall. *Reorganizing Canadian Libraries: A Step Back from the Front. Library Trends* 46: 564-580.

3   Henty, M. 1995. Resource sharing ideals and realities: the case of Australia's distributed national collection. *Advances in Collection Development and Sharing, 1*, 139-152.

4   Koontz, Christie. 2002. "Stores and Libraries: Both Serve Customers." *Marketing Library Services* 16(1); Jan/Feb. www.mls.com. Lovelock, Christopher H. 1991. *Services Marketing* (2nd ed.). NJ: Prentice Hall, pp. 22-34.

5   Line, M.B. 1989. *National Library and Information Needs: Alternative Means of Fulfilment, with Special Reference to the Role of National Libraries*, UNESCO, Paris Melot, M., Ed. 1996. *Nouvelles Alexandries:*

les Grands Chantiers de Bibliotheques dans le Monde. Editions du Cercle de la Librairie, Paris.

6   National and Kapodistrian University of Athens, *School Libraries Work Evaluation: Statistics and Results of Evaluation.* Athens: 2003.

7   Nicholas, J. "Marketing And Promotion Of Library Services. Library and Information Services in Astronomy III: ASP Conference Series". 153. 1998. Date last accessed: 17 June 2005. http://www.eso.org/gen-fac/libraries/lisa3/nicholasj.html.

8   MacDonald, Martha. Fall 1991. *Post-Fordism and the Flexibility Debate. Studies in Political Economy* 36, pp. 177-201.

9   Orava, Hilkka. 1997. "Marketing Is an Attitude of Mind." Proceedings of the 63rd IFLA General Conference, August 31September 5, 1997.

10 Shapiri, Beth J. and Kevin Brook Long 1994. *Just Say Yes: Reengineering Library User Services for the 21ˢᵗCentury.* The Journal of Academic Librarianship, November, pp. 285-290.

11 Webster, Frank. *Theories of the Information Society.* London: Routledge, 1995.

Intercultural Dialogue in the Public Library: The Experience of the District 2 Library in Terrassa, Barcelona

Maria Gental Morral
The District 2 Library in Terrassa

Abstract

Terrassa is a city with a population of 200,000 inhabitants, 30 kilometers away from Barcelona. It has six districts. The library is in the quarter of Ca n'Anglada, in district number 2. This district has a population of about 18,000 inhabitants, and the quarter concentrates 13,000, of which 25% are foreign immigrants, mostly Moroccan.

The Library in District 2 (BD2) has drawn up a project with the aim to "stimulate intercultural dialogue and favour cultural diversity" making it easier for foreign immigrants living in the quarter of Ca n'Anglada to use the library.

This offer from the library comes from the reflections over a specific social reality that is becoming more and more common and that cannot be ignored: the immigration phenomenon. This fact gives rise to social and cultural conflicts, coexistence problems and new needs that can be detected from the library.

With the implementation of this project we intend to present the library to the citizens as a meeting place and as an opportunity of cultural exchange. The several actions designed to promote integration of immigrants include helping neglected children outside school time, Catalan lessons and a section for language self-learning, job information and CV writing, the creation of a library working team about immigration, being a member of UNESCO and providing information about legal proceedings. To attain all this, a new working method is started with the participation of different equipment, professionals and associations of the quarter, based on transversality.

The library is a citizen-proximity service and, as such, an excellent resource to work on social cohesion. However, a project like this cannot work successfully without the involvement and sensitivity of a human team.

1. Nature of the Population of District 2

Terrassa is a city of 200,000 inhabitants located 30 kilometers from Barcelona and divided into six districts. The library is located in the area of Ca n'Anglada, within District 2. There are a total of 18,560[1] inhabitants living in the district, with 14,000 concentrated in the Ca n'Anglada area. Over 26% of these are foreign immigrants, mainly from Morocco.

64% of the population of Ca n'Anglada has completed primary education and 50% of the population is aged between 17–45, meaning many residents are no longer of school-going age and have a high degree of illiteracy.

After analysing education levels we have discovered that the highest levels of illiteracy were found among the Moroccan population. The so-called local population is made up of immigrant nationals from the rest of Spain who arrived in Terrassa in the 60s, when there was a wave of industrial expansion in the textile sector. They arrived as young, uneducated citizens and went straight to work; today the population is old and demonstrates high levels of illiteracy.

2. The District 2 Library

2.1. bct xarxa: Terrassa's network of public libraries

Terrassa Town Council, under its Pla municipal de biblioteques[2] (Municipal Libraries Plan), which proposes "to configure a network of public libraries in Terrassa based on the model of a central library with a public library in each district", opened the District 2 Library (BD2) on 20 October 2001.

In terms of structure BD2 depends on the Central Library of Terrassa, and together with 4 other libraries it makes up bct xarxa (The Network of Public Libraries of Terrassa).

2.2. Basic information about the BD2 service

The library receives an average of 500 visits per day and performs 250 loans. It is open 34.5 hours a week.

In 2005 a total of 107,300 people visited the library and borrowed 54,700 items. Currently (February 2006) there are a total of 5,200 library card holders; this means that 30% of the population of the area has a library card.

2.3. Personnel

There is a fixed workforce of 4 people: 1 service worker, 2 administrative assistants and 1 librarian/director.

There is a support staff of part-time workers who work in the evenings. The 4 additional workers are: a security guard who controls the level of noise, behaviour, use of services, etc.; an IT student on work experience who takes care of the Internet service and office IT services, provides IT help for registration services, organises personalised training sessions, controls connection hours, etc.; a teacher subsidised by the Union European under the scope of the Law of Neighbourhoods, and a mobile worker who offers support in terms of technical tasks, depending on the municipal network.

2.4. Activities

BD2 is a very dynamic library. Over the course of 2005 it hosted a total of 46 school visits from 1,100 children, and 28 educational and vocational workshops for 320 participants. Normally volunteers or library workers give the workshops. In addition there were 15 story-telling sessions that were attended by 565 people.

111 activities took place in 2005, and 2,370 participants got involved.

There are Catalan classes running two evenings a week, with 20 students in the class.

3. Detecting New Needs

The proposal for intercultural dialogue in BD2 responds to a social reality that is gradually becoming clearer: that is, the issue of immigration.

The immigrant population has new needs. The library is one of the public services that citizens have easy access to and it offers them a way to overcome their lack of resources. It should also be noted that like any institution we represent a board, in this case, the Town Council of Terrassa.

Currently the library's work and its team goes a lot further than processing documentation or simply providing information to users. We have found that in today's world we have to be multi-qualified (multi-professionalism), that is, we play a more social role and act as educators.

Therefore it is clear that the library should continue to act as an intercultural meeting point and a point of contact, where immigrants feel that "natives" understand their situation and welcome and accept them. Local authorities require a good hosting policy to orient newcomers in our society. Many immigrants in the area are searching for employment, and as Catalan is often a requirement, they want to learn the language.

4. Our Services

BD2 is a public service that offers free access to everyone. There is no charge for the service and we are open to cooperating and collaborating with entities in our environment (inter-professionalism), and with motivated personnel who have experience dealing with the phenomena of immigration. These three aspects help us perform and maintain our work over the long term. We are at the citizen's service and for that reason we are equipped with the best tool to advance social cohesion: the library.

Below we have listed the main fields of activity of the library and the entities with which we work. Our objectives are defined by the aforementioned needs.

4.1. Citizen's advice

The Terrassa Town Council is decentralised in such a way that each district has an office that performs similar tasks.

BD2 addresses newcomers to the OMD (Municipal Office of the District). It helps them register and informs them of how the registration process works. To obtain a library card a person has to show proof of registration and a passport, residence permit or any other official document. The library also collaborates with the Ciutadania de l'Ajuntament service to welcome newcomers, offering them the possibility of filling out arrival forms to request the services of this department.

The service is verbal and is provided on the spot when a user makes a request. However in general immigrants do not want to complete forms, etc.; they prefer to be accompanied by a guide from their country who has been living in Terrassa for a while.

4.2. Achieving understanding between immigrants and the library

BD2 relies on the support of Moroccan mediators (immigration service of the Town Council). A mediator is requested when the user and library worker fail to understand one another, either for language, behavioural, or cultural reasons, etc. We are currently visiting Moroccan mothers to get parents involved in their children's leisure time and in the use of the library. Visits are organised in collaboration with the school for adults, Moroccan mediators and social services.

Another tool targeted at achieving communication is a police presence in the surrounding area. Police agents are there to observe the level of compliance with usage norms and regulations. Agents have incorporated a visit to BD2 on their route, which also takes in other public services in the area. From time to time they visit the library, always ensuring respect for the authority of the personnel working there.

4.3. Help in the search for work

The library is going to define cooperation parameters with the Foment de Terrassa (a municipal employment orientation organisation) to help users search for employment. We have established four main objectives: to train a library worker according to the guidelines of the organisation, to present Foment work offers in BD2, to help users formalize a job request in Foment, and to provide users with support when drawing up curriculum vitae, based on a template. To date there has been a lot of interest in creating curriculum vitae, which has led us to draw up a model C.V. in Word format, which users can access, print, save and send directly by Internet.

In September 2003 a worker from the library did a training course at Foment, however the two institutions have yet to sign an official contract, mainly due to a change in management.

4.4. Learning the language

Catalan is the official language of Catalonia and is a pre-requisite for finding work.

The library actively collaborates with the Servei de Normalització Lingüística de Terrassa (Language Normalisation Service of Terrassa) and lends its installations to this body to house classes.

The 7th edition of basic Catalan will begin in September this year. Classes are run on a Tuesday and Thursday from 19.00 to 20.30 h. The course is free and if the student passes the final exam he or she will receive an official certificate.

4.5. A sense that the library includes you

4.5.1. Collection

Municipals libraries have decided to adapt their resources to the inhabitants of the particular district.

The objective of the library network is to unite all the books in the city in one common catalogue. Users are free to borrow items from one library and return them to any other library in the network. Often if a physics book is missing from BD2 the user will find it in the Central Library. He or she may request the book from the Central Library and the next day the user is free to come and pick it up at no extra cost and without having to travel to the Central Library.

BD2 is specialised in resources on immigration and self-guided language learning.

4.5.2. Services: Link to UNESCO

In June 2003 the Group of Catalan Libraries linked to UNESCO approved BD2's application to join the group. BD2 currently enjoys the support, experience and help of other libraries. It is important to have a reference group on a similar trajectory that performs work via teams that share common goals.

4.5.3. Immigration work group

The libraries in the Comarca del Vallès Occidental have organised themselves into work groups, and one of these focuses on the issue of immigration. BD2 forms part of the latter group.

The group promotes experience-sharing between libraries of a similar nature. The result of these work sessions has been the creation of a document that unites all the resources for immigrants in the region, and it benefits from collaboration with the Pla Comarcal de Ciutadania i Immigració del Vallès Occidental (Regional Citizenship and Immigration Plan of Vallès Occidental).

4.6. Monitoring child users

The majority of child users are Moroccan immigrants.

Their parents do not accompany them to the library nor do they play an active role in their free time. In Morocco when a child acts out of line, society in general teaches him or her the correct way to behave. If an acquaintance of the family sees the child behaving badly, he or she directly informs the family or the parents of the child. This means that parents know whether their children are behaving themselves or not, without leaving the house.

When Moroccans arrive in Spain they find that society fails to play a similar role in the education of their children and no information concerning their children's actions reaches them. This leads to a sense of "freedom" on the part of the young person. However, the library has assumed the role of neighbour, friend, and family member, who informs of the child's behaviour.

This is one reason the library works with social educators in the area. And it sets up meetings to discuss how to deal with specific cases. When a child fails to make proper use of the library we set up meetings with the child's family.

District 2 is going to receive a European subsidy to improve the area at the structural and co-existence level. The library has a small budget that allows it pay a part-time educator who carries out the following functions:

- To establish guidelines governing behaviour, respect for the surroundings and hygiene.

- Help children search for information.
- Promote interest in learning and reading: introduce young children to the habit of reading, promote parents' involvement in their child's education and reading.
- Coordinate reading activities.
- Provide support in workshops and story-telling in the library.
- Organise educational workshops.
- Perform library service functions: loans, ordering books... and providing support to library personnel.

Given the specific nature of the library users, the educator will also:

- Ensure compliance with the normative framework.
- Reduce the level of conflict.
- Guarantee peaceful co-existence.
- Be a welcoming agent and an agent of social integration.
- Make the library into a social education space for the district.
- Make the library into a space for dialogue between cultures.

5. Evaluation

5.1. Errors and corrections

Our services need to be directed to *everyone,* not explicitly "immigrants," in order to avoid positive discrimination and a feeling of displacement on the part of locals who feel the library does more for those from "outside" than for "them".

We draw up usage norms, which we can consult and on which we can base decisions, as opposed to making decisions purely on "personal" opinions.

We promote inter-professionalism (collaboration with other professionals), which is not the same as multi-professionalism (a single person acting as mediator, educator, father, policeman, and so on ... librarian). A person working alone tends to achieve a lot less than a group of professionals working in the same area.

Working transversally is difficult. It implies significant changes in how we think and act: calling at many doors, holding lots of meetings, and implementing new work guidelines, but it is an extremely gratifying and fulfilling experience. Most collaborators are from the area, and as such they share the same users, the same problems, shortages, and hurdles—and draw on our support, understanding, professionalism and a spirit of teamwork.

We undertake each objective with an end goal in mind. As we perform a lot of work in collaboration with other entities it is difficult to come up with achievement rates. However, achieving an objective does not mean terminating an action; on the contrary, we continue to promote work relations with other services and professionals when a project ends. Our work is ongoing and our objectives may be redefined and extended.

We believe that a positive work method is to promote exchange with the surrounding area. This is also a very enriching method. However we should bear in mind that the project will only last if the team wants it to. Participating on the project means more than performing a functional role. Many of the tasks to be undertaken will fall outside the worker's employment profile and as such will have to be assumed voluntarily.

Notes

1   Anuari estadístic de Terrassa 2005.
2   Pla municipal de biblioteques http://www.terrassa.org/laciutat/pmbiblio. htm.

References

1   Ajuntament de Barcelona. Pla municipal per a la interculturalitat. Barcelona: Ajuntament de Barcelona, 1997.
2   Ajuntament de Terrassa. Anuari estadístic de Terrassa 2005 [en línia]. Terrassa: Ajuntament de Terrassa, 2005. http://www.terrassa.org. [Accessed: 15 March 2006]
3   Bartolomé, M. Identidad y ciudadanía: un reto a la educación intercultural. Madrid: Narcea, 2002.
4   Blooomfield, Jude. Franco Bianchini. Planning for the Intercultural Ci., Stroud: Comedia, 2004.
5   Carta de serveis de les biblioteques públiques de Terrassa [en línia].
6   http://www.terrassa.org/mes_facil/cartes_serveis/biblios.htm. [Accessed: 16 March 2006]
7   Centre UNESCO de Catalunya. Les biblioteques públiques: espais d'integració social. Barcelona: Centre UNESCO de Catalunya, Grup de Biblioteques Catalanes Associades a la UNESCO, 2003.
8   IFLA, Sección de Servicios Bibliotecarios para Poblaciones Multiculturales. Comunidades multiculturales: directrices para el servicio bibliotecario [en

línia]. http://www.ifla.org/ VII/s32/pub/ guide-s.htm#2. [Accessed: 15 March 2006]

9   Kymlicka. Ciudadanía multicultural. Barcelona: Paidos, 1996.

10 Maaluf, A. Les identitats que maten. Barcelona: La Campana, 1999.

11 Pla de biblioteques de Terrassa [en línia]. http://www.terrassa.org/ laciutat/ pmbiblio.htm. [Accessed: 16 March 2006]

12 Rodrigo Alsina, M. Comunicación intercultural. Barcelona: Anthropos, 1999.

13 UNESCO. Manifest de la Unesco sobre la biblioteca pública: 1994. Barcelona: Col.legi Oficial de Bibliotecaris-Documentalistes de Catalunya, [1994].

Dynamics of Marketing Library Services to Disadvantaged Communities: Promoting Knowledge Seeking Behavior

Muhammad Kamran Naqi Khan, Muhammad Anwar Ejaz, and
Aamir Ghafoor Ch.

Hamdard University, Islamabad, Pakistan

Abstract

The modern world is moving rapidly towards knowledge acquisition and information seeking, key variables for well rounded progress. This situation calls for seeking innovative techniques that convey the value of library service in developing countries. An outgrowth of this cognitive field is the promotion of tolerance, acceptance, and inclusion of diversity. In other words, a closed mind breeds intolerance and extremism. The question, therefore, is how to transform a culture to one where knowledge seeking becomes internalized. While the need for a higher rate of literacy is generally recognized, little attention is given to building a supportive system in the society to inculcate the need for knowledge and, thereby, a major driving force for achieving developmental goals of the society. This paper empirically tests the contention of Khan (2004, 2005a, 2005b), who has proven conclusively that when target groups use group dynamics in the process of social marketing, appreciable results do accrue — desired behavioural changes and mobilization of communities to improve their lives. An empirical study was conducted in the north of Pakistan to test this proposition. The study is still in progress and has demonstrated some impact, particularly in promoting a program where knowledge acquisition gains acceptance through group dynamics. This, in turn, has created a supportive system at the grass roots level so that the community is equipped with the predisposition towards seeking knowledge. Integrating group dynamics, the missing link, serves as a social mechanism to create a supportive system at the grass roots level.

1. Introduction

Ours is essentially an age of information, and the knowledge explosion is on a scale that history has never witnessed before. It is, therefore, a significant problem that the underdeveloped world, which constitutes the major portion of humanity, is not only impoverished in terms of physical needs but also the quality of education is much too limited. The knowledge gap between the developed and developing world is widening. While the need for a higher rate of literacy is generally recognized, little attention is paid to how to build a supportive system in a society in order to inculcate the need for knowledge as a major driving force of the nation.

As advocated by Larry Page, co-founder and President of Google, "… you had to deliberately seek out the toughest challenges because that was where the greatest opportunity lay." In support of his philosophy he also argued that "You might as well do some social stuff because that is where the big problems are," he said, "if a lot of people come out of poverty that is a tremendous business opportunity." (Thornhill 2006).

Needless to say empowering disadvantaged communities is one of the biggest challenges. Unless these impoverished segments are brought to a respectable level there is no concept of real development and growth. In the words of Kofi A. Annan:

> We will have time to reach the Millennium Development Goals— worldwide and in most, or even all, individual countries—but only if we break with business as usual.
>
> We cannot win overnight. Success will require sustained action across the entire decade between now and the deadline. It takes time to train the teachers, nurses and engineers; to build the roads, schools and hospitals; to grow the small and large businesses able to create the jobs and income needed. So we must start now. And we must more than double global development assistance over the next few years. Nothing less will help to achieve the Goals.

In Pakistan, as in most of the underdeveloped countries, more than 65% of the population live in rural areas, which lack avenues to learning and library facilities, resulting in community members' not developing the reading habit and having their experience widened through exposure to books, journals, newspapers etc.

Effective implementation of any organizational strategy demands that it must define the challenge. The challenge of marketing library services in the words of White (Besant & Sharp, 2002, cited in Kumbar, 2004) is that "What we need to tell people is not how wonderful our public libraries are but rather how wonderful they could be. The awakening of these dreams are marketing." The aim of this paper is to elaborate on this challenge to better understand this perspective and help in persuading the attendees of the conference and other stake holders in re-orienting their approaches to marketing library services, particularly at the grass roots level. The basic tenet is that without establishing a supportive system we cannot truly initiate and sustain a reform process among the most deprived segment of our society. This supportive system, in turn, builds a culture where knowledge seeking becomes valued and people develop and practice positive habits. This will help to facilitate social and economic progress, besides addressing the values of IFLA to ameliorate the conditions of knowledge and information services.

1.1. Dynamics of marketing

The scope of marketing and its relevance for accelerating human and social progress has been acknowledged, besides the role it plays in the promotion and progress of commercial and economic activities. The role of marketing in promoting social causes, services and products has been recognized. But the potential of the field, particularly in the area of social marketing, has by and large remained untapped. Therefore, achieving effectiveness through social innovation remains a very neglected area in the developing economies and particularly in Pakistan with the result that investment in building infrastructure for library services and other commercial and public ventures failed to deliver appreciative performance because of attitudinal impediments, which hinder innovative approaches to advance the good of the community. In other words, what is needed is to see how a community 'ticks,' to determine what the positive and negative aspects are. The lack of communication between the planner and the beneficiaries creates a vacuum and grossly affects the outcome.

This challenge could be addressed through the concept of social marketing and its tools and techniques. Social marketing is no longer a hit or miss affair. It is a scientifically determined approach based on a systematic and logical process, selecting appropriate marketing tools and techniques to organize and implement its strategies (Andreasen, 1993, 1994, 1997, 2002, 2005; Brenkert, 2002; Kotler, 2005; Kotler and Zaltmann, 1971; Bloom and

Novelli, 1981; Willkie and Moore, 1999, 2003; Khan, 2005a). According to Susan Kirbys (Hasting, Mac Fayden, and Stead 2000): "social marketing is a program planning process which promotes voluntary behavior change based on building beneficial exchange relationships with a target audience for the benefit of society." This area of marketing supports the promotion of library services if we review the history and evolution of library marketing and its movements in the USA and Europe. Moreover, it can better serve the perspective of those who came before like Samuel Swett Green, who gave an address at the American Library Association (ALA) conference in 1876 in which he strongly advocated, "improved personal relations between librarian and readers"; "ideas of reaching libraries to common man" and "Library movement in India" (Kumbar, Fall 2004). In Pakistan, there was a commendable effort by Shaheed Hakim Mohammed Said to institutionalize the library movements and the founding of the Pakistan Library Association. He was on the forefront in advancing the good of the community. Needless to say, Pakistani libraries are at a crossroads where they have to meet enormous challenges respecting library services. However, one of these major challenges is professional acumen, not only understanding the concept of marketing, but also the effective utilization of the concept for improving library services.

Some of the important research done in the area of social marketing is to promote social products. When the topic is library service, the surveys undertaken indicate a marked indifference to the values that affect community behavior (Costanzaco et al., 1986 quoted in McKenzie-Mohr, 2000, p. 1). Moreover, the many barriers that exist for any sustainable activity means that information campaigns alone will rarely bring about behavior change. McKenzie-Mohr (2002) also contended that a variety of studies have established that by merely increasing knowledge and creating supportive attitudes had either little or no impact on behavior. The inadequacy of these techniques in bringing about the desired changes in behavior and attitude was brought to light by Rangan et al. (1996). The lessons were learned from the experiences of telecenters in many developing countries (Oestmann and Daymond, 2001; Mahmood, 2005). This myopic view is the basic impediment in pursuing the basic principles of marketing, particularly social marketing of any concept, idea, product or service in developing countries at the grass roots level. In other words, marketing of the library to the common person in disadvantaged communities in developing countries requires a methodology that suits the social forces for inclusion of the concept and promoting the idea in a logical manner; as rightly said, "Libraries are both a creation and a servant of society . . . operates on trust" (Kumbar, 2004).

In the context of Pakistan, Khan (2005a, 2005b, and 2006) has empirically verified the crystallization of library services in one community under study, in addition to other initiatives taken by community members in the village Mera Bagwal, Islamabad, Pakistan. This study has also revealed that through group dynamics the community members did change their behavior pattern— the community members perceived the criticalness of gaining knowledge in order to fulfill their potential objectives. Moreover, in a very short span of time, they became positive achievers by changing their quality of life as well as influencing those who did not initially participate in the study.

He has also argued (Khan, 2004, 2005a) that previous researchers in the field of social marketing have, by and large, mainly adopted one-way communication from the source to the target, which has not yielded the desired results. It is assumed that by incorporating psychosocial variables at the micro-level the change process could be facilitated and the techniques of social marketing could be used. This would generate a force which has to be channeled for sustainable growth, socio-economic improvement, acquisition of knowledge and people-centered political activities and a climate of overall societal development. In other words, one can refer to the underutilization of the concept of the "Telecenters" in developing countries for several reasons (Oestman and Dymond, pp. 6-7, 2001). Initially it was introduced in Sweden to serve the knowledge need of disadvantaged communities and the idea has been very successfully used in other communities in the developed world. Therefore, to deliver more value to this idea requires a supportive system to generate a critical mass. In other words, in the developing world one of the major impediments is a lack of attitudinal predisposition of the society for knowledge and information seeking behaviors, particularly at the grass roots level. Without understanding and defining theses challenges we cannot achieve maximum effectiveness from a venture like telecenters. This supports the contention that the focus of research in marketing was merely on changes in attitude since often attitudes do change, but behavior appears to resist change.

In order to inculcate reading habits among community members it is, therefore, necessary that they discuss their problems with respect to their own empowerment. The facilitator will only engage them in discussion while remaining objective. The facilitator will not intercede.

Once the community realizes the need for some essential services like health, education and communication, through the process they will likely realize a need for a social institution like a community or information center. This sharing of minds within the group through mutual discussion on a regular basis will serve as an effective mechanism to establish a facility that serves as a place for community interaction as well as a stepping stone to inculcate the need for knowledge and information services. Once this occurs, the community members will perceive the importance of gaining knowledge to fulfill their potential aspirations, objectives and goals. Enlightenment is the incentive and motivation to become a knowledge worker. When the group or community members require help, guidance, and assistance they may take initiative themselves to consult agencies, institutions, and universities to meet some of their needs, such as books, journals, and newspapers.

1.2. Extending the methodological domain of social marketing

The present research brings into focus the modality of social marketing strategy to facilitate IFLA's efforts targeted to promote knowledge development, particularly in disadvantaged communities, to facilitate and sustain their development initiatives through a participatory paradigm, and also to help support and reinforce new millennium goals at the grass roots level in a sustainable manner.

Social marketing is thus the required strategy to initiate the change process by community members. In other worlds, the group through participation seeks solutions to the problems that they encounter. Someone rightly said that between an idea and reality there always remains a shadow. To reduce this shadow, social marketing is an effective tool, as it breaks the community resistance and mobilizes its potential for betterment.

The distinctive philosophy of group dynamics, espoused by Kurt Lewin, is that an individual rises above his own self interest for the good of the community. Wiener (1993) very rightly observes that social marketing is essentially the recognition that social problems cannot be resolved by any single individual. Therefore, social marketers and academicians have come to realize that community goals could be achieved by taking collective action. To this may be added that group dynamics provides the necessary mechanism for realization of the core objectives of any social marketing campaign—gross behavioral change along with attitudinal change within the target group.

2. Empirical Study and Results

The study tests Khan's proposition to promote group dynamics as methodology to promote social marketing in order to create a supportive system at the grass roots level to effectively combat obstacles to the development and progress of the community, as well as barriers for promotion of knowledge and information seeking behaviors. Once the value of knowledge seeking is internalized through a system based on equality and making a decision through a process of consensus, the group and community members perceive the instrumentality of gaining knowledge in order to fulfill their objectives. This way the group and other members of the community can see value for knowledge and information needs and an imperative for their sustainable development.

The study concentrates on the small group as the unit of analysis. The group interacts in a manner that identifies the problems and also takes steps toward resolving them. A facilitator only coordinates the discussion but makes no intervention on his/her own.

2.1. Problem statement

Planned change, no matter how well intentioned it may be, through one-way communication and persuasive techniques, is very often resented by people. Social marketing through predetermined modalities tends to be perceived as a relatively manipulative act.

2.2. The hypotheses

H1 Free and uninhibited interaction creates attitudinal changes among the group members, who on account of long deprivation and neglect by society have, by and large, remained reconciled to their fate with a sense of helplessness. Interaction may help overcome these inhibitions by gaining confidence and the ability to resolve problems through commitment and cooperation.

H2 There will be a substantial measurable change, which could be recorded and observed.

H3 In addition to attitudinal and behavioral changes conducive to the resolution of problems, the participants may also develop a greater affinity to promote a paradigm of co-existence, leading to curtailment and resolution of past hostilities.

3. Method

Through group interaction comprising 15-20 members of the same community there will be a great sense of involvement and commitment to get over the crises as speedily as possible. The underlying assumption is that if the group members participate in a free and unhindered manner they will gain insight into the reality of the situation and through a process of consensus undertake measures which are necessary for effectively dealing with the situation. In other words, the coping mechanism, which is a vital imperative of the situation, will be evolved, which, in turn, will also help in reducing the impact of anxiety and sense of helplessness. For an effective and productive outcome of group dynamics, a facilitator was counseled and trained on how to conduct the process of interaction so that the group themselves evolve modalities of adjustment and coping with the situation. The facilitator would not intervene or impose his ideas. The process will also insure the use of grants-in-aid in a very effective and efficient manner and adhere to standards of accountability.

3.1. Measures

3.1.1. Feedback—participants

Feedback was also obtained through 13 items to determine the impact of group interaction as perceived by the participants themselves (Appendix-I).

3.1.2. Facilitator

The facilitator was also briefed to keep a mental note of patterns of behavior and attitudes, reflected in the process of interaction as much as possible. It is pertinent to mention that the main objective of the study was observation of gross behavioral changes and not merely attitudinal changes, for the reason highlighted in the literature review. Moreover, the facilitator remained totally detached and unobtrusive in the discussion process and the decisions made by the group members. The primary idea was to ensure authority/autonomy of the group in analyzing problems as well as taking remedial measures without outside intervention.

3.1.3 Independent observer

To see and measure the impact of the intervention and sustainability of the program the opinion of the independent observer was also sought to empirically verify the effects.

4. The Study Promoting Knowledge Seeking Behavior

The study was the result of the initiatives by Hamdard University to facilitate disaster relief efforts. The study was conducted in two phases. In phase I the recovery of the victims was undertaken through the support of government efforts. Like other institutions, the faculty and students of the university engaged in the disaster relief efforts and reached affected remote and distant destinations. The group centered approach helped students and faculty to effectively coordinate the activities. The principal investigator of the research had planned to further promote the idea in some of the disadvantaged communities to test the efficacy of the mechanism in rebuilding of these communities and to facilitate relief efforts in a sustainable manner.

4.1. Phase II

In phase II, some disadvantaged communities were selected north east of Batagram that are located in an isolated area and have very little opportunity for interaction and access to the main town of Batagram on the Silk Road.

Following were the objectives of the study:

- It is important that the people affected get out of the dependency syndrome and passively waiting for help and support to come from the outside.

- Integrating them into the mainstream of life should be the central objective of crises management.

- Once the situation is comprehended, the impact of the shock will gradually diminish.

One-way communication and a media strategy will not alone achieve the desired results. It has to be augmented through a group dynamic method so that the requisite activity is generated and channeled for the overall welfare of the community. Crises intervention through group dynamics requires the following:

- Understanding the problems so that comprehension is gained by providing adequate support to face the situation.

- Once the understanding of the situation is comprehended in a logical and rational manner without too much rhetoric and pontification, there will be a considerable reduction in stress preparing them to find the best possible coping mechanism to determine future action and rehabilitation. The coping mechanism of different groups of individuals will depend on the level of education and other dimensions of their psycho-social make-up.

- After the coping mechanisms are clearly understood the victims will re-gain their confidence to restore a balance that had been disturbed from the intense shock and anxiety.

4.2. Empirical study—Habib Banda (Batagram)

The researcher selected village Habib Banda situated north east of Batagram. The chosen community was not easily accessible and was close to the epicenter of the earthquake. The village Habib Banda consists of approximately 510 families. All of them were severely affected by the earthquake. One community member had been selected as a facilitator and was given training to conduct the process. The members (nineteen in number) voluntarily participating in the study, filled out a questionnaire prior to the interviews, were interviewed twice a month, and had feedback after each interview. The initial results of the group interview at Habib Banda have been very encouraging as reported by the facilitator.

4.3. Results

The following are the main observations as functions of group dynamics, as recorded by the facilitator:

- The initial stage of shock and disorientation is subsiding and there is a general feeling among the community members that the situation could be managed with collective efforts, insight and understanding.
- Quality of life could be improved.
- Instead of a self centered orientation the group is promoting a sense of sharing and togetherness like distributing ration supplies and securing shelter for the homeless.
- A feeling of joint dependency has markedly improved with each trying to help others such as protecting animals which are the economic assets and their source of income and support. As an example they have constructed shelters so the remaining animals could be protected.
- Similarly other measures were taken care of so that help could be provided to women, children and the elderly, the destitute, and other vulnerable members of the community.
- Overall there is a will to survive the adversity even as after-shocks of the earthquake are still being felt. The fear element is progressively subsiding.
- Through consensus small groups have also been formed to re-build houses on a self help basis including the design, keeping in view the vulnerability of the location and persistent seismic activities. A list of families and other details were completed.
- The consistent interaction has generated dynamism and a force among the members to meet the volatility of the situation and the challenge the community is confronted with and provides insight to help adjacent communities, particularly widows, the poor and disadvantage families.
- There is considerable evidence that through group interaction there is a marked change in negative attitudes and approaches, a sense

of commitment developed to collectively engage in alleviating community problems. In this regard they have taken the initiative to build one community school (Madarsha) and a place for a library. For this purpose group members are exploring other possible, desirable actions. For this purpose, through consensus, a small group has recently been formed to explore the re-building of schools and learning facilities.

- Group dynamics have reinforced the core values. Negative ideas and thoughts are gradually reduced through free and fair interaction. It is this understanding and insight that becomes instrumental in changing cultural attitudes, reflecting a measurably more positive behavior. As a result of group interaction the members take decisions through a process for consensus and the explicit understanding that all members participating in the group interaction are equal. This can be seen from the feedback of the group members shown in Appendix I.

- The members expressed great satisfaction with the efficacy of the method used and felt that if it were continued on a permanent basis it could help improve the quality of life of the people in the community. It can be seen from the feedback as shown in Appendix I.

4.4. Feedback of the group members

Feedback on the questionnaire was needed (see Appendix I), to determine the nature of the changes that occurred in attitude and behavior through discussion with the subjects. The result (see Appendix I) conclusively proves that on a number of points, the members felt marked changes of attitudes and a willingness to implement the plan. For all items on the feedback questionnaire, there was significant improvement. The quality of interaction can be verified from the feedback of Q.1, group discussion was considered extremely useful. In Q.3, they were of the opinion that it did enhance collaboration and cooperation that resulted in desired behavioral changes. It is also important to mention that in all questions, particularly in Q. 12 where 73% expressed that it provided a fair and free opportunity to express their ideas, there was a clear indication that being a member of the group restored their confidence after the shock. Group dynamics did help develop a coping mechanism to deal with the situation. It also shows that this technique started the process of creating a supportive system and building a climate of collective action in a positive direction.

4.5. Independent observers

The report from an independent observer was also taken. According to him:

- The methodology has had considerable impact in promoting a sense of togetherness with a sense of commitment to manage the affairs on a self help basis. Prior to this they were, by and large, afflicted with a self-centered attitude before and after the earthquake. But this participatory model has provided a new understanding to the group members, which, in turn, is serving as a catalyst for change for this community and causing their fellow community members to meet the challenges by sharing.

- A consensus does emerge on some difficult, pressing issues faced by the communities when studied in a natural field setting. They not only identify problems but also seek their solutions through well deliberated operational modalities. Once they start, the feedback from their results further reinforces them to improve upon the implementation strategies.

- Once the group makes the decision to identify not only un-met needs but also the modalities that produce desired results, there is a likelihood this will deliver greater satisfaction among the group members and community in general.

- This participatory model has substantially improved their attitude towards knowledge generation. They have felt some cause and effect relationship which has generated the requisite enthusiasm, sense of direction, and realization of the objectives.

- Another important effect of group dynamics is that now the members of the group are meeting on a regular basis, at least twice a month, where they evaluate the progress and actions taken, and prepare a future course of action and team building.

4.6. Conclusion

Human society encounters several challenges of various dimensions. The mere doling out of money and technology is not enough unless it is dovetailed with creating an attitudinal climate for alleviating problems through mutual cooperation, consensus and support. In this respect social marketing is an effective method, through use of group dynamics by empowering community members to get beyond the crises and channel their productive efforts toward re-building the community. Group dynamics have a therapeutic effect as well as building resilience to withstand challenges and take initiatives to create a supportive system, which, in turn, generates social and economic avenues that could greatly be facilitated through this approach.

5. Discussion and Implication

Unlike other studies in the field of social marketing where planned behavioral/ attitude changes, by and large, have received wider acceptance, this study is free from any imposed intervention. The real empowerment comes when people feel that they are themselves responsible in bringing about the desired change, so that the quality of life could be improved. Through group dynamics they not only become motivated but also gain insight and a sense of direction on how to accomplish a social marketing plan.

The rationale, therefore, for using group dynamics in social marketing is that it involves every member irrespective of their background, cultural status or social prejudices so that they can discuss problems without any inhibitions. The studies did reveal that consensus was achieved through understanding each other's point of view and coming to a joint solution. The success of their actions caused further reinforcement and commitment to the participatory process.

The study, though on a small scale, lent ample support to the idea that people could be very effective change agents provided they are given the opportunity to be integrated into the mainstream of development.

The concept of social marketing is not disputable, it has attained acceptance. What is significant in this research is demonstrating the efficacy of group dynamics as a social mechanism to promote knowledge seeking behavior, which through positive direction and the sense of group commitment shows that they can be successful in attaining their potential objectives. Third world countries need to adopt this approach in order to effectively harness the efficacy of social marketing, and particularly to overcome some downsides of marketing. The idea is to reduce the fatalistic viewpoint and over-reliance on external change agents. This mindset must be changed so that effort and self reliance become the determinants of achievement. A culture of deprivation tends to breed extremisms in thought and behavior, which, in turn, causes social prejudices, violence, and terrorism. Group dynamics also serve as a therapeutic measure in curtailing these maladies and promote democratic values that give respect to diversity, tolerance and acceptance for people of diverse values, which are the quintessential norms of a pluralistic nation.

References

1   Andreasen, Alan R. (1993), "Presidential Address: A Social Marketing Research Agenda for Consumer Behavior Researchers," in Michael Rothschild and Leigh McAlister (eds), University of Connecticut, *Advances in Consumer Research*, Vol.20, pp.1-5.

2   Andreasen, Alan R. (1994), "Social Marketing: Its Definition and Domain", *Journal of Marketing and Public Policy*, Spring, pp.108-114.

3   Andreasen, Alan R. (1997), "Challenges for the Science and Practice of Social Marketing", in *Social Marketing: Theoretical and Practical Perspectives*, M. E. Goldberg, M. Fishbein and S. E. Middlestadt (eds), Mahwah, NJ, Lawrence Erlbaum Associates.

4   Andreasen, Alan R. (2002), "Marketing Social Marketing in the Social Change Marketplace", *Journal of Public Policy & Marketing*, Vol.21(1), Spring, pp.3-13.

5   Andreasen, Alan R. (2005), "Marketing Scholarship, Intellectual leadership, and the Zeitgeist", *Journal of Public Policy & Marketing*, Vol.24(1), Spring, pp.133-136.

6   Annan, Kofi A. (2005), "What are the Millennium Development Goals", UN Millennium Development Goals, Retrieved February 17, 2006, from http://www.un.org/millenniumgoals/.

7   Bloom Paul N. and Novelli, William D. (1981), "Problems and Challenges in Social Marketing," *Journal of Marketing*, Vol.45, Spring, pp.79-88

8   Brenkert, George G. (2002), "Ethical Challenges of Social Marketing", *Journal of Public Policy & Marketing*, Vol.21(1), Spring, pp.14-25.

9   Hastings G. Mac Fayden, Lyun and Stead Martin, "Social Marketing", The Marketing CIM, 2000, pp.562-592.

10 Khan, M.K.N.(2006), Empowerment Trough Social Marketing, AMDIP Conference on Management Education and Practices—Challenge of Relevance, Convention Centre, Islamabad, May 5-6, 2006.

11 Khan, M.K.N. (2005b), Alternative Dispute Resolution Through Social Marketing; A Conference on Arbitration "Privatization of Justice", Islamabad, November 15, 2005.

12 Khan, M.K.N. (2005a), Social Marketing: Creating Synergies through Participatory Paradigm; Marketing and Public Policy Conference, American Marketing Association; Washington D.C, May 19-21, 2005, American Marketing Association.

13 Khan, M.K.N. (2004), Promoting Group Dynamics as Strategic Tool for Social Marketing, Marketing and Public Policy Conference, American Marketing Association; Salt Lake City, Utah USA; 20-22 May, 2004.

14 Khan, M.K.N. (2003), *"Dynamics of Marketing-Social Welfare in a Community"*; Productivity Journal, National Productivity Organization, Islamabad, pp. 39-41.

15 Khan, M.K.N. (2002), *"Productivity: What triggers it?"* First National Productivity Conference, May 2002; National Productivity Organization, Islamabad, Pakistan.

16 Kotler, Philip and Zaltman, Gerald (1971), "Social Marketing: An Approach to Planned Social Change", *Journal of Marketing (pre-1980)*, July 1971, Vol.35, pp.3-12.

17 Kotler, Philip (2005), "The Role played by the Broadening of Marketing Movement in the History of Marketing Thought", *Journal of Public Policy & Marketing*, Vol. 24(1), Spring, pp.114-116.

18 Kumbar, Rajashekhar D. (Fall 2004), "The Importance of Marketing and Total Quality Management in Libraries", *Electronic Journal of Academic and Special Librarianship*, Vol. 5 (2-3), Retrieved January 5, 2006, from http://sourhernlibrarianship.icaap.org/content/v05n02/ kumbar_r01.htm.

19 Mahmood, Khalid (2005), "Multipurpose community telecenters for rural development in Pakistan", *The Electronic Library*, 23 (2005): 204-220.

20 McKenzie-Mohr, Doug (2000), "Promoting Sustainable Behavior: An Introduction to Community-Based Social Marketing", *Journal of Social Issues,* Fall, pp.1-2.

21 McClelland David C., "The Achieving Society", D. Van Nostrand Company, Inc., (1961).

22 Oestmann, S. and Dymont, Andrew C. (2001), "Telecentres—Experiences, Lessons and Trends", in *Perspectives on Distance Education: Telecentres: Case studies and key issues*, Colin Latchem and David Walker (eds), Vancouver, The Commonwealth of Learning, pp. 1-15.

23 Thornhill, John. (2006), "The View of the Future from Davos," *The Financial Times.* January 30, 2006.

24 Wiener, Joshua L. (1993), "What Makes People Sacrifice Their Freedom for the Good of Their Community?" *Journal of Public Policy & Marketing*, Vol.12(2), Fall, pp.244-251.

25 Wilkie, William L. and Elizabeth S. Moore (1999), "Marketing Contributions to Society", *Journal of Marketing*, Vol.63 (Special Issue), pp.198-218.

26 Wilkie, William L. and Moore Elizabeth S. (2003), "Scholarly Research in Marketing: Exploring the "4 Eras" of Thought Development", *Journal of Public Policy & Marketing*, Vol.22 (2), Fall, pp.116-146.

Appendix I

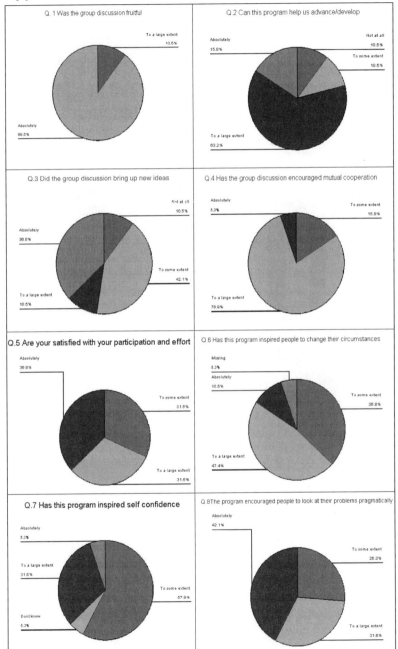

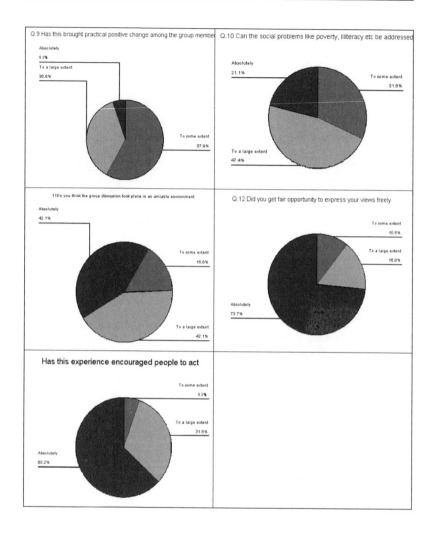

The Public Library: Environment for the Formulation of Risk Indicators in the Information Society

Ana Pérez-López, Javier López-Gijón, and Carmen Gálvez
Library and Information Science Faculty, University of Granada,
Granada, Spain

Abstract

The beginning of the third millennium confronts us with a set of changes that are the culmination of processes generated from the second half of the 20th century and are directly linked to information and communication technologies (ICT). The information society, through the Internet, is encouraging globalization and simultaneously promoting social paradigmatic changes such as sustainable development and the risk society that are slowly being outlined as an alternative, feasible, and necessary change. The indicators of risk management are considered strategic for their application to the evaluation, control and adjustments of the process of sustainability prompted in the world environment, in which public libraries become laboratories of multicultural measurement of the information society. With this paper we intend to contribute to the formulation of new indicators, within the environment of public libraries, to characterize and measure the risks that exist in regions and countries, as much inside as out of the information society. Our proposal will be focused on two basic points: (a) from a systems perspective, that advances come from the need to undertake new work methodologies that include levels of uncertainty, which, at present, accompanying risk is stated and decisions are made; and (b) by means of a holistic, interactive, flexible, and participatory perspective, just as it is being achieved in environmental risk management. These approaches will be investigated within the framework using the instruments of strategic social management, such as the indicators proposed in the Manual of Lisbon for the Information Society, and then formulated inside the management of risks proposed by Ulrich Beck.

1. Introduction

The beginning of the third millennium confronts us with changes that are the culmination of processes generated from the second half of the 20th century and are directly linked to information and communication technologies (ICT). The information society, through the Internet, is encouraging globalization and simultaneously promoting social paradigmatic changes, such as sustainable development and the risk society that are slowly being outlined as an alternative, feasible, and necessary change.

Following are the two major points of this work: first, the role the Public Library (PL), as a democratic institution, must allow access to information in all formats, areas, and times, in the information society (IS) and secondly, the definition for the conceptual basis and the methodological contributions of the proposal to formulate indicators of risk management caused by the IS.

2. The Concept of Risk Society

The risk society is a modern concept; Beck (1998) claims that it is somewhat new in the history of humanity, and implies that today there are ghosts of different social conflicts representing different historical events. Thus, according to Beck (1998) with the rise of the risk society, the conflicts on the distribution of the 'wrongs' are superimposed on the conflicts of the distribution of the 'goods' (income, work, social security) that constituted the basic conflict of the industrial society, and prominent institutions have attempted to solve these conflicts. These conflicts on the distribution of wrongs can be interpreted as conflicts on the distribution of responsibility. They arise around the distribution, prevention, control and recognition of the risks that accompany the production of goods.

The idea of "risk society", according to the German Ulrich Beck (1998, 2002), has to do with the fact that in modernity risks have grown in magnitude, have been globalized and are more difficult to calculate, to manage and to avoid. For this reason, modernity turns into reflective and critical modernity from progress, which becomes more problematic when producing goods that have some negative consequences. About the concept of "risk society", Gandásegui (2000) explains that the central element of the presentation of Beck (1998) is exactly the concept of "reflective modernity" and that this notion

implies that modernity introduces a critique of its own processes of modernization: whereas modernity was seen as a supplier of indefinite progress and
well-being without limit, at the present time, (post)modernity is producing
many risks or negative experiences that threaten the daily life of people (environmental deterioration, unemployment, diseases). The main institutions of
(post)modernity—government, industry and science—are identified as the organizations responsible for the production of these risks.

Nowadays, we live in a society of high risk: present technology has created new forms of risk and imposes a danger qualitatively different from the
ones in the past. According to Beck, we even directed ourselves toward a
new society in which the axis that structures our industrial society is no longer the distribution of goods but of wrongs. In fact, it is not the distribution
of wealth, but rather the distribution of risk which mobilizes numerous social
groups today (the fight against nuclear energy, toxic pollutants, huge public
works, food additives or genetically engineered foods). We will discuss "risk
society" by trying to assess how risk is perceived in our present "informed"
world.

The United Nations Program for Development (UNPD) has a program
titled the International Strategy for the Reduction of Disasters (ISRD). As it is
established in the World-wide Report of the UNPD (2004) on risk reduction
of disasters (see table 1, column 1), it states that disasters limit human development, especially the economic and social aspects. On the one hand, human
development could be understood as a process through which opportunities
for individuals are extended and these can be a long and healthful life, access
to education, quality of life, political freedom, guarantee of human rights and
respect for himself or herself (United Nations Program for the Development,
UNPD, 1990). On the other hand, for those people who are vulnerable, this
development can cause a greater risk of disaster and therefore cause them to
reduce their risks.

At this point in the discussion on the global risk society, it can be accepted that threats generated by industrial technological development—measured according to existing institutional criteria—are neither calculable nor
controllable. A real global challenge arises here, from which can be 'shaped'
new critical global conflicts and even wars, but also supranational institutions of cooperation, regulation of conflicts and development of consensus.
In this sense, we admit that the distribution of positives and negatives has to
be equitable. We cannot permit the benefits going to the first world and the
disadvantages to the second; this policy would cause conflicts, as mentioned
above.

Table 1. Disaster-Development

(Source: World-wide Report of the UNPD (2004). "The Reduction of Risks in disasters. A Defiance for the Development", p.20.)

	Economic Development	**Social Development**
The disasters limit the development	Destruction of fixed assets. Loss of productive capacity, access to the market and material goods. Damage to the transport infrastructure, communications or energy. Deterioration of life means, savings and physical capital.	Destruction of the sanitary or educational infrastructure and loss of human resources. Death, incapacity or emigration of important social actors, with the consequent deterioration of the share capital.
The development causes risks of disaster	Practices of unsustainable development that enrich some at the expense of others' work or unhealthy living conditions for others, or of deterioration of the environment.	Decisions in matters of development that generate cultural norms that promote social isolation or political exclusion.
The development reduces the risk of disaster	Access to drinking water, food, safe dwelling and elimination of pollutants, enlarging the adaptation capacity of the people. Commerce and technology can reduce poverty. Investments in financial mechanisms and social security that can protect against vulnerability.	Promotion of social cohesion, recognition of people or social groups excluded (as women) and opportunities of greater participation in adoption of decisions. Better access to education and sanitary services, that increase the capacity for advancement.

3. The Information Society as Risk Society: The Need for Control Mechanisms

The IS could be characterized, according to Fritz Machlup (1933), as the number of jobs that are based on the manipulation and management of information which is greater than the ones related to some type of physical effort. Therefore, the product is the information. From the perspective of the contemporary globalized economy, the IS grants to information and communication technologies (ICT) the power to become the new engines of development and progress. In the development of the IS the following features have been observed: a) the privatization of the telecommunications industries; b) the deregulation of the telecommunications market; and c) the search for global access to ICT. Many critics have indicated that the term "Information Society" is only an updated version of the cultural imperialism exerted by the rich countries toward the poor ones, especially because the plan for technological dependence is favoured.

Those who are in support of the IS claim that the incorporation of the ICT in all productive processes facilitates entrance into the global markets, where the intense competition requires a reduction in costs and almost immediate adjustment to the changing conditions of the market. In any case, even optimists about the "Information Society" admit that the digital gap is one of the main obstacles in this developmental model. For many characteristics, this phenomenon applies to all those sectors that remain, for very diverse reasons, on the margin for the benefits and associated advantages of the ICT.

The IS is not limited to the Internet, although it has played a very important role as a means to facilitate access and exchange of information and data. *Wikipedia* is an excellent example of the result of the development of this type of society. The weblogs have recently been considered as tools that encourage the creation, reproduction and manipulation of information and knowledge. According to the statement of principles of the summit of the IS carried out in Geneva, Switzerland in 2003, the IS should be centered in the person, integrative and oriented towards the development, in which all can create, consult, utilize and to share information and knowledge, so that people, communities and towns can fully employ their potential in the promotion of their sustainable development and in improvement of their quality of life, on the basis of the purpose and principles of the Letter of the United Nations.

As main characteristics of the IS we would be able to emphasize:

- Multi-focus—supports that all people with access to the network become the focus of opinion and influence.

- Terciaritation—50% of the workers of the advanced companies corresponds to the tertiary sector, and inside this group the workers dedicated to products and services linked to the information represent a greater proportion than those of other professions.

- Automation—understood as the intensive use of the ICTs.

- Globalization—understood by vague borders; already the world doesn't have boundaries defined by governments.

- Complexity—as capacity to produce, to create, to modify and to consume simultaneously inside the interactive network.

- TeleLIFE—understood as the possibility by which everything can be done at a distance: health, education, sex, banking, leisure, economy, democracy.

As all unfinished transitions, the IS generates restlessness and loss of the future vision. To reconstruct this vision and to find new alternatives which make life sustainable, mainly those who have been marginalized of the IS should constitute a commitment by political authorities and above all by information professionals. In this context, information professionals are called upon to have a proactive position that places us in new spaces and to create control mechanisms. The PL represents itself as a privileged observatory of the IS and of the inherent risks. The question, now, is to consider what the PL needs and what new competencies librarians need to acquire in order to answer the challenges we have mentioned. In relation to this, we consider:

- The PLs and institutions of information will be charged to support through new and better services the educational process just as the classical educational institutions assumed specialized training and postgraduate qualification.

- The PLs and information literacy programs will be essential in the digital environment just as virtual information access systems are for education (e-learning).

- The information professional will need the know-how on learning theory and pedagogical methods, as well as abilities and teaching experience, to design programs for training users and also effective information literacy programs.

4. The Public Library as a Key Institution in the Information Society

We propose that the PL, as a proponent of literacy, is one of the institutions that can help us advance toward the information and knowledge society. According to the human development paradigm advocated by the United Nations Program for the Development (UNPD), the development goal is not expressed exclusively by economic growth. This is considered a means but not an end to the development of opportunities for all: extended life expectancy; better quality of life; freedom; and access to education, culture and other fields that would allow them to fulfill their total personal accomplishment (UNPD, 2004).

We also consider that human development must be sustained through the conservation of the natural resources for the next generation and through sustainable social development in order to insure that the achievements of the present are consolidated to avoid backward movement. Public libraries are conceptually oriented to serve societies through democratization of information, access to knowledge, information without discrimination due to gender, ideology, or any other social and human difference. It also provides access to culture and leisure and to continuing education (literacy, self-learning). Therefore, the PL plays a vital role in the information society as well as promoting equality of opportunities and social integration. Besides, the PL fosters literacy and generates "information literate" readers.

With this objective, the PL should focus on two major goals. First, the PL should be a force for literacy. Second, the PL, as the guardian of the IS, assesses the potential for censorship and its inherent risk to society.

4.1. Information society promotion:
Reading of public library materials

At the present time it is quite common to hear that use of public libraries is needed to create a critical citizen with the capacity to generate knowledge. Some authorities state that the IS was going to be a more democratic society with integration, cooperation and social synergy, in which resources would be shared and dedicated to welfare improvement in order to put an end to social inequalities. Nevertheless, with the dawn of the new century, what we observe in general is a dominant society where resources are concentrated in the ones who have the power, exacerbating the process of inequality. Generally the people who form the disadvantaged groups belong to low social, educational, economic levels, etc., and they are not informed; these people are called the 'info-excluded' (Contreras, 2004). It is a fact that the access to information, a constitutional right in democratic societies, can be provided only through the PL as the only institution capable of guaranteeing the democratic fulfillment of this right, the same as hospitals do for health.

The PL would position itself as one of the basic pillars to advance the IS and the knowledge society, putting in practice the following functions:

- Group and collective socialization
- Access to information
- Access to education and informational literacy
- Top-level cooperation

4.2. Information society observatory: Innovative propositions

The PL from the perspective of "risk society" (Luhmann, 1998) becomes a perfect observatory for the IS. It will allow us to detect what social sectors are included ('info-included') or excluded ('info-excluded'). Disinformation can mean the lack of information, but it can also mean "information censorship," incorrect information, manipulation of information; this could all take place in a society that is incapable if discerning and critically evaluating it, and, consequently, unable to make favourable decisions for its own future. On this point, we wonder in what sense the PL has become an IS observatory. The idea here is to create a place to collect data, to process them, to produce information on the IS in order to propose guidelines to follow its development and also to know the 'radiograph' of the current situation defining the risk.

We consider that, due to the social development in which we are involved, the PL must assume new functions and tasks to complement the ones mentioned in the previous section. Some of our proposals are the following:

- Dissemination of information produced by various user groups.
- Disseminating cultural objects created by different user groups.
- Collaboration on the second (virtual) level.

5. The Public Library as the Environment for the Formulation of Risk Indicators: Proposals

In general terms, it is the denominator indicator in an empirical observation that synthesizes the aspects of a phenomenon that are considered important for one or more analytical and practical applications. Although the term "indicator" can apply to any observable characteristic of a phenomenon, it is usually applied to those that are capable of numerical expression (CEPAL, 2001). The indicators are criteria used to value, to analyze and to evaluate the behaviour of variables, that is to say, the characteristics, components, factors and elements that are taken into account for study reasons, planning and for making decisions. Also they differ from a list of data processed statistically, since the statistics are indicators directed toward a theory that supports the results, which is one reason why they are defined in advance (Tosics, 2002).

An indicator is more than a statistic. It is a variable which depends on the value assumed at a certain moment. It conveys meanings that are not immediately apparent, and that the users will decode beyond what is directly shown, because there is a cultural and social bias that is associated with it (Tau, 2001). The application of social indicators attempts to translate abstract dimensions or concepts on social reality to ones measurable and classifiable by using a process resulting in the assignment of a category or amount to each observational unit (SIISE, 2000).

Assuming that the definitions we have just brought forth on what an indicator is are understood as a 'measurement of facts', we contribute this first proposal of possible indicators to measure both the IS and its underlying risks.

5.1 Indicators of application in the determined geographic areas: Countries, regions, cities, etc.

Indicator 1. Level of development of the IS in a country.

- *Definition*: measures the degree of IS development in a country.
- *Indicator calculation:* % of workers related to information—% workers related to physical efforts =
- *Interpretation*: the positive values correspond to countries that are in the IS; the more positive the value, the more advanced is the IS. Values of 0 would mean we have just reached the IS, that is to say, the threshold of the IS. Negative values correlate to countries that have not reached the IS; the more negative the value, the farther from the IS.
- *Improvement*: increasing the number of workers related to information. If the number of workers related to the physical effort diminishes, the indicator must improve.

Indicator 2. Collective and social groups included/excluded from the IS.

- *Definition*: attempt to show what groups or collectives are included or excluded from the IS.
- *Indicator calculation*: isolation of the collectives or groups that make use of the PL and the groups that do not.
- *Interpretation*: the collectives and groups that do not make use of the PL are the groups at potential risk to be excluded from the IS.
- *Improvement*: as the number of users of the PL increases, the number of people excluded diminishes.

Indicator 3. Information literacy.

- *Definition*: ability to apply information.
- *Indicator calculation*: necessary that an international organisation define a standard of informational literacy.
- *Interpretation*: result of the application of the standard.

- *Improvement*: with programs 'CMI' (Capability for Information Handling).

Indicator 4. Indicator of the level of use of public libraries.

- *Definition*: % of the population that states it reads materials from public libraries.

- *Indicator calculation:* survey made by a statistical agency in the country among people who state they have read materials from a public library and those who have not.

- *Interpretation*: we think this indicator would correlate with the degree of development of the IS. The more reading of public library materials, the more human capital (HC) of a country, region, city, etc.

- *Improvement*: increase the number of public libraries (PL).

5.2. Indicators of the application for public libraries

Indicator 5. Use of the public library per capita.

- *Definition*: virtual and physical use per capita that a library has.

- *Indicator calculation:* total number of uses divided by the population of the library. (no. of uses / population).

- *Interpretation*: the more uses per capita, the more the population is of the IS, and is better prepared for the changes and adaptation, more human capital, more sustainable societies.

- *Improvement*: increasing the virtual and physical services of the public library.

Indicator 6. Indicator of cultural production of the different groups—users of the library.

- *Definition*: ability of the library to issue and spread the information produced by its user groups (blogs, ipod, cms . . .).

- *Indicator calculation:* number of cultural objects produced divided by the population of the library (no. cultural objects / population).

- *Interpretation*: the more objects produced per capita, the more productive wealth of the library with a more actively involved population in the IS, up-to-date, ready for change and adaptability, more human capital, more sustainable societies.

- *Improvement*: increase the production of cultural objects.

Indicator 7. Indicator of degree of primary and secondary cooperation.

- *Definition*: capacity of the library to interact with other libraries and with the user community (shared collections, reference at the library, interlibrary lending, virtual collection, more circulation). It is considered first level when it is related to onsite interaction, and second level when it is related to virtual interaction.

- *Indicator calculation:* number of cooperative programs a library has divided by the library staff (no. programs/staff).

- *Interpretation*: cooperation increases the information services of the library. The more cooperation, the less risks.

- *Improvement:* increasing the production of cultural objects.

6. Final Considerations

We are convinced that the public library is an ideal measure to determine the level of the information society in different geographic areas of the world. With this work we have theorized and tried to prove that taking risks does not always have to result in disasters, but that the risk observed, studied and analyzed becomes a means of innovation by redefining itself as the engine for social development. In this sense, we have proposed a bold series of indicators that offer interesting lines of study. We are conscious that the public library is in "an initial phase of its development" in the new information society. The current public library is open to thousands of possibilities to introduce new services, new tools, new skills by its professionals, and new functions and tasks. The only thing we need to know is how to recognize them and to create them. We have a sufficient budget, a sufficient technology, but we lack imagination.

References

1   Beck, U. (1998). *La sociedad del Riesgo*. Barcelona: Paidós.

2   Beck, U. (2000). *The Brave New World of Work*. Cambridge: University Press.

3   BISER Indicators. (2002). The Emerging Information Society. Accessible at http://www.biser-eu.com/results.htm [12/02/2006].

4   Castells, M. (1998). *La era de la información. Economía, sociedad y cultura. Fin de milenio*. Madrid: Alianza Editorial.

5   CEPAL (2001). Accessible at http://www.eclac.cl/publicaciones/ DesarrolloProductivo/7/ LCL1497P/LCL1497.pdf [16/01/2006].

6   CEPAL (2001). Estadísticas. Accessible at http://www.eclac.cl/cgi-

bin/getProd.asp?xml=/revista/agrupadores_xml/aes18.xml&xsl=/
agrupadores_xml/agrupa_listado.xsl [16/01/2006].

7   Coll, C. (2005). Lectura y alfabetismo en la sociedad de la información.
    UOC papers. Accessible at http://www.uoc.edu/uocpapers/1/dt/esp/coll.
    pdf.

8   Contreras, F. (2004). Bibliotecas públicas: espacios de inclusión social.
    Bibliodocencia: Revista de Profesores de Bibliotecología 1(2). Accessible
    at E-Lis http://eprints.rclis.org/ archive/00005309/.

9   Gandasegui, M. (2000). *Cultura, Riesgo y el Canal de Panamá. Modernidad
    reflexiva e Irresponsabilidad Organizada*. Ponencia. Conferencia IV
    Encuentro de Prospectivas. México, D.F., 24-26 May.

10 Gill, P. (2002). Directrices IFLA/UNESCO para el desarrollo del servicio
    de bibliotecas públicas. In Cabrera Bohórquez, J. (Eds.). *México: Consejo
    Nacional para la Cultura y las Artes*. Accessible at E-Lis: http://eprints.
    rclis.org/archive/00006318/ [13/05/2006].

11 INFOLAC (1999). *Declaración de Caracas sobre la biblioteca publica*.
    Accessible at http://infolac.ucol.mx/documentos/bibliotecas/prin2.html
    [13/05/2006].

12 Luhmann, N. (1998). *Sociología del Riesgo*. México: Triana; Universidad
    Iberoamericana.

13 Machlup, F. (1933). Zur Frage der Ankurbelung durch Kreditpolitik.
    Zeitschrift für Nationalökonomie. Accessible at http://es.wikipedia.org/.

14 SIISE (2000). Sistema Integrado de Indicadores Sociales del Ecuador.
    [Human Development Department; Latin America and the Caribbean
    Region] Ecuador Crisis, Poverty and Social Services (2 vols.) Volume
    1: Main Document. Accessible at http://www-wds.worldbank.org/
    servlet/WDSContentServer/WDSP/IB/2000/09/01/000094946_
    00082305314080/Rendered/PDF/multi_page.pdf [13/05/2006].

15 Suaiden, E. J. (1999). La biblioteca pública y la sociedad de la información;
    globalización y escenarios. *Revista El libro en América Latina y el Caribe*
    no. 87 (Jan–June 1999) pp. 28-38.

16 Suaiden, E. J. (2002). El impacto social de las bibliotecas públicas. *Anales
    de Documentación*, no. 5, 2002, pp. 333-344.

17 TAU (2001). Indicadores Ambientales, una propuesta para España.
    Accessible at http://www.eclac.cl/publicaciones/DocumentosPublicacion
    es/7/LCL1607P/lcl1607e_4.pdf [12/02/2006].

18 The Lisbon Handbook (2004). Accessible at http://ricyt.centroredes.mine.
    nu/ricyt/lisboa/ manual_lisboa.pdf [13/05/2006].

19 Tosics, I. Measuring and Evaluating Transition: The Blessing and Curse of

Indicators. Accessible at http://www.worldbank.org/transitionnewsletter/ mayjune2002/pgs44-46.htm [13/05/2006].

20 United Nations Program for the Development (UNPD) (2004). *Informe Mundial del 2004. Reduciendo el riesgo a desastres: un desafío para el desarrollo.* Accessible at http://www.undp.org/bcpr/disred/espanol/ publications/rdr.htm [13/05/2006].

21 UNESCO (1994). *Manifiesto de la UNESCO sobre la biblioteca pública.* Accessible at http://www. ifla.org/sg/unesco/spain.htm [13/05/2006].

With Multiculturalism as a Backdrop, the Re-positioning of Digital Information Services in Chinese Public Libraries

Tong Zhang
The Information Department of Tianjin Library

Abstract

The formation and structure of global multicultures has put an end, once and for all, to the traditional role and services provided to society by the public library. Digital information services provided by Chinese public libraries are now causing a great reform. This paper discusses the challenge to reposition digital information services in Chinese public libraries.

Since entering the 21st century, people have been anticipating the rapid development of science and technology through information technology, and the culmination of civilization by the expansion of communication to become the "global village." Through dialogue and cooperation and communication and harmony between communities, there is a movement in China to learn from the creation of a global world culture. In the Chinese public library, the information technology department employs the Internet and digital technology to meet the ever increasing need for information by providing multiple services ever trending toward more digitization. All agree that the fairest way to obtain information is by sharing information resources and closing the "digital gap". Through network opportunities, public libraries are now acting to safeguard the interests and rights of people to access public information. So in public libraries, we can't only concentrate on increasing the number of readers on site, we should also place an emphasis on increasing the number of readers in our community from among those who have not used the services of public libraries, especially digital information. Tianjin Library, which is one of the largest public libraries in China, has created and adopted the latest digital information services during the ten years since 1996. In light of specific circumstances, the author re-thinks the focus of information reference work within the concept of multiculturalism and modern information processes, redefining the role of digital information work in the public library, and presents ideas from her own experience and that of colleagues.

1. The Goal of Digital Information Services in a Chinese Public Library

The public library is not only a great treasure house of knowledge; it is also a collection and distribution center of information resources. The change in public expectations leads to changes in functions and patterns of information service, helping readers locate information from a vast global information sea, and satisfy many demands by providing on-line service. The librarian has moved gradually from the beginning to the end by providing Internet advisory services, instead of bringing the readers to information and service. At present, a variety of processes have created many new ways to express and convey information. By learning and applying new systems and methods, it is convenient and efficient to exchange knowledge and information. Especially through the use of the Internet, the acquisition of books in a public library has created the new phenomenon of document delivery, intellectual property, and information networks. These have all been created by using new digital information technologies.

2. Rapid Adoption of Digital Information Service in the Chinese Public Library

In 1993, America raced to build the "Information Highway". In 1994, it opened the first "Global Information Highway" to the entire world, and there was a response from many countries. The Chinese government and the Chinese library circles paid attention to the role of Chinese public libraries during this information trend. The authorities held the view that digital format is the inexorable trend for the future development of the Chinese public library. So the government quickly invested funds to do basic construction of digital libraries. In 1995, the Chinese National Library was the first to set up an electronic reading room, and then the other provincial public libraries followed one after the other. The first wave of electronic information created by Chinese public libraries was from 1995 to 1998. Many of these libraries are located on the east coast, having a major impact on opening up to the outside world.

Then the wave reappeared in the provincial public libraries. The electronic reading rooms of all the provincial public libraries are almost completed, including the relatively isolated western and remote areas. Those libraries that had already set up a reading room have further expanded their services and perfected their public services. At Tianjin Public Library the government invested 30 million RMB to build an electronic reading room with 24 computers and seats; in 1996 it opened for users. Due to the demand for electronic information service, in 2006 the fund for buying various electronic or Internet data bases reached 800,000 RMB. Many provincial public libraries have already set up their own web sites on the Internet. The computer work stations—more than several dozen—let users of digital information access every department of the public library and through those, the global network of document information systems.

3. Digital Information Service in the Chinese Public Library

At present, there are two major digital information services in the public libraries; they are local service and long-distance service.

3.1. Local service

This service focuses on those who use digital documents including standard Internet service, media viewing, speech and hearing services, and specialized subject consultation service. It not only saves human resources but also space. Readers can enjoy all the digital electronic services they want in one place conveniently and quickly. Readers do not have to come to the library in person to locate information. They may not have a high level of computer skills. They should also be familiar with information resources and have some retrieval skills and a foreign language. Due to economic circumstances, some people may not even have a computer, or understand how to operate one. Some libraries don't have internal networks or access to the Internet, but they have a strong desire to access information. The general public at the present time is unable to access and use digital resources of the public library, even though there is growing popularity of digital information services.

3.2. Remote information service

Because of the current reality of full-text searching on the Internet, e-mail has become a popular way to access and exchange information resources.

It has already become an important part of distance information service by making full use of the Internet by quickly providing them electronic document information from other libraries who own it. For example, in 2003, Tianjin Library signed more than 30 agreements with libraries of national universities and institutes. Readers can send their request to the information service center of their local public library through e-mail, and receive the full text the same way within a day. So the readers can get the documents quickly instead of going to the library in person. This service is very popular and is welcomed and appreciated, and the use of it is growing rapidly. Distance education is one of the new offerings of the public library's remote information service.

4. The Study of the Digital Information Service in the Chinese Public Library

After reviewing the *Public Library Manifesto* issued by UNESCO in 1994, the challenge is how to accomplish the public library's mission "Reading for All." The services of the public library should be geared to the need of all the citizens in the community. It's not only for a few, especially after the development of digital information service; it should be an all-encompassing, multicultural service, that is to say, as the Chinese proverb goes: "It should be as the spring snow is fertilizer to the poor farmer," bringing benefits to all people. Using Tianjin Library as an example, the readers are generally divided into two groups by their digital information needs, namely the digital document reading service which is called positional service in the library, and the digital document searching service which is called the Internet service. There are no restrictions on use of the digital databases for those readers who come to the library in person. They are welcomed as long as they hold a Tianjin Library card and have the required credentials; also we especially provide free digital service to the elderly, children, city labor workers and the other needy groups. For readers who use the library without coming to the library, we promote the library through its Internet homepage, the media, and news releases, etc., and by providing "Internet Joint Consulting Services"—Internet expert consultants who answer questions and find digital documents on-line. The public libraries jointly co-distribute electronic book cards within the 18 district or suburb libraries and all the community libraries in the city. We do our best to popularize the use of digital information among citizens.

4.1. Individualized service

As a result of the constant and newly emerging changes caused by new social phenomena, national marketing for economic development, vendors'
sharp competition, economic prosperity and great interest in science, numerous readers are expecting more for their own use or that of a spouse. To accommodate the special needs of a reader, some well-supported national public
libraries, such as Shanghai or Tianjin, have organized special departments and
transferred a few qualified librarians to provide special services. As the Chinese proverb states: "Fit the appetite to the dishes and the dress to the figure";
whatever they do must be done according to the real need. It also includes
providing reference materials throughout the entire research process, from the
time of signing an agreement for the project, to the different research stages,
resulting in the academic researcher's publication, and even the final step of
providing market access throughout the world. This kind of service is changing individual service images of the public library among readers. This has
been identified as "a crown jewel" for information special services of the national public libraries.

4.2. Service for special social groups

Chinese authorities are putting into effect the policy of "strengthening the nation through science and education"; we are adopting various ways of running
schools in order to raise the quality of the nation. These students don't have
the study resources provided by a university, so they place great expectation
on the public library. They come to the public library and form a special group
of the readers. We think it is an opportunity for the public library to serve continuing education. We immediately began to revise searching resources and
methods; held computer training classes; taught skills for searching digital
electronic documents; etc. We distributed preferential library cards to those
students and we do our best to meet their needs. The public library can become the major resource to support continuing education. Many readers became skilled and trained persons with the help of public libraries. With the rise
of material living standards, the average life-span has been lengthened more
than ever. Many healthy elderly are still eager to pursue new knowledge; with
major construction in the city, more and more rural workers are becoming a
main source of labor for this construction. So the handicapped, the elderly,
and city labor workers are now formed as another special community group.
At present, we have set up special reading-rooms and provide special computers for them in most of the national public libraries. A series of preferential

measures and universal education lectures are provided for the elderly and the city labor workers, and we try to provide enriched free-time cultural activities, help them solve some legal issues such as legal policies and procedures, material benefits, etc, by allowing digital service in the public library to accommodate the ordinary person, especially that the disadvantaged groups have access to digital information by providing it free of charge.

4.3. Internet joint consulting service

Digital consulting service, which has broken through space restrictions, reaches people who are distant and provides them with service. This service that bridges the space distance is accomplished through the Internet. There is a column for reference consulting service on the homepage of every public library. The reference consultant librarians not only answer the various difficult questions that are raised by the readers on-line, but also indicate to them how to access and use the Internet digital systems. Meanwhile, to meet the readers' needs, they do their best to gather appropriate information from many different digital databases, then re-package it, and finally transmit it to the readers through the Internet. We wish that all of the local public libraries, college libraries and other professional libraries would join together and combine resources to provide 24 hour on-line service, thereby enabling digital consulting service to span a greater distance.

4.4. Information education service

Information Education Service is the service to assess the readers' abilities to use information, focusing on using the computer and remote on-line information, to understand the contents of various digital information resources, to learn retrieval methods, and finally to improve their ability to acquire and utilize digital information. So the librarian is also called a "knowledge navigator", and has the responsibility to instruct and help users understand the types, distributions, structures, and searching methods of various on-line digital information data bases, and finally to increase the efficiency of digital data consulting. We regularly hold lectures on special topics such as "Internet On-line Digital Document Retrieval" or "Http Instruction" and so on, to satisfy different readers' demands from the multicultural perspective.

The public library is a large classroom and is not restricted by one's educational background, position, or age. Even though the public library has the responsibility to provide open access to information, the separate nature of the public library contributes to its ability to be fair distributors of information. We should provide the superior service of "The Spring Snow" and the universal popular service of "The Song of the Poor Farmer" as well. Through the utilization of today's modern high technologies, an international tide of digital library creation has been adapting digital information consulting service as a dominant factor in China's reform. Outside policy requires that the Chinese public library eventually approach the world level. This can be accomplished through the creation of the Chinese digital library, by promoting the development of the national economy, by raising the level of education in the nation, by realizing the link between science and culture to eventually achieve the reality of a harmonious society.

Beyond Promotion—The Destination Library: The National Library of Singapore Case Story

Wee Pin Wan

National Library Board, Singapore

Abstract

It is believed that marketing is the elixir to promote the usage of library services; however many fail to see the huge gap that exists between telling everyone you have the best collections and them using it.

More than promotion is needed if people are to come to use library services. There is a need to change the mindset in terms of what a patron can experience or do each time he makes a trip to the library. The Destination Library strategy thus adopts a 3-pronged approach to catalyze this new paradigm shift.

No. 1: Libraries cannot be passive; they must actively create opportunities where the usage of services is embedded within activities or programmes that can attract the masses. In this instance, services are the means to an end; patrons can for example use the library's collections within the context of creating new historically based characters in a Comics competition.

No. 2: The multi-tiered model utilized in the strategy ensures a variety of programmes and activities that differentiates in terms of participation and interactivity. This ranges from tier-one programmes that adopt a populist approach to attract patrons to tier-three workshops where the participants are involved in the creation process with tangible outputs.

No. 3: As a Destination Library, the emphasis is to provide visitors with an enriching experience encompassing different dimensions like exhibitions, workshops, seminars and performances. This is achieved through a monthly thematic scheme that is represented by an icon or topic that is accessible and interesting. Like the seasonal collections of fashion houses, each month the library will showcase activities and programmes that fall under the overarching general theme.

This paper will discuss these three aspects as well as highlight other issues and related ideas from the NLB perspective.

Libraries have traditionally not been known as places that the general public would visit other than to borrow books or to enquire for information. As societies change and with the advent of the Internet as the now preferred source of enquiry for many people, libraries can no longer sit back and expect that our customers will continue coming to us. Libraries can no longer afford to be passive; rather we must change our tack to attract the people back to our building.

In the past, library programmes have been seen as the accompanying component to the books that libraries have; we use programmes like storytelling or book launches to highlight the collections. However in today's societal context that is no longer enough. We need to seize the initiative to create programmes of a new and different nature in order to compete with the many attractors fighting for the limited leisure time an individual has.

What I am about to share with you is the strategy that the National Library in Singapore has embarked on to successfully reconnect with the public and to change them from being our readers to our "audience".

The main thing that we have done is to adopt the concept of being a "Destination Library," defined as a place that people can spend their entire day exploring rather than just the time that they usually take for borrowing or returning their books, and conducting their research. Programming is at the forefront of recreating the library as a destination that people would specially visit. We want to present a holistic experience for any person that walks through our doors.

The Destination Library strategy adopts a 3-pronged approach to catalyze this new paradigm shift.

- The library cover story

As a Destination Library, the emphasis is to provide visitors with an enriching experience encompassing different dimensions like exhibitions, workshops, seminars and performances. This is achieved through a monthly thematic scheme known as a cover story which in turn is represented by an icon or topic that is accessible and interesting. Like the seasonal collections of fashion houses, each month the library will showcase activities and programmes that fall under the overarching general theme.

- Multi-tiered programming model

The multi-tiered model utilized in the strategy ensures a variety of programmes and activities that differentiates in terms of participation and interactivity. This ranges from tier-one programmes that adopt a populist approach to attract patrons to tier-three workshops where the participants are involved in the creation process with tangible outputs.

• Applied librarianship

Libraries cannot be passive; they must actively create opportunities where the usage of services is embedded within activities or programmes that can attract the masses. In this instance, services are the means to an end; patrons can for example use the library's collections within the context of creating new historically based characters in a Comics competition.

1. The Library Cover Story

Similar to other industries like the fashion houses or the museums, we centre our programmes along a particular theme—known as a cover story, just like that of a monthly magazine. These cover stories are linked each month to a particular collection within our library so as to generate coherence, and this creates a sense of excitement and anticipation for the public. Much like how one would wait for the launch of Prada's or Armani's new collections, so are the programmes introduced in a similar manner.

We understand that the manner in which our libraries classify our collections and the related headings may not be appealing to the public, thus it is important for us to select an icon on which to hang all the programmes. We usually utilize the guiding principles of People, Place, Event and Object and these are usually linked to pop culture references that most people can identify with.

• People refer to the personalities, or characters that are interesting and engaging from a historical as well as modern perspective.

• Place refers to certain areas, countries, cities, or even civilizations that are rich and intriguing.

• Object would refer to the physical entities that either have great significance or meaning.

• Event refers to certain incidents or happenings that have a lot of resonance from a historical and social perspective.

For example, the National Library used the Chinese classic *Dream of Red Chamber* as the cover story for our programmes in January 2006. This was linked to our Chinese collections and in relation to the cover story; there were programmes, talks and even a world-first exhibition that displayed all the rare and private collections of several local collectors to showcase the richness and diversity of this novel.

With this cover story, members of the public found it very easy to identify with the programmes that are curated in relation to it. With twelve cover stories that revolve around the multiple collections, we ensure that there will always be something for the public to look forward to.

That is not all; we also support our programmes with collaterals that serve to introduce to the general public our collections and resources. We position these as the accompanying materials much like how catalogues and exhibition guides are to fashion houses and museums.

We always have a resource guide that is produced in relation to the cover story, with the purpose of allowing those who found the subject interesting and would like to explore it further, the links and titles available in our library. We also give out a programme guide at each programme that usually covers the main topics discussed and even speaker recommendations. Thus the interests in the topics are sustained and the experiences extended beyond the lifespan of the programmes themselves.

2. Multi-Tiered Programming Model

Now that we understand the philosophy and concept of the Destination Library, let us examine the format of how this scheme is being carried out.

Essentially, this is done through a three-tiered format that covers different natures of programming and different venues or physical spaces. Allow me to introduce them. For tier-one programmes, these are usually held in our plaza where there is a large space for the gathering of crowds. These programmes are usually catered for mass participation; they are entertainment-based and there really is little to no audience interaction. Events such as exhibitions, cultural performances, and even movie screenings are part of the repertoire of tier-one programmes.

Tier-two programmes on the other hand pertain mainly to sessions such as talks, panel discussions and conferences. There is some interaction between the speaker/expert and the audience because the latter is encouraged to take part in the discussion and there are facilitation segments such as a question & answer session. More than just public education, the talks and discussions are meant for presentations that intrigue and catalyze thinking and reactions.

In a way, conferences are meant as avenues for participants to share and to exchange ideas; we work a lot with different communities and organizations to co-organize these events to ensure a certain level of expertise and standard. Amongst the speakers we have invited are ambassadors, overseas professors and even a NASA astronaut.

There are in fact two approaches here when it comes to the talks; on the one hand, we aim to promote the quality and depth of content when it comes to the talks and the speakers. We want the talks to go beyond the general—rather than educate, we want to provoke.

On the other hand, we also adopted a populist approach. We know that not all of the speakers and the topics will be able to attract the audience that we want so we also organize other series where the invited guest speakers are real personalities that can attract the numbers. Through the talks, we then aim to let the participants know about the richness and quality of the collections that we have through the guides that were mentioned earlier.

The main aim of this approach is to attract into the library a particular clientele and segment of society that otherwise will not come to the library either due to their own perceived ignorance of what the library has or deterred because of the image of the word "library".

In this vein, we have created a very successful series called Directing Asia where we got prominent Asian directors to talk about issues and topics that revolve around Asian societies that also cropped up in their films. This has attracted crowds of more than 500 at its peak and created a real buzz for the library. Amongst the speakers we have had included Jackie Chan, Pan Nalin, Stanley Kwan, Peter Chan and our local filmmaker Jack Neo.

3. Applied Librarianship

Finally we arrive at tier-three programmes, which are programmes of an interactive and creative nature. These usually take the shape of workshops or creative sessions where the audience is expected to participate in the discussion and a lot of times, the experiences generated include hands-on activities.

In these instances, what we have done is to integrate the usage of the library's resources and collections into the process of the workshops themselves in a subtle and covert manner. The main purpose is to get the participants to use the library as part of the process. As an example, the National Library and a local comics company worked together to create an event called the 24 hours Comics Jam that was meant as a talent search creative competition as well as to introduce their launch of a new line of comics.

What was included in the competition was a prize called the research prize and this was given to the artist who was the most accurate and extensive in his research so as to portray historically correct details such as costumes, scenery and even hairstyles. As a result, the participants referred to the books and resources available in our reference libraries as materials for their works. In this way, the participants would have already used the library in a natural and unobtrusive manner, at times even without them knowing it. This proved to be more effective in allowing and introducing the library to the public rather than user education courses or info-literacy classes.

Another new concept that we have introduced is to subtly include our librarians into the workshop format and process as well. In the past, what we tried to do was to explore the possibility of inserting the librarian into the world, i.e., trying to get librarians to be involved in the creative processes and work plans of organizations in order to demonstrate what the librarian can offer or contribute in a real and tangible manner. While logically sound, the implementation process proved too difficult.

Thus instead what we have done now is to include the librarian as part of the experts involved in the workshops and discussions so that they can provide their perspectives and knowledge and make real tangible contributions in the creative process. This has allowed a real-life environment whereby librarians can interact with both industry experts as well as members of the public from all walks of life and display the value-add that their profession allows.

This leads me to my final point which is the fact that libraries today need to face up to reality. We are now competing for time together with so many other options that people have to spend their time and if we remain stuck in the old paradigm, then our survival will be seriously threatened. Thus when we do good work in our libraries by organizing events and curating programmes, we need to market and advertise them properly, tapping on the advertising channels that are normally used by commercial companies. We need to do a better job of reaching out to the masses and the most effective manner is through the mass media. Thus we need to be savvy about this aspect of work that did not come to play in the past.

I hoped to have shared with you the story of how the National Library in Singapore attempted to recreate and revamp the way in which programmes are being organized and the manner in which they are used. Likewise I hope this would inspire all of you here today to rethink about your processes and to come up with your new ideas on how this can be done. Do share with me your success stories in the coming future ahead.

Part IV

**Changing Libraries
in a Multicultural World**

Librarians' Professional Values and Perspectives in the Era of the Digital Library

Keqian Xu

Nanjing Normal University Library

Abstract

As a result of the rapid development of information technology in the past decade, technological factors are playing much more important roles in today's library. Nevertheless, the value and the position of librarians as the experts of information management and consultancy have not been replaced by technology. In this paper, some traditional and also permanent values and perspectives of librarianship have been emphasized and reiterated in the environment of the digital library, combined with the introduction and discussion of the practice and the experience of Nanjing Normal University Library during its pursuit of modernization and new technology in the past few years. The paper shows that in the time of the digital library, traditional librarians' values are still very important in adding humanistic concerns to the technological operation of the digital library, and librarians should never shirk the responsibility of promoting information literacy and information democracy. Under the new situation of digitization and globalization, librarians should be more aware than ever of their responsibility of protecting and preserving human heritages and cultural diversity. As managers of both knowledge and communication, librarians may possibly contribute more of their wisdom and perspective in the dynamic and collaborative process of knowledge creation.

1. Introduction

As a result of the rapid development of the technology of computer network and information communication, IT factors now play more and more important roles in the work of libraries. In the past decade, the rapid development of information technology has been vigorously and irresistibly pushing libraries towards the era of computing, networking and digitization. The "digital library" has recently become the most frequently mentioned term in almost any discussion related to librarianship. However, most research concerning the digital library today mainly emphasizes the technological aspects of library science, while the roles and values of librarians in the digital library have not been fully discussed (Sloan, 1998). There is no doubt that the emphasis of technological aspects is reasonable and necessary. However, some traditional and permanent values and perspectives of librarianship, which so far have defined the vocation of a librarian, are still very important and should never be neglected.

Some scholars have correctly predicted that "In the future, the librarian's roles will shift from an emphasis on acquisition, preservation and storage to an emphasis on teaching, consulting, researching, preserving democratic access to information, and collaborating with computer and information scientists in the design and maintenance of information access systems" (England & Shaffer, 2004). In my opinion, this shift will not mean that the librarian will disappear from the oncoming digital library. Rather, it indicates that librarians will play more important roles in the digital library. The ways and methods that librarians use to do their jobs may be changed, but the essence of librarians' social function and core values as the experts of information management and consultancy will remain the same. And more importantly, some traditional librarians' values will be indispensable in adding humanistic concerns over the technology mechanism of the digital library.

In the past 10 years, the Library of Nanjing Normal University (NJNU), as an epitome of many ordinary college libraries or academic libraries in China, has experienced huge technological renovation and revolution. Libraries have been shifting from the simplest self-designed computer-controlled circulation system to the advanced all-in-one library management system; from a single-medium library with printed materials as its main collection, to a hybrid library with multi-media and multi-genre collections; from merely providing on-site reading and circulation services to today's variety of information service based on computer technology and the Internet. Our librarians have witnessed dramatic changes happening in the library every year, every semester, every month, and even every week.

The great higher-education expansion of China in the past years, combined with the newly developed and ever-changing library technology, has stimulated and accelerated the governmental investment in many academic libraries. As in the case of the NJNU Library, the library's annual budgets in recent years have been roughly 6 to 8 times that of early the 1990s. In 1997,

NJNU was fortunate to be included among 100 universities covered by the national "211" project, which means that with other universities on the list, NJNU would receive extra investment from both the central and local governments. And in both the first and second 5 year terms of this project, the library of NJNU has been undertaking a sub-project with the goal of promoting library modernization. The sub-project of the second 5-year term, which began in 2002, is especially concerned with the construction of the "digital library". With the strong financial support of the project, our library has become much more modernized, networked and digitized, in terms of library buildings, library facilities, or in its forms of collections and its way of providing services. In the past years the sharpest outlay increase had occurred in those expenses related to new library technology and newly emerged sorts of library collections, such as the electronic reading rooms, computer network and storage hardware, all kinds of digital resources such as CD-ROMs, mirror site databases, and licensed on-line accessible databases.

However, on our road towards the so-called "digital library", we have found that whether in a traditional library or in the oncoming "digital library", the most important factor that has defined and will decide the nature and future of our profession is not just technology, but some of the traditional librarian's values and perspectives. Without these values and perspectives, no matter how well a library building is equipped with modern information technology and connected with the gigantic digital database network, it will still be anything but a library. Well educated and qualified librarians as the human resource are still the most important factor in a digitized library.

In the following parts of this paper, I would like to reiterate some of the basic values and perspectives of librarianship as a profession, which will still be very important in the digital library and, in general, in the contemporary information society. Some practices and experiences of the NJNU Library will also be discussed and shared.

2. The Role of Human Interaction Between Information, Technology and Their Users

Although the technology and tools used in the library have been changing so quickly during the past decade, the essence of the librarian's mission remains the same, that is, to help the user find the right information and help the information reach its intended user. Technology itself can never completely replace the humanistic concern and human interactions that happened in traditional libraries. Just as some experts have pointed out: "A connection between the information system and the end user built with the support of the information specialist is often stronger than the direct connection from system to user" (Tenopir, 2006). In the environment of the Internet and the digital library, the librarian's role as a bridge is even more important. While in a traditional library, our users faced only relatively limited types of resources, now they are facing a much wider range of information, which is in a variety of media, from various sources, kept in quite different types of storage and retrieved in quite different ways. At the same time, it is likely that some information may reach the users more easily for any reason, but its academic value and veracity might be questionable. Sometimes academic users even complain that the new information technology only resulted in piles of more information rubbish along with the real, valuable information they wanted. Therefore, the librarian's function of information guiding, filtering and evaluating becomes more necessary and crucial.

After several years of construction, our library now is providing many new services based on computer network and digital databases, such as self-help online searching, guiding and tutoring, etc. But one of our recent questionnaire surveys shows that the first choice of more than half of our clients when they need help in using the library or finding information is still "ask a librarian face to face". This rate among the senior professors is 62.1%, among the other faculty and staff is 55.6%, among the postgraduate students is 58.1%, and among the undergraduate students is 72.2%. Our questionnaire also asked our clients if it is necessary for the library to set special librarians with certain academic backgrounds as the link person between the library and the clients of different specialty areas. 56.9% of the senior professors, 28.9% of the other faculty and staff, 42.4% of the postgraduate students and 17.8% of the undergraduate students thought it is "very necessary". Only less than 3% of all those surveyed persons thought it is "not necessary". This survey shows that in the environment of a quasi-digital library, our users still need the personalized service of librarians, and this need is considered to be more urgent by those who mainly concentrate in academic research (senior professors and postgraduate students).

Electronic or digital publication is a revolution in the history of publication. However, digital publication has not fundamentally changed the dialectic relation between the publishers and their consumers. In the digital era, the librarian's role as a bridge between knowledge creators and knowledge users is still valuable and necessary. The frequent conflicts and contradictions between the owners and the users of digital intellectual property rights have made the big electronic publication companies eventually find that they still need librarians to connect their products (especially those big academic databases) with their terminal users.

A few years ago, the NJNU Library bought a couple of Chinese e-book systems, which were sold to the library in whole packages. However, our users' response was not as enthusiastic as expected. Some users, especially the professors and the postgraduate students, were disappointed with the un-selected contents of some e-book databases. They complained that there were few books of real academic value that were relevant to their teaching and re-search. This shows that without the traditional acquisition process conducted by the experienced librarians, the quality and relevance of the digital collec-tions will not be guaranteed. Afterwards, we managed to cooperate with one of the e-book companies. Our librarians provided the book list, and the company was supposed to find these books, get the copyrights and then digitize them for us. This way we have greatly improved our e-book collections.

Librarians should keep a balance between promoting free access to in-formation and respecting intellectual property rights, and between the ben-efits of information (databases) providers and those of library users. Our li-brary has bought most of its databases as a member of the consortia led by CALIS (China Academic Library & Information System) or JALIS (Jiangsu Academic Library & Information System). We know that our representatives always have a tough time when they negotiate with those commercial data-base companies for a favorable price and for minimizing the restriction in ac-cess. So we want to let our users get the maximum benefit from these digital resources. Librarians play a very crucial role in promoting and instructing in the access and usage of new databases. Nevertheless, librarians also play an important role in keeping the access and usage legal and complying with the agreements, thus protecting the property rights and the benefits of the database companies.

3. Librarians' Role in Promoting Information Literacy and Information Democracy

Just like any other technology, the technology that is used in the digital library may have both positive and negative consequences to a society. One of its possible negative consequences is that the rapid development of new technol-ogy might enlarge the inequality between the information-rich and informa-tion-poor. It is the librarian's humanistic concern and duty to avoid or reduce those negative consequences. Librarians should never shirk the responsibility of promoting information literacy and information democracy.

A statistic provided by Mr. Vint Cerf, the senior vice-president of tech-nology strategy at MCI, in his keynote address in JCDL (Joint Conference of Digital Library) 2004, shows that among the currently estimated 745 million Internet users in the world, 31% of them are in Asia, and the growth trends indicate that the majority of Internet users will eventually be from Asia (Cerf, 2004). This statistic seems quite optimistic at first. However, 31% of the 745 million Internet users only constitutes about 6% of the total Asian population of 3,800 million. That means the majority of Asian people at this moment have not been able to benefit directly from the Internet. In an information society, the capability and the right of access to information mean opportunity and fortune. However, the advancement of information technology has not benefited every-one equally, due to the unbalanced development of economies and education. While information technology has greatly empowered certain social elites, the lower classes might still be in a state of information illiteracy. Consequently the gap between the rich and the poor is deepening. It is the librarian's profes-sional duty to promote the equal and free access to information for everyone. We even have tougher tasks in the digital era to reach this goal, since in addi-tion to our traditional endeavor we also have to help people to overcome the technological barriers that did not exist in the traditional library.

China's economy has been developing quickly in the past decades, and the Jiangsu province, where our university is located, is one of the most quickly developing provinces in China. Yet the economic development in this prov-ince is not balanced, which has obvious consequences for our students, who are from different parts of this province. While some students from the rich southern urban areas are quite sophisticated in computers and networks, other students from some of the northern poorer rural areas have seldom touched a keyboard in their middle and high school education. This difference has deep influence on their capability and attitude in using the modernized library, and even has further influence on their personal development in the university. With professional and ethical consciousness, our librarians have created sev-eral countermeasures to deal with this situation, such as providing more tutor-ing for those students who need more help than the new students' orientation program gives; providing more convenience in using on-site library facilities to those students who have no personal computers and are not able to access library resources in their dormitories; giving more part-time library jobs to those students who come from the poor families, etc. But what is most im-portant is that our librarians should be alert to find out that sometimes a us-er's difficulty in using a digital library resource may just be caused by some very simple technical problems, and our librarians should be more patient with those students who have little knowledge about computers and networks when providing them with troubleshooting help.

Free access to information is very important in promoting information democracy and social democracy in general. Protecting the privacy of information users is crucial in achieving this goal. However, due to the openness and vulnerability of computer networks, library users' privacy is more endangered in certain aspects than in traditional libraries. Protecting the users' right and privacy of free accessing to information is an important library value which is promised in the code of ethics of libraries in many countries. This value should also be seriously considered and realized in designing and managing the digital library.

Due to the influence of certain aspects of traditional Chinese culture, the privacy of library users was seldom emphasized for a long time. However, in the first Chinese Librarians' Ethic Code issued by the China Society for Library Science in 2002, there is an article about respecting users' privacy. In today's networked library environment, it is easier for a well trained librarian to check any user's personal data, such as book borrowing history, net browsing record, etc. Traditionally we didn't consider this as important private information. But today, it is necessary to make our librarians be aware about this. As librarians we don't have the right to disclosure our users' data to a third party. A couple of years ago, two marketing persons from a software company, who claimed that they had some half-official background, came to our library and suggested we install software in our library system to filter, monitor and record any user's trying to access either porno or politically sensitive websites. However, this suggestion was politely turned down.

4. The Mission of Preserving Cultural Heritage and Diversity in the Digital Era

Preservation has ever been one of the important functions of traditional libraries. If the digital library is still a library, it should keep on undertaking this mission. Under the new situation of digitization and globalization, librarians should be more aware than before of their responsibility of protecting and preserving cultural diversity. The long-term preservation of digital information is facing both organizational and technological challenges. It is doubtful if the digital form is a reliable medium of permanent preservation for all the valuable human cultural heritage. Some people believe that any storage medium has a finite lifespan, and that digital objects may have only a much shorter lifespan than some other media, such as bamboo slips or paper.

As more and more printed materials, such as the old books and back issues of bound periodicals, have been digitized by some commercial database companies, our library users can access these materials by network service. Consequently, quite a lot of our paper media collections seem to lose their storage value and are hardly used. Since our library is only an ordinary college library, preservation is not our main mission, and our storage space has always been very limited. Consequently, we really don't have to keep all the old paper media collections. However, our librarians should be extremely cautious when we try to give up any of our old collections. No one thinks that we should give up all of our old paper collections and rely only on the digitally stored versions. Experienced librarians demonstrate their important professional values and perspective in judging what kind of paper collections are worth permanent preservation. According to the suggestion of some senior librarians, in the past years we had arranged a team of senior librarians to reorganize our old collection of educational documents dated before 1949. Although these documents have had almost no users in recent years, our librarians still considered them as our special collections and suggested permanent preservation.

The Internet and information digitization will surely accelerate economic, social and cultural globalization, which will certainly influence various aspects of the cultures of different peoples in the world. However, different cultures are not equally represented in the digital world. According to Ethnologue, there are about 6,800 languages in existence today in the world, but how many languages are represented in the digital form and on the Internet? We should not expect the technology to provide equal protection for all cultures automatically. It is librarians' responsibility to rescue and preserve as much as possible cultural diversity and cultural alternatives that are still in existence today, whether in digital or in other forms. Librarians from all over the world, at different levels, can make different contributions in preserving special local human cultural diversities in the era of digitization.

5. Cooperative Activities of Intellectual Research and Innovation

In traditional academic libraries, some librarians were also engaged in the process of academic research activities as collaborators of those professors and research fellows of different specialty areas. In the era of the Internet and digitization, it is possible for librarians, as a special sort of intellectuals, to contribute more of their wisdom and perspective in the creation and accumulation of human knowledge. As some scholars have pointed out, in the era of digitization and networks, knowledge and information are no longer considered as something simply fixed, there for distribution or retrieving; it is also the process of finding, inquiring itself, and the process of communicating among collaborators. Research and innovation will more likely be an interactive and collaborative activity rather than individual exploring. "Knowledge and information in all areas and in all applications are increasingly produced, distributed and used collaboratively" (Kuhlem, 2003). In the process of academic communication, librarians will be able to participate more deeply in the creative activity by means of both knowledge management and communication management.

As an academic library with nearly a hundred years of history, the NJNU Library has a tradition of encouraging academic cooperation between librarians and the professors in their research, but this kind of cooperation usually happened in those traditional humanistic disciplines, such as history, classic literature and archaeology. However, recently there is a trend that some professors of other disciplines also rely on our librarians' cooperation in their research. This is because of the following reasons: first, in recent years our library has recruited some new young librarians who have the educational background of certain disciplines besides library science. Second, many new databases and new services are still strange to some professors, especially to the old professors; they need to spend some time to get familiar with them, and they find that the librarians can do some basic searches more efficiently. Lastly, some of our librarians are simply eager to make some contribution in academic activities. The library gets acknowledgment from the professors for the help they got from our librarians. In some cases, a research program is almost half done when all the help from the librarians has been provided. The question now is how to limit a librarian's engagement in a professor's personal research, lest the librarian spends too much time on it, thus neglecting his or her own duty. It also seems necessary to make clear the duty and right of both the librarians and the professors in a cooperated research project. Anyway, this phenomenon shows that although the digital library provides an unprecedented quantity of resources and many more choices of searching, librarians' personal help is still considered valuable and necessary by the academic community.

The cooperative virtual reference service system (such as the QuestionPoint) provide a totally new arena for experienced and specialized librarians to use their knowledge and skill in academic activities. Breaking through the physical wall of library buildings, librarians are able to provide more personalized reference services in cyberspace, which will likely be more specialized in subject areas and contents. This trend is both a big challenge and a big opportunity for the development of the profession of the librarian.

The "China Academic Library & Information System" (CALIS) and the "Jiangsu Academic Library & Information System" (JALIS) now are developing their own virtual cooperative reference system. As a member library of both CALIS and JALIS, what we should consider is not only how to equip our library with advanced hardware and techniques in order to fully enjoy the big achievement of CALIS and JALIS, but also how many excellent librarians, who are supposed to be real experts of information management and communication of the digital era, will come forth from our library, and make their unique contribution to the cooperative online reference service with the librarians from other colleges and universities.

6. Conclusion

It is obvious now that even in the digital library, we still need librarians, who may be called "digital librarians". Their roles have been described by some scholars as "to be the guardian of the information superhighway, the guardian of the universal digital library, a symbiotic human-machine guru, an expert in navigation/browsing/filtering, an expert in indexing, knowledgeable regarding data mining, an expert searcher, and an intermediary between users and technology" (Sreenivasulu, 2000). Others predict that the roles of librarians in the future may evolve into one or more of the following: "knowledge manager/ worker; internet and intranet content manager; individual information consultant; analyst/organizer for value-added products; trainer/teacher; and system designer" (i-DLR, 2003).

In order to play these roles in the era of the digital library, librarians are facing many challenges, especially those challenges related to the advanced information technology. However, just as some scholars have pointed out: "By itself, technology—however marvelous or powerful, whatever its potential—is cold and sterile. It will remain so unless someone adds the ability to bring the right information to the right user at the right time. If technology is a great force multiplier, the digital librarian can be a great force" (Matson & Bonski, 1997). Anyhow, no matter how advanced and how well we have been equipped with the new technologies, we should never forget that we are professional librarians rather than professional technicians, and we should forever adhere to our professional values and perspectives.

References

1 Sloan, B. (1998). Service Perspective for the Digital Library Remote Reference Services. *Library Trends,* Vol. 47 No. 1, pp. 117-143. available at: http://www.lis.uiuc.edu/~b-sloan/e-ref. html.

2 England, M. & Shaffer, M. (2004). *Librarians in the Digital Library.* available at: http://www. csdl.tamu.edu/DL94/position/england.html. accessed 2004-6-10.

3 Tenopir C. (2006). Building Bridges. *Library Journal.* Apr 1, Vol. 131, No. 6; p. 32.

4 Cerf, Vint (2004). *Keynote Address at JCDL2004.* http://digitallibrarian. org/. accessed 2004-6-9.

5 Kuhlen, R. (2003). *Change of Paradigm in Knowledge Management - Framework for the Collaborative Production and Exchange of Knowledge.* Paper of 69th IFLA General Conference and Council. http://www.inf-wiss. uni-konstanz.de/People/RK/Vortraege03-Web/rk_ifla03_for_publ300803. pdf.

6 Sreenivasulu, V. (2000). The Role of a Digital Librarian in the Management of Digital Information Systems (DIS). *The Electronic Library,* Vol. 18, No. 1, pp. 12-20.

7 DLR (2003). *Introductory Paper: Roles and Responsibility of Digital Librarians.* available at: http://www.coe.missouri.edu/~DL/iDLR/viewpaper. php?pid=23, accessed 2004-6-10.

8 Matson, L. D. & Bonski, D. J. (1997). Do digital libraries need librarians? An experimental dialog. *Online,* Vol. 21 No. 6, pp. 87-91.

Think Multiculturally, Recruit Nationally, Relate Locally: Library Campaigns in the Netherlands and Denmark

Marian Koren
Netherlands Public Library Association, The Hague, Netherlands

Abstract

Do national library campaigns make sense for local libraries? The local library has the closest contacts and best knowledge of its users and potential multicultural user group. Campaigns for recruitment of new users and relation marketing therefore seem only appropriate on the local level. At the same time, libraries, especially public libraries, present themselves as networks. Their library association works for the branding of the public library at the national level in many ways, including national campaigns. How do these campaigns interact with local marketing and promotion?

In the Netherlands a joint marketing and promotion policy and campaign has been launched by the Netherlands Public Library Association, including recruitment of new members of libraries, keeping the current membership, and knowledge sharing for library marketers, to start in 2006.

In Denmark, a national campaign on libraries has been prepared for 2006 by the Danish Library Association, as follow-up of its 100th anniversary.

Focus, funding and management of these campaigns will be studied, in relation to the local library in a multicultural world. The paper will make a comparison between these two current national campaigns in the Netherlands and Denmark and formulate some recommendations for future local-national marketing activities.

"*The library is at the heart of the information society*" is the slogan of IFLA's campaign in the framework of the United Nations World Summit on the Information Society, WSIS (2003-2005).[1] In similar ways, local libraries present themselves at the core of the community, or as the heart of a vital society.[2]

The time has passed that libraries are such self-evident elements of a society, that it is unnecessary to speak about them, or to draw the attention of the general public and politicians to them. Even in countries with a long tradition of public library services, such as The Netherlands and Denmark, one has to lobby for enough political weight and public attention, in order to have adequate resources for libraries to meet the user needs of today and, preferably, also tomorrow. At the local level, it has become a core task of the librarian/director to collect data on the use of the library and potential user groups, including multicultural groups. Increasing time is devoted to talks with the municipality and local authorities. On top of that, modern directors and libraries have excellent contacts with the local media and appear in the press on a regular basis. As the public library in Spijkenisse has demonstrated, a local campaign called 'We miss you' can even reach the international level: the International Marketing Award 2006.[3]

Library associations, operating at the national level, have extended their work to public affairs, marketing of their policies, and lobbying for the benefit of libraries as a whole or network. Different types of campaigns are undertaken, which in one way or another should also benefit the local library and its users.

As national campaigns in general are a costly affair, broad support of the membership, local libraries, is necessary, both for commitment and funding, and in many cases also for execution of the campaign.

What types of national campaigns can be beneficial to local libraries? How do library associations take into account the local aspects in national campaigns? What choices do they have to make? And which campaigns are more effective?

These are some of the questions which come up when learning about the library campaigns in Denmark and the Netherlands. As there is a number of similarities between the countries and their respective library landscapes, it is interesting and a learning experience to study these campaigns undertaken in 2006. Both small countries have a long-standing tradition of public libraries, operate in socially responsible democracies, and are moving into the 21st century with digital innovations in the library field. Furthermore, both have a library association which consists of (at least partly) public libraries' institutions as members, which allows for political decision making in the field. Differences in size and composition of population make The Netherlands more heavily (16 vs. 5.3 million) and multiculturally populated. In both states, the formal administrative structure of municipalities and regions is undergoing a process of restructuring, mainly into larger units. This affects and includes also the libraries' organisational structure. At the same time, after restructuring and elections, new politicians come to the scene, often unaware of the transformations public libraries have made in recent years. Against this background, national library campaigns were organised.

This research exercise might bring the best of both national campaigns to the surface; it may also pave the way for a model to present national library campaigns for further analysis, exchange, comparison and benchmarking for best practices: a noble aim for IFLA's Management and Marketing Section.

This study is structured as follows: after a brief introduction of both library associations, an explication of the studied campaigns is given along the lines of the reasons for the campaigns (Why?), content of the campaigns (What?), aim and target groups (What for?), how the campaign was done (How?), their partnerships, funding and effects or evaluation.

1. National Library Associations, Players at (Inter)National Level

The *Danish Library Association* describes itself with the aim to further public library development. The objective is to ensure that public libraries can further enlightenment, education and cultural activity to the highest standard for the good of the community. The Danish Library Association is unique because it counts politicians as well as library staff among its members. This leads to a fruitful collaboration and ensures political backing as well as interest. Membership is either personal or by local authority. Eighty percent of the Danish population is represented in the association through local authority memberships. The DK-Library Association is the advocate for libraries at all levels of government as well as internationally. The association is entitled to be heard in matters concerning library legislation. It sits on several influential committees on all levels of government as well as on international committees. It aims to reflect the geographical and political variations of its members. It is organised on the basis of library county associations, which work at the county level. These associations elect representatives to the Council of the central association. The Council sets up an Executive Committee with ten members including a president, always a politician, and two vice presidents, one a politician and the other a professional.

The Danish Library Association was founded in 1905, celebrating its first centennial in 2005. It has had and has a great influence on the development of public libraries and on educational and cultural policies. The Association has been the driving force behind government select committees, the formation of co-operation on the local government level as well as influencing library legislation.

The office in Copenhagen has about 7 staff members.

The *Netherlands Public Library Association* aims at bringing coherence in the public library services, to the benefit of a learning, well-informed and democratic society. In other words: the Association supports the local libraries in their societal task and advocates for the interests of libraries and their users in general. All 450 public library organisations—representing 1,100 public libraries/service points and 60 mobile libraries—are members of the NL-Association, establishing a maximum for legitimate representation. Members form the General Assembly, meeting twice a year, deciding on budget and strategies proposed by a Board of at most 7 persons, elected by them. The Association members have adopted agreements and commitments in various fields, e.g. service level, digital information, RFID, including a standard quality system and a certification scheme.

The Association stands also for advocacy in the field of copyright, public lending right and legal aspects of digital content and IT-services; it represents the interests of public libraries, and works for their recognition at ministries, councils and other bodies. Other tasks developed for public libraries are staff and organisation development, knowledge sharing, research and development of products and innovative services, including services to schools and learning at large, services to immigrants, community information services and reading promotion programmes.

The NL-Association is represented in a number of professional organisations, such as the main library supplier NBD/Biblion, the academic field, and the international field, in the same way as Denmark, especially in EBLIDA and IFLA.

The annual membership fees and additional contributions are used for library promotion campaigns, national digital services for the library portal bibliotheek.nl and a basic digital content package.

The Association receives, apart from its membership's income, also national subsidies from the Ministry of Culture, based on a 4-year cycle, in order to perform tasks as a National Public Library Authority (to some extent comparable with the separate Danish Library Authority, Biblioteksstyrelsen). The NL-Association cooperates with the associations of Dutch municipalities and of provinces, and with the Ministry of Education, Culture and Science for high-quality development of libraries. A Covenant has been agreed to, result-

ing in a major project addressing restructuring of library governance, investments in staff and IT and of service innovation jointly undertaken until 2007.

The Netherlands Public Library Association was founded in 1908 as
the Central Association (CV) and transformed into a library support centre
(NBLC) in 1972. It is now the professional sector association of public libraries in the Netherlands (VOB).

The NL-Association has an executive office of about 30 staff members for
all, also nationally subsidised, tasks.

Both library associations demonstrate strong lobby awareness and library
policy activities for the benefit of the public library network. They underline
that libraries are part of society. They support libraries in marketing policies
and in reaching their target groups. Nationally organised campaigns are undertaken in the perspective of working on new ways to put libraries on the
political agenda and have them firmly positioned in their societies. In what
context are these campaigns taking place, and what are the main aims and arguments?

2. Putting the Aims of Campaigns in Context

National reading programmes in *The Netherlands* have a long tradition and are
even internationally well known and copied, e.g. Children's Jury. Working on
a better library position in society, the NL Library Association organised image campaigns around a theme, with appropriate partners (environment, travel
etc.). Other campaigns addressed specific target groups, especially young people. The local libraries as members of the Association pay an additional fee
for joint promotion campaigns, proposed and executed by the Association.
In 2005, the set-up of promotion was revalued. Furthermore, libraries see a
decrease in loans and memberships (2% net), resulting in less income from
membership. (In the Netherlands, public library membership is, in general, not
free, but fee-based, the amount of the fee being subject to local decision making.) At the same time, local funding authorities are pushing harder to have
quantitative output of their funding. How can libraries increase customer relations with 4 million members? They therefore stress the need for actions for
recruitment of new members and keeping the current ones. Can this be done
on a national scale?

At the same time, the need for more coherence in marketing policy at the
national level is felt, after many libraries have been struggling with Product
Market Combinations (PMC's) for effective outcomes.

Combined efforts of working groups and the librarian-in-residence, working on marketing policy, led to a *Marketing programme 2006-2007*, adopted by the Assembly in 2006.[4]

This programme aims at the sector itself, focussing on cooperation within the sector and with partners; improvement of competencies and skills; and addressing the audience: campaigns. Local, regional and national levels are described in terms of basic conditions, knowledge and facilities in order to create a coherent marketing policy. Pilot projects in two regions are testing various concepts and instruments. One region, Groningen, has already done a successful recruitment campaign, with broad commitment from the staff for an internal campaign among users and an external one with the help of local VIP's, resulting in 3,000 new members.[5]

Competencies at the local level, where data and knowledge about users, non-users, transactions and trends can be gathered best, are reinforced by introducing *relation marketing*. Studies[6] show that those who borrow seldom and little, and young people (15-22 years of age) are the largest groups of non-renewers of memberships. By informing these groups, sending a voucher and informative materials within 6 months, a quarter of this group can be retained. Informing members by letter or postcard is often considered expensive; that's why most libraries use e-mail, but only 10% of the library members have an e-mail address. Relation marketing and especially retention marketing require local activities. The NL Library Association will set up training for these competencies, and also organise theme-based courses on marketing aspects, every quarter.

The NL marketing strategy is based on the broadest possible interest, the best possible product, in as many libraries as possible. Membership still means for most people being able to borrow materials. Those materials are mainly books, preferably non-fiction; reading for pleasure, to relax, is still the most important reason for membership. In the portfolio analysis the physical library with its easy access and service can be improved and receive additional value through tailor-made services and communication, demand-driven collection development, exclusive membership benefits, introduction offers, alliances, etc. The basic thought is to use opportunities and do smart investments—many readers are buyers and borrowers! A numbers of libraries work already along these lines with partners as local bookshops, e.g. in Deventer, Rotterdam, and Amsterdam. These local initiatives are implemented at the national level through cooperation with the CPNB, the Foundation for Collective Promotion of the Book. This has resulted in two campaigns in the Netherlands for 2006.

The NL national membership recruitment campaign is an action-oriented campaign with an exclusive offer for direct recruitment; at the same time the campaigns will present a broad profile of the library. The member-oriented campaigns include reinforcement of local membership activities and an attractive offer for members.

The aim of the *Dutch* campaign is recruitment of members and keeping current members. The target is set at recruiting 40,000–60,000 paying 18+ members before the end of 2007. The profile of membership (imago) will be strong and visible, telling: *"This is what I want to be part of"*.

Keeping members will work on profiling and making known that "Members get extra benefits". The campaign will create conditions for local, exclusive membership-focused activities.

3. The Danish Library Campaign

Four out of five Danes use the library at least one a year. The library campaign is not so much aimed at recruiting new members, as about informing members and policy makers about new library services, away from the book, into the digital web services.

When did you lately visit your library? Is the challenging question to update information on the modern library? Are the libraries sacred halls of books or blind followers of information and electronics? Can libraries use modern forms of communication in the service to citizens, or should they go back to paper and stamps when users need to know about their reserved books? The debate around these questions in autumn 2005 marked a new route.

The Danish Library Act 2000 states the equality of media, so libraries should have a broad choice of new media in the same way as they always had done for books. The big chances, away from the classical book based library, were the starting point for the Danish campaign to point to the 21st century's e-library. So the information campaign focuses on the offerings of the modern public library, to create a better knowledge about current library services, and to make the library portal and digital libraries and services known.[7]

At the same time, the Danish Library Association works in a highly political field, especially in the current years as local and regional administrative reforms even affect the very statutes and structure of the Association itself. As the number of counties has been reduced, likewise the county-based representation in the Association had to be revised. In the same way municipalities merger with larger communities with a new council and newly elected members. The new representation of councillors with culture in their portfolio in the Association likewise caused a strong need for thorough briefing on the values of the library, its new services and potential role in society. This is not only important for the Association work, but of course also for maintaining a firm library basis in the local communities and politics.

3.1. Content

The general slogan in Denmark, to get away from the book-based library and to demonstrate the creation of the 21st century modern e-library, is *Is there something you want to know, just come—24 hours a day.*

3.2. Target groups

The library campaign in Denmark therefore addressed two groups. The broad general public, ranging from children to adults, is the target group for drawing their attention to the libraries' activities, especially in the newly formed municipalities and the members in the new councils: *'The library has useful offers for all'.*

At the same time, decision makers are addressed in order to have positive political attention and understanding for libraries' contribution to society, and create good working condition to achieve this: *The municipality can make use of the library* for this and this . . . on condition that you provide the library with good working conditions.

3.3. Organisation

In Denmark well known people from various backgrounds—sports, politics, literature—are presented and tell how the library is part of their lives, demonstrating: the library has something for everyone.

With the help of a PR bureau, the briefing by the DK-Association was transformed into ideas regarding the message to the decision makers: politicians should be informed, in order to be able to decide on matters regarding the future of the library. New elections and newly formed municipalities require updating on libraries' modern perspectives and their new landscapes. At the same time new politicians are facing the challenge of creating a new cultural identity for the newly created municipalities. A well functioning library with many or multicultural offerings and activities would be able to play a role in that identification process. Instead of saying directly what the modern public library is, the DK campaign takes the road of *Myths and Facts about libraries.*

3.4. Media plan

The DK-Association worked from the draft campaign in April 2005 to January 2006 when the campaign started. It had a clever presentation of the posters with famous Danish VIPs at its centennial celebration in November 2005.

After one of the two selected PR-bureaus was contracted, a media plan was drafted for weeks 4 to 10 in 2006, including advertisements in newspapers and magazines, outdoor posters, web banners and press releases.

The communication about the campaign and presentation of the modern library was done through a new URL: www.e-bibliotek.nu.

3.5. National celebrities and VIP's

The 9 national VIP's with backgrounds in sports, politics, music and theatre were selected to give information and experiences, not to sell a product in the commercial sense. They should be reliable in relation to the message. Among them is the Minister of Culture, with the comment: *Already as a child, Brian discovered that the library was enormous.*

These nine faces were presented in national press coverage.

The Danish Library Association wondered whether local well known faces would get more attention in the local community. Libraries were asked to give their ideas about local VIP's and they responded very positively and were willing to have a local campaign running, on their own costs for a short period of four weeks, resulting in about 40 local faces and almost the same number of municipalities.

An attractive approach to local politicians were not only the posters, but also the booklet: *Myths and Facts about the library: An introduction to the modern public library, and as such a tool for all municipal politicians and civil servants who are co-responsible for libraries.*

The idea behind it was the conviction of the DK-Association that all municipalities should work and elaborate a strategy for the local library services, for example as Århus has done.[8]

Talks with the Minister helped to get this part of the campaign sponsored, so 4,000 hardcover books were sent to all local politicians.

3.6. Newspaper inserts

The good attraction and short messages of advertisements, posters and web banners were backed up by the introduction, gradually added to the media plan, of two newspaper inserts, for some more in-depth stories about libraries. The first insert in the main newspaper *Jyllands-Posten,* released in February, addressed the general public; the second one, in March, addressed primarily politicians.

The first one contained an interview with a newly educated librarian about the many new library services and the library services for the blind. It also has articles on library transformations and the Readers Book Award, and the main sponsor Danish Library Centre. The second one set focus on the library of the future, the new municipal landscape, and also presented the music services via the web and network.

3.7. Local perspective

The local libraries were supported by tools from the Danish Library Association, for example a model for a press release, which can be completed with local assets to address the local media, stating:

"Why have a campaign for public libraries?

Everyone already knows what they can use the library for, or don't they?'

… in the library of today exactly the same shift takes place as we have seen in our use of media and expectations of the information society: modern people wish to have information which they can use, when they see fit, and in a form they like. The library knows that, the library can deliver it, and we in the Danish Library Association think it is good to have this told to all."

On the website of the DK-Association the local activities were showcased, encouraging further best practices.

3.8. Funding

The Danish Campaign made use of the good will towards the Association on the occasion of its first centennial celebration. It also managed to attract a major sponsor, and to gain the interest of both the Ministry and the local tax fund. In this way, the campaign, which cost about 1.7 million Danish kroners (250,000 euro), could be financed. The local posters with celebrities were locally financed for about 200,000 DK.

4. Library Campaign in The Netherlands

Based on the aforementioned marketing programme, not one, but in fact two library campaigns are launched by the Netherlands Public Library Association, including recruitment of new members of libraries, keeping the current membership, and promoting reading as a demonstration of the socially responsible role libraries play in modern society. The two campaigns are scheduled in spring and autumn of 2006: a campaign related to the generally known Book Week: 15-25 March; and a new concept in the Netherlands: The Netherlands Read: 10 October-17 November.

The campaigns are described consecutively.

The Book Week is a reading promotion activity with a long tradition, organised by the CPNB, the Foundation for Collective Promotion of the Book. The NL-Library Association is a partner in this Foundation, contributes substantially, thereby assuring that libraries are included in all publicity and actions. Every year a well known author receives the honourable task to write the Book Week Present, a short novel, etc. All those who buy a book during the Book Week receive a free copy of the Book Week Present. Annually, about 750,000 people come and get their present in the bookshop.

The library campaign to recruit new members is attached to this Book Week, making efforts to demonstrate that the public library has fantastic offers, the whole year round, so a library membership is a valuable asset, worth the money.

4.1. Content

The author who wrote the Present for the Book Week 2006 is Arthur Japin. The campaign focused on the fact that also libraries are giving away the present, or the author. The author carries the Book Week publicity, and also therefore the library campaign. The slogan reads:

> Also the library gives him away!
> Arthur Japin wrote the Book Week Present this year. You receive it when you register as member. Including a book voucher of 5 euro. Go today to your library.

In the days before and during the Book Week, Arthur Japin will draw much media attention. He will, thereby, also be the face for the library campaign.

About 90% of the libraries participated in the action. They ordered more than 36,000 vouchers for the Book Week Present and 100,000 Book Week Tests, a device to test literature knowledge.

The national library recruitment campaign started just before the launch of the Book Week.

4.2. Target group

Readers of literature are the main target group. They are characterised by the following features: more women than men, aged 20-34 and 50+, 40% of them are singles, highly educated with a relatively broad interest in culture. In total at least 472,000 households buy literary novels. [9]

4.3. Organisation

The division of tasks in this campaign was as follows: the CPNB developed the Book Week campaign, created connection between the library recruitment campaign and the Book Week; it also produced the Book Week Presents, the Book Week Test, publicity materials and a commercial. The NL-Library Association worked on specific campaign communication, whereas local libraries worked on local communication and distribution of vouchers.

4.4. Media plan

The media were chosen according to their function to transfer an action message: quick and visible. Timing is important, as in a few days a large group would be addressed.

The national campaign had the following media, focussing on the period 13-20 March:

- Station spreads (posters at the railway stations, 13-26 March)
- Advertisements in main newspapers, broadcast magazines and the free tabloids *Metro* and *Spits*

- National library websites: Literatuurplein.nl, Bibliotheek.nl and al@din.

Through partnerships additional media attention could be drawn. Additional publicity could be connected to the famous Book Ball, a literary and VIP festival no media would miss. Furthermore, the national railways NS, as sponsor partner of the CPNB, organised a radio campaign, announcing that people could travel free on 19 March, when in possession of the Book Week Present.

The CPNB communicates the Book Week Present in radio commercials, including reference to libraries.

4.5. Local perspective

The NL-Association encouraged libraries to contact local and regional media, which cover 40% of literature readers, whereas the national campaign would reach 51% of this group with on average 1.5 contacts. Combined efforts should lead to increased results. Local advertisements and/or activities were supported with a toolkit provided by the NL-Association, to be downloaded from www.debibliotheken.nl/boekenweek.

- promotional materials which libraries could order and use for activities in the street, at stops and stations, and in places with a lot of traffic.

- advertisements used for the national campaign could be used or completed with local addresses and logo and placed in local newspapers, etc.

- free publicity through press releases and interviews in local media. The model press release reads: "The Book Week Present 2006 is during Book Week also available in the public library for every member over 18 years of age who registers as new member. The new member receives a voucher with which he can receive the present *The Big World* by Arthur Japin in the bookshop, including a discount book voucher of 5 euro." Additional information to be found at the partners website: (www.cpnb.nl, click Vakinformatie).

- banners are available for website promotion.

- as a recruitment action, current members can be encouraged to recruit new members, with a discount as compensation.

- current partners and contacts can be used for further cooperation, distribution of information, press releases, etc.
- regular Book Week activities can be expanded by attractive actions for new members.

Communication with the local libraries is established through a digital newsletter.

5. The Second Dutch Campaign: The Netherlands Read!

Following the American example of *One book one city*, the second campaign organised by the NL Association was transformed into One country—one book, encouraging people to read the same book and discuss it. The aim was still to recruit new members and keep the current ones, especially by making membership attractive through exclusive benefits.

5.1. Content

The title of the campaign is: *Nederland leest* (The Netherlands read). The message that is transmitted translates as "For reading you have to go to the library', and 'We value your membership.' And to the policy makers and opinion leaders 'The library takes its role in stimulating social awareness.' In this way, they continued the message of the first campaign under a different angle.

5.2. Organisation

The set-up of the campaign consists of a National Campaign, called *The Netherlands read,* carried by a well known Dutch person, who marks a national period of reading the same book in the Netherlands, which culminates in a big final evening in all libraries. It is hoped that in the future the final event will be broadcasted also on television.

The criteria for the choice of the book are that it should be easily available and attractive for a large audience; relevant for literature, politics, society; and allow connection with a theme or subject.

The well known Dutch person should be charismatic, a verbally strong character with a professional and or personal reference to the theme.

The campaign will make use of the free publicity around the VIP reader, the public debate about nominations and selection, and thereby create opportunities for local actions.

CPNB and local libraries will arrange an evening, with national and/or local publicity.

The main message: Netherlands has a big reading adventure invented and presented by the library.

5.3. Media plan

The campaign was presented at the National Library meeting, December 2005. The selection of the featured book and author were revealed just before 23 April 2006, World Book Day, starting publicity. A well-known journalist serves as ambassador for the campaign, which was launched by the Secretary of State for Culture. In June, a cultural event in preview of the Reading Month reminded readers of the upcoming campaign. The real reading event takes place in the time from 20 October until 17 November: four weeks of reading by all Dutch finalised by evening events organised in local libraries. The final evening of 17 November all libraries can organise as they see fit, with debate, dinner, discussion.

The NL-Association organises four marketing workshops, as part of the marketing policy programme. At these workshops, local activities around the Reading Campaign are discussed, trained and prepared, so a wealth of creative ideas and activities have been the results. The first 60 participants showed enormous interest for the Reading Campaign, so the workshop had to be repeated.

The Reading campaign means that all people in the Netherlands are encouraged to read the same book, which, in a special edition, will be distributed freely to members of the public library. Libraries will invite readers to discuss the book, in this case *Dubbelspel* by Frank Martinus Arion. And the reading period will cumulate in a final event on 17 November in the libraries.

5.4. Local perspective

The campaign is organised by the CPNB. The VOB organises a campaign to support local and regional activities and publicity via local media through national publicity.

Local activities are encouraged, also in cooperation with partners, and allowing the creation of an exclusive membership event. A Toolkit for local actions and background information are available via www.cpnb.nl/vakinformatie.

5.5. Funding

These types of campaigns are mainly financed by the libraries through an extra fee to their Association membership fee. By associating with strong partners in the field, national media exposure is feasible, relating to the partners' media connections and the cooperation by celebrities.

The Book Week has a budget of 70,000 euro; the reading campaign about 170,000 euro.

6. Results

The campaigns have not yet been evaluated by the library associations themselves. The second part of the Dutch campaign still has to take place. Nevertheless, some results are already available.

The *Danish* campaign has been well received by the members and partners of the Association. The enthusiasm to come forward with local celebrities and pay for local VIP-posters demonstrates the good local connection. The DK-Association reported halfway through the campaign that in general the local press had been very good, but the national media had been less convinced in taking up any news, apart from a radio broadcasting. The local perspective has been well taken care of and proved to be successful. The DK-Association will evaluate the other aspects like advertisements, web banners, inserts and the website www.e-bibliotek.nu in autumn 2006. It will discuss the question of 'How to "sell" the modern library'. The theory says, it is easier to sell if there are 1) conflicts; 2) breaking news; 3) special target groups and 4) relation to other news subjects. Libraries, however, are seldom at the core of real conflicts; according to journalists, they seldom cause groundbreaking news. Libraries are for everyone, but the national campaign has at least a well-elaborated local element. Another news subject is the municipal reform, which was the reason the Danish campaign focused on the new municipal council members, etc. This campaign can be considered as a good experiment. In the near future, the DK campaign might be drawn closer to its strategy, for example to set focus on the consequences of the municipal reform for the individual citizens; to profile digital services and come with a statement to make the modern library understood by many more citizens and politicians.

The first *Dutch* campaign, focusing on recruitment of membership in relation to the Book Week, encouraged many libraries to order vouchers—in fact three times as many as the final number of new members: 11,000. The CPNB director had estimated about 10,000, so he had a good guess. But libraries could send back the vouchers, so no harm was done. In fact, libraries were just enthusiastic.

One of the remarkable actions undertaken by libraries is to start calling members up when they are in arrears with membership payment. This telemarketing has worked very well and resulted in 20% renewed memberships in Almere.[10]

On the whole the libraries enjoyed participating in this type of actions for the first time. And as it was the first time, they were not shocked by limited results.

The autumn campaign is still come. But the interest in the marketing course shows a rising awareness in professionalism when it come to all types of campaigns.

7. Final Remarks

As could be known from the beginning, it is not easy to compare campaigns, not even campaigns in the same country. Nevertheless, it seems that at least different types of campaigns can be distinguished, all of which in the end are meant to contribute to strong library development and profile in society.

Library associations can at least be involved in three types of campaigns:

1. Image of the library
2. Recruitment of membership
3. Promotion of reading.

The Danish campaign focused most on the first type, with a strong emphasis on practical knowledge to be achieved by the general public and new local politicians and decisions makers. The Dutch ones combined the latter two types in one year in joined and consecutive campaigns.

Although we distinguish the campaigns in this way, the Danish one has a number of references to book reading, especially in the messages given by the national VIPs.

In earlier years, the Dutch Association had worked on image campaigns and target group campaigns, very costly operations, without any satisfying results, except for the campaign of the digital reference service, Al@din.

Another element should be mentioned. The Danish campaign includes information for local politicians. Similar information was produced in the Netherlands, to inform local politicians. Apart from a more formal agreement, a *Guideline for the local library agenda* was formulated. Furthermore a short film, *Look, The library!* (8 minutes), was produced and distributed on DVD to tell new politicians and partner organisations about the modern public library. These materials are used in local agenda-setting and administrative renovation, a process taking place between 2000 until 2007 and probably beyond. It would be interesting to compare these specific materials more thoroughly, as they include formulations of library values and arguments for local library policies.

In general, all marketing of the library portal and digital services is done separately by the (marketing) staff of Bibliotheek.nl. In a similar way, Biblioteksstyrelsen in Denmark was central to launching Bibliotek.dk and other web based services to the general public. It now also works with reading campaigns, such as *Laeselust*.

7.1. Model

In general, setting up campaigns takes place as a structured activity. This structure includes:

1. Aim
2. Content, incl. target groups
3. Organisation
4. Media plan
5. Funding, incl. partnerships
   (In the case of national campaigns, especially initiated and or executed by national library associations, it is important to add the element of the local perspective to the analysis model.)
6. Local perspective

Promising to discover the best of both national campaigns, it seems attractive to adopt the thorough marketing plan and strategy developed in the Netherlands, as an overall framework for improving awareness among the public and politicians, create opportunities for local library activities and profiling and enhance competencies and skills of library workers.

Likewise, it seems attractive to adopt the Danish approach to include local VIP's in posters, as they seem to have worked very well, and showed the commitment of local library staff. In fact, the good result of, e.g., the region of Groningen, NL, was also due to dedicated local library staff, *and* the library promotion through local celebrities.

The Danish idea of inserts on library issues in newspapers might also prove to be useful and effective. There is always a need for a good story. The advantage of these inserts is that the text and presentation are done by the library community itself, avoiding bitter or negative tones, which sometimes pop up in interviews and articles written by general journalists.

These materials are valuable also for future actions. The same can be said about the arguments used to counteract myths about the library. It seems a strong Socratic approach to argue with hard facts about the library. In this way, politicians will already have a communication and dialogue model for local practice in hand.

7.2. Partnerships

Both campaigns show that only with strong partnerships are such campaigns feasible and fundable. The Danish one stays close to the Library community, but involves a media partner and the Ministry for some aspects. The Dutch campaign partner is in fact a very skilled one, with a long tradition for publishers and book sellers, but is still young in explicitly addressing library audiences and working with libraries as equal partners. As in many countries, for a long time booksellers, libraries, and publishers have mixed feelings on their relationships. Nowadays, the overall and common need to encourage reading and create a climate of books and reading makes widely profitable alliances possible. That is why the premises for the second campaign—many readers of literature are both buyers and borrowers of books—is such a promising one for a new era of cooperation.

Notes

1 Libraries @ the heart of the information society, IFLA, The Hague/Geneva, 2003, http://www.ifla.org/III/ wsis.html.

2 Mulder, B., In het hart van een vitale samenleving, Procesbureau Bibliotheekvernieuwing, Den Haag, 2005.

3 www.ifla.org; www.bibliotheek-spijkenisse.nl.

4 Marketingprogramma 2006 – 2007: Campagnes, kennis en samenwerking, VOB, Den Haag, 2005.

5 www.biblionetgroningen.nl.

6 Jansen, M., Deelproject Relatiemarketing, VOB, Den Haag, 2005.

7 Library portal: www.bibliotek.dk and services like www.nettbibliotekerne. dk.

8 Århus strategy plan: www.aakb.dk/sw47814.asp.

9 Source: Cendris TPG.

10 See www.bibliotheekalmere.nl.

The Impact of Globalization on Library Management and Marketing

Ronghui Su
Hunan Library, Changsha City, Hunan, China

Qingming Yang
Central-south University, Changsha City, Hunan, China

Abstract

This paper deals with the new changes and tendency of library management in the context of globalization, and its influence on library strategy and marketing measures. The authors think that on the basis of the globalization of knowledge management and service, the library must guarantee the difference of cultural diversity and marketing, which is a necessary option in the sustainable development of the library.

The development of the library industry in the 21st century is facing the "transition from a stable and par mechanism to an unceasingly diversifying dynamic mechanism speeding up the change". The present tendency is the ever-increasing globalization in economy, science, technology and culture. The undertaker of knowledge resource is moving from printing type to digital type, and the way of knowledge-obtaining and the habit of utilizing library book collections are changing to relying on the Internet. The library is an important social institution undertaking and spreading world civilization. We need to examine and analyze the background of the library industry in the historical and liberal perspective, and also the far-reaching impact of it on 21st century library management.

1. The Impact of Global Identity and Multi-cultural Difference on the Library

If developed transportation enhances the integration of the world economy, then the development of the Internet and information technology speeds up the globalization of information and culture. Some dominating cultures spread throughout the world, which are very much likely to assimilate and swallow other cultures. To address this problem, UNESCO summoned several global conferences, and in the 2001 world multi-cultural arena adopted a world multi-cultural announcement—the UNESCO Universal Declaration on Cultural Diversity—to prevent the cultural hegemony in the process of globalization.

In fact, though the phenomenon of multi-cultures has long existed, the advocated idea of "multi-culture" results from the trends of cultural globalization. The relationship between globalization and multi-culture is the unity of opposites. They are opposite because "globalization" refers to the trends of unity, while "multi-culture" means the difference. They are opposite, which is reflected in the conflicts between overemphasized "cultural hegemonism" and "cultural isolationism". In terms of unity, it refers to multi-cultural differences and the fusion of global cultures accompanied with the appearance, exchange and development of human civilization. They are unified and synchronic. Unity means the co-existence of multi-cultures and the relationship of promoting each other through integration. Therefore, multi-culture is by no means the splitting of culture, but joins individuals, societies and nations all over the world, so that people can share their history and experience in the past and hope in the future.

In the 21st century, the trend of globalization and the advocacy for multi-culture provide new historical tasks for the library—one of the most important social institutions undertaking and spreading world civilization. These tasks are as follows: how to make every country and nation enjoy the multi-cultural prosperity brought by globalization; and how to protect the brilliant traditional culture of every country and nation so that it will not die out. Under the trend of globalization, the management of the library has been changed and challenged, which in turn brings two major effects on the library.

1.1. Globalization and diversity of the library's information resource

The development of the Internet, the evolution and progress of the knowledge information undertaker, and its way of collection, access and preservation make it possible for the library to gather and provide information on a global basis. It is a tendency to share literature resources based on the Web in the scope of the whole globe.

The "UAP Plan" made by IFLA in 1978 aims to promote the concerned nations to establish a national system with a combination of publishing, issuing, purchasing, processing, storing, protecting and inter-library borrowing, to build a system of domestic bibliography and the net of inter-library borrowing, to provide the readers with needed publications to the largest extent and to share the world-wide literature resources.

In the context of globalization, an individual library cannot be regarded as a starting point in the construction of literature resources, and it becomes a common understanding that libraries must build up the regional, even national, ensuring system in the liberal perspective. So in recent years, China has built up the shared system on the basis of common construction, such as establishing library union, sharing out work and cooperating with each other, and strengthening the construction of the digital library. The work we did was active and effective.

Take Hunan Provincial Library as an example, in which the authors work. In the past, Hunan Provincial Library focused its collection mainly on the gathering of physical literature resources, wishing to possess as large a collection of books as possible. But the fact is that the number of printed publications is ever-increasing and the funds for purchasing books are comparatively limited. Therefore, we have to consider and discuss the rule for the construction of library document resources. That is, we should emphasize the collection or the utilization. Is it necessary for us to pursue the numbers of the library book collection?

From the end of the 20th century, especially in recent years, with the rapid development of information technology and the wide spread of the Internet in China, both the construction and utilization of document resources in our library have shown the tendency of diversity and globalization. Meanwhile, the constituents of the document resources are also being changed from printed publications and non-printed to electronic publications and network databases. At present, besides over 340 million printed publications, our library owns 48 resource databases available which cover every field and extend to various types. Among them are 24 Chinese databases, which include Chinese Social Science Citation Index (CSSCI), Chinafobank, Chinese Doctoral Master's Dissertations & Full-text Database (CDMD), Chinese Core Newspaper Database (CCND), VIP Database, Wanfang Data (China Info), China National Knowledge Infrastructure (CNKI), Hunan Celebrities Database, Hunan Opera Database, Hunan Historical Picture Database, Hunan Genealogy Database, etc. There are also 24 foreign databases, which include ISI-Proceedings, Spring Link, EI, ACM, IEL, PQDD (A) (B), DII, PQDD, BP, ASP, CA, CCC, AC, Elsevier, AIP, IOP, Kluwer, OCLC, INSPEC, BSP, Nature, WSN, e-Science, Netlibrary, etc.

Once the document information becomes digital, the collection and delivery of document resources will stretch to every corner of the globe conveniently and quickly. Therefore, the rapid development of the Internet and information technology results in the trend and possibility of the globalization of document information. Under this situation, a requirement arises, that the thousand years of multi-culture of different regions, countries and nations should be protected. As a provincial public library, in order to meet this requirement, we set up a website named Hunan Cultural Information Website under the leadership of the Cultural Department of Hunan Province in 2002. As a central web of Hunan, this website belongs to "the Share of the National Culture and Information Resources Project", which aims to serve the masses, including the people in the community, remote mountain areas and the base unit of the sentry post. Through opening a channel of cultural transmission not limited by time and space, the website aims at eliminating the digital gap and improving the situation of the lack of information, and economic and cultural backwardness, especially in central and western and poorer regions in China. The web has abundant information which includes every aspect of Hunan, such as local conditions and customs, the cultural publications, the cultural geography and so on. In addition, ever-increasing attention is paid to the collection, compilation and digital processing of the documents of local culture in Hunan. Until now, our library has built several databases which include Hunan Celebrities database, Hunan Opera database, Hunan Historical Picture database and Hunan Genealogy database. Our work contributes to the protection, dissemination and globalization of Hunan's multi-culture.

1.2. Globalization and diversity of the reader groups and library service

Similarly, take Hunan library as an example. Readers and the services of the library gradually moved to globalization and diversity. In the past, few foreigners came to the library, and mainly just to visit. However, in recent years, more foreigners come to the library as common readers. They use the "electronic reading room". Additionally, in our library, we hold an 'English corner' and a 'French corner' for the purpose of offering a chance for foreigners and foreign language learners to watch videos together or just communicate with each other. Now, foreigners come to our library not only for visiting but also for utilizing resources in it. Especially on the weekends, we always see many foreign readers, some of whom we are familiar with and some are strange to us. Referring to this trend, when introducing the situation of the library and notices to readers, we begin to provide bilingual signs and multilingual signs for the sake of helping international readers to utilize the library more conveniently.

The physical library is facing the change of reader groups. Meanwhile, the spread of the Internet helps readers from different regions overcome difficulties. By means of the Internet, it is possible for readers to utilize the library at a far distance. For example, when writing professional theses or consulting materials, we want to familiarize ourselves with the latest information about the development of recent research in our own field or when helping readers to consult materials and foreign publications, we will land at some foreign library websites and other websites with some foreign databases, etc., which our country has already imported, in order to get some related information. Currently, we are becoming the international user of a certain foreign library from a long-range distance.

At present, over 100 million readers have visited the website of the Hunan Library for searching bibliographies, skimming and utilizing the library resources. On the BBS of our library, many long-distance readers communicate with librarians. On the "Reader's Arena", readers can express their thoughts and offer advice. On "Reader's Advice on Purchase", they can list the books and magazines they need so that the purchaser of the library can take their advice into account. On "the Consulting Union on line", readers consult all kinds of problems and ask the librarians to help consult materials. As the provincial public library, our website also set up a sharing project of BBS that can help solve problems of libraries in the county and city. So the libraries and readers all over the province, who can communicate with each other, search information, read electronic books, and have become the long-distance readers of the Hunan Library.

In a word, with the development and application of the Internet and information technology, the reader groups and services of the library transcend the region, reaching every corner of the earth, which accelerates the tendency of globalization. It is visibly realistic and predictable.

With the globalization of readers, the service of the library becomes diversity. That is to say, the reader groups and services of the library become diverse, both in their types and in the need for service. For example, spatially, there are local readers and long-distance readers. According to the type of library, there are physical library readers and digital library readers. Meanwhile, the multi-cultural differences and social backgrounds of different regions, countries and races make the reader groups and services of the library more and more diversified.

2. Library Management and Marketing Measures

In the digital age, with the influence of globalization, library management and marketing strategy should be dealt with in the following aspects.

2.1. International management vision

In the process of development in the new century, how to adjust and innovate in the management idea determines the public library's development and its social value. Facing the challenge of management in an environment of global integration and diversified differences, the administrator needs an open and international perspective, which covers different levels of management. For example: (1) In strategic management, the administrator must acquaint himself with the worldwide library's development trends, and combine the library management with the worldwide management system in working out the development strategy and managing the library. (2) In manpower management, the library's globalization needs international library management talents. Therefore, recruit and train them, encourage the library staff to improve their foreign languages, computer-using skills, and their professional faculty, and keep them informed of the development in their own fields. Broaden staff's vision, and make them not only be competent for the traditional library work, but face the challenges of digitalization and globalization in library work. (3) In information resource management, the direct influence of dramatic changes in the information environment on the library is the globalization of document resource construction and management. Strengthen the international, regional, and trans-trade cooperation and collaboration in resource construction actively. Try to eliminate the "digital gap", and dig out, organize and protect the local distinctive cultures. Strengthen the management and construction of local document resources to ensure the development and transmission of the multi-culture of human beings. (4) In professional management, speed up to conform to the international library practices and standards, and try to avoid standards and regulations that are incompatible with aspect of documents and data of the library, and eliminate the obstacles in information exchange and transmission. (5) In service management, a library open to the world should try to be more liberal, meet readers' requirements and serve global readers with multi-cultural backgrounds. It should follow the obligations and regulations in the convention of the International Library Association, and act according to international practices in library service in content, style and cooperation, etc.

2.2. Market-oriented marketing strategy

Marketing is a customer-oriented philosophy, regarding the corporation's operation as a continuous process to satisfy the customer's demand. Since the

1980s, the international library industry has begun to apply and create traditional marketing theories to guide public library management. After China's opening up, the planned economy has been transformed to a market economy. The idea and concept of marketing gradually spreads, and slowly extends to library management and other social non-profit fields. The reason that marketing theory and methods are widely used in non-profit industry is that it can also bring efficiency to them. The unique difference is bringing economic efficiency to enterprises and social efficiency to non-profit industry. The public library's marketing management is just like this. The core idea of a "market and consumer center" is also suitable to the "reader and consumer market center" of library marketing management as well. Its management is to analyze characteristics of the reader group and its demand for information, to organize and supply readers with various service styles and information products, and eventually complete the management process of realization of library value and its social efficiency.

With globalization and digitalization, the new features and changed requirements of the users' market and service of the library in the 21st century should be concerned with the process of marketing management of the library. For instance, there exists the distinction between local readers and long-distance readers when the users' needs are subdivided and a marketing strategy is established. And the distinction between library users and suppositional library users exists too. Moreover, the various social foundations and varied cultures of different districts, countries and nations will lead to diverse readers and services of the library. The application of the skills of marketing and the marketing management of the library should achieve mastery through the global library management system, link the international related laws and practices and respect social foundations, cultures and customs for the purpose of erasing the information gap and equally offering information to everybody in society.

2.3. Work standardization

The global library demands the assurance of work standardization of the library. Generally speaking, work standardization includes the collection, management, processing, protection of the library books, the knowledge service, etc. However, the library in the 21st century, which integrates various kinds of printed and electronic or local and long-distance information and references, provides global readers with the "Compound Library" of knowledge service. It emphasizes the obedience to the international and national norms and standardization in the construction of the digital library for the sake of facilitating the global information service and providing management means with compatible integration and retrieval.

In China, the second program of the national library, the program of the digital library, has been underway since the end of 2004. It signals that the norms and standardization for the systematic construction and improvement of the digital library have been launched.

The historical experience and lessons teach us that the norms and standardization of the library should avoid acting blindly in the changing digital times. We should continuously pursue the development of the Internet and information technology to enable the study of the global knowledge service of the library and the construction of the global digital library to come into contact with the document resources on the Web. And we should pay attention to the compatibility and extension of the skills and norms of information storage, management, and communication capability.

2.4. Distinctive service

The distinctive service of the library should be highlighted under the global marketing management of the library, which is expected of the library by the multicultural environment. What is the distinctive service? Huang Enzeng once defined it in the following way: "The distinctive service refers to the certain distinctive collection of books, certain distinctive service, and certain reader group." Hence, we extend it to the fact that the contents of the distinctive service can be listed as follows.

2.4.1. The distinctive resources of collections

A local culture is infiltrated into its life styles and customs. The provincial public library represents its local cultures and is absolutely responsible for collecting, classifying, and serving Hunan local document resources and the digital processing of distinctive resources. Traditionally, this is what we value in collection and service. The Hunan Provincial Library provides the local distinctive resources and service including Hunan Geography Digest, Hunan Life Styles and Customs, the important information research of local papers, Literary Talent World, newly edited provincial column, Xiaoxiang Art Gallery, Local Almanac, Local Life Styles and Customs, Local Periodical Contents, Sanxiang Overlook, Local Document Database, Local Drama, Local Paper Database of Document Study, Internet Hunan, Surname Source of Hunan, etc.

2.4.2. The specified service target

The specified service is intended for the specified readers according to their needs by applying marketing and subdividing the users' needs. For instance,

"Readers' Club", "Film Club", "Children's Reading Room", "Foreign Language Club" and others are built for the specified people, which can satisfy some readers' urgent needs and achieve the maximal benefit.

2.4.3. The distinctive service style

For satisfying the diverse needs of readers, some irregular distinctive service style needs to be established. For example, books can be renewed by telephone, borrowed by post, sent home for the blind, incapacitated people and important users. Lectures and training are offered regularly, etc.

2.4.4. Diverse library-opening modes

The diverse library-opening modes can show the distinctive service of the library. For instance, we have the mobile library, the library for the blind and the disabled, the branch library in the remote countryside. Moreover, the distinctive service of the library is formed through the coexistence of multiple management systems. The construction of the library is funded by the government, library and collection of money. The library is jointly run by society communities or enterprises or sponsored by individuals.

2.4.5. Share of distinctive resources

Being a provincial public library, the Hunan Library should have an overall plan and share resources with libraries of every region, every municipality and every county. It should enhance the cooperation with local cultural organizations including the district museums within the province and the People's Art Gallery, etc., under the leadership and coordination of the Cultural Department of Hunan Province.

2.5. Active international exchange in professional and academic fields

Actively launching international professional work and academic exchange of library and inter-library exchange are efficient ways of improving the overall management and quality of library staff, and are demanded by the linking of the global world management system of the library. It is beneficial that the development of the Internet and information technology makes both library users and librarians transcend spatial boundaries. The competitor's work and academic exchanges become easier and more efficient via the Internet. The assistance column from municipalities and counties of BBS of the Hunan Library has become an efficient place for developing the professional training and academic exchange among public libraries within the province.

The library administrator and the academic leader should acknowledge the new tendency of international communication and cooperation of the 21st century libraries, and actively organize bilateral international and inter-library communication, which is communicative and pragmatic. "Bilateral" requires us to reach an agreement actively on the cooperation of bilateral communication. "Communicative" means the sense of communication and image in international communication. "Pragmatic" refers to the positive international communication and cooperation for library work, which aims to improve the overall management of the library, its international position and social value, the norms and standardization of library professional work, and the service and study of the library.

3. Conclusion

The rapid development of new information and the spread of technology speed up the process of globalization, which is not only a challenge for the library management, but also provides new conditions and opportunities for the positive participation of the library in the world library system, jointly promoting the protection and development of our ancient and colorful human civilization.

With the vision of internationalization, the full application of the concept and means of marketing depends on the constant advancement of information technology, attaining the goal of the global delivery of knowledge, and eliminating the "digital gap", while keeping the diversified marketing concepts for respecting and protecting multi-culture in different areas, countries and races. Such management strategies and marketing concepts are an inevitable choice for the sustainable development of the 21st century library in the age of globalization.

Developing Future Library Leaders in the Context of Globalization with an Analysis on Cultural Intelligence (CQ)

Xuemao Wang and Chang Su
The Johns Hopkins University Sheridan Libraries, Baltimore, Maryland, USA

Abstract

Leadership development is such an imperative topic that it cannot be overstated in any management discussion for any industry or field. According to a recent survey conducted by professional associations, nearly 50% of senior American library leaders, including those at the director level, will retire by 2010. Findings of such surveys confirm and raise strategically important issues. Is the library profession ready to pass the torch to the next generation of leaders? How are the next generations of leaders to be assessed, selected, and developed? What are the core leadership attributes or the ideal profile for future library leaders? How can we develop future library leaders with global perspectives?

U.S. libraries have pioneered in library leadership development. A number of leadership development programs across all segments of the library profession have been established. Experience from those programs with highly influential outcomes may be applied to libraries elsewhere in the world. The increasing globalization in business practice has a great impact on leadership development in all industries. Cultural Intelligence (CQ) has been identified as one of the most important leadership attributes in addition to Emotional Intelligence (EQ) and Analytical Intelligence (IQ). The increasing dependency of global resource sharing in library and information services has created demands on libraries and fostered the new frontier of global collaboration. A new concept of Global Library is emerging. Future library leaders with global perspectives will be highly sought.

"I feel about globalization a lot like I feel about the dawn... I didn't start globalization, I can't stop it..."

—Thomas Friedman, from *The World Is Flat*

"The Jack Welch of the future cannot be me. I spent my entire career in the United States. The next head of General Electric will be somebody who spent time in Bombay, in Hong Kong, in Buenos Aires. We have to send our best and brightest overseas and make sure they have the training that will allow them to be the global leaders who will make GE flourish in the future."

—Jack Welch, former CEO, GE

1. Introduction

Leadership development is such an imperative topic that it can never be overstated in management research for any industry. Leadership development is facing a more urgent demand in the profession of librarianship. Statistics have shown that librarianship entered an aging workforce and library leaders are becoming more "graying". Younger leaders need to be developed and educated to take the torch.

The world is flattening. Globalization has an impact on every industry, and library and information service is not an exception. The emerging global library operational environment creates demand for new leaders possessing highly cross-cultural management skills. Accordingly, library leadership development needs to add new dimensions of global library leadership development. The practice of current library leadership development has focused on local and special segment needs with less updated curriculum.

Cultural Intelligence (CQ) has been identified as one of the most important leadership attributes in addition to Emotional Intelligence (EQ) and Analytical Intelligence (IQ). However, in the literature of library leadership development, there are no discussions and applications of CQ yet. In this paper, we use Chinese culture as an example to explore the value of CQ in library leadership development.

2. Globalization and Its Impact on Librarianship

2.1. What is globalization?

In Friedman's (2006) book, *The World Is Flat,* he described globalization as the interweaving of markets, technology, information systems and telecommunications systems in a way that is shrinking and flattening the world. Globalization enables us to reach around the world farther, faster, deeper, and cheaper than ever before.

Rikowski (2005) describes four contradictory dimensions in which globalization manifests. The first dimension is the cultural dimension. In globalization, we must acknowledge the diversity of various cultures in the world; on the other hand, we have to face the challenge of homogenizing different cultures. The second dimension addresses the vanishing of national power in the global economy, with the appearance of so many transnational organizations, such as the World Bank and the International Monetary Fund. These transnational organizations set up the standards of the field in the world and greatly influence the national organizations. The third dimension is capital's expansion, which describes the individual lives in the global market. The last and most important dimension is the global labor value. With globalization, employers can hire the best value labor across the world to maximize profit. These four contradictory dimensions demonstrate that globalization brings opportunities as well as challenges to us.

2.2. What is the global library?

We used to say "the end of the stand-alone library"; soon we shall say "the end of local library", and the beginning of the "global library".

Globalization, the most progressive global movement since the industrial revolution, has brought enormous impact to every single continent and every single industry. As libraries are increasingly obtaining resources and providing services to users all across the world, a new model of library service and operation emerges, which is referred as Global Library in this paper.

The Global Library (GL) can be defined with the following key characteristics: 1) is globally accessible in either a virtual or physical library environment; 2) serves global public or institutional users with 24/7 services; 3) hosts global-focused library collections and resources; 4) employs global talents; 5) operates globally with headquarters in the home country, and activities in regional and national areas; 6) is actively engaged and involved in library-related activities among global communities.

The benefits of the Global Library are as follows:

- Integration of resources
- Have equal access local and global to all resources
- Maximized productivity and minimized operational cost
- Leverage local and specialized talents
- Promote and spread an international library standard while respecting and preserving local civilization and culture

The challenges of the Global Library:

- Make the local culture diminish
- Deal with various cultures in management
- Understand local religion, ideology, political systems, etc.
- Require new managerial skill sets in a global and cross-cultural management environment

Some typical existing global library or global library-like services examples:

- OCLC virtual reference QuestionPoint (http://www.oclc.org/ questionpoint/about/default.htm)
- Global distance education with library services (http://www. logintolearn.com/nextdistance.html)
- Global Library Initiative (http://www.globallibrary.org/en/index.php)
- Multi-National Corporate (MNC) global library services (http:// www.online-information.co.uk/2004proceedings/thursam/ heye_d.pdf)

3. Overview of Leadership Theories

3.1. Definition of leadership

Leadership is a popular topic in many fields, such as management studies, behavior studies, and so on. Such discussions can be found not only in western literature, but also Chinese traditional literature which was written over a thousand years ago.

Different definitions of leadership emphasize various aspects of leadership. Maxwell (1999) defined leadership as follows: "Leadership is influence—nothing more, nothing less" (p. 17). For a leader, influence is the most important thing. A manager needs a position to empower him, but a leader does not need such a position. "Leadership is also a performing art—a collection of practices and behaviors—not a position . . . thus we define leadership as the art of mobilizing others to want to struggle for shared aspirations" (Kouzes and Posner, 2002, p. 30).

Just as Lao Tse mentioned, a leader is the catalyst. "Leadership is communicating to people their worth and potential so clearly that they come to see it in themselves" (Covey, 2004, p. 122). Leaders empower the followers to reach their potential, which may be even beyond the followers' abilities that they realize. "Leadership is creating an environment in which people want to be part of the organization and not just work for the organization. Leadership creates an environment that makes people want to, rather have to do" (Covey, 2004, p. 217). In an organization, a true leader can create an exciting and encouraging culture which attracts followers to devote themselves to the organization and to make contributions with passion. The followers work for the organization not only for making a living, but for the hearty love for the job. Mason and Wetherbee (2004) summarized the key characteristics of leadership compared to management (*Table 1*).

Table 1. Leadership versus Management
(Mason and Wetherbee, 2004, p.191)

Leadership	Management
A leader does the right things.	A good manager does things right.
Leadership is about effectiveness.	Management is largely about efficiency.
Leading is about what and why.	Management is about how to do things.
Leadership is about trust and about people.	Management is about systems, controls, procedures, policies, and structure.
Leadership is about innovating and initiating.	Management is about copying, about managing the status quo.
Leadership looks at the horizon, not just the bottom line.	Management is about the bottom line.

3.2. Leadership theories

There are eight recognized universal leadership theories in the field, including great man theory, trait theory, behavioral theories, participative leadership, situational leadership, contingency theories, transactional leadership, and transformational leadership (http://changingminds.org/disciplines/leadership/theories/leadership_theories.htm), as shown in *Table 2*.

Table 2. Leadership Theories

Types	Assumptions
Great Man Theory	Leaders are born and not made. Great leaders will arise when there is a great need.
Trait Theory	People are born with inherited traits. Some traits are particularly suited to leadership. People who make good leaders have the right (or sufficient) combination of traits.

Types	Assumptions
Behavioral Theory	Leaders can be made, rather than being born. Successful leadership is based on definable, learnable behavior.
Participative Leadership	Involvement in decision-making improves the understanding of the issues involved by those who must carry out the decisions. People are more committed to actions where they are involved in the relevant decision-making. People are less competitive and more collaborative when they are working on joint goals. When people make decisions together, the social commitment to one another is greater and thus increases their commitment to the decision. Several people deciding together make better decisions than one person alone.
Situational Leadership	The best action of the leader depends on a range of situational factors.
Contingency Theory	The leader's ability to lead is contingent upon various situational factors, including the leader's preferred style, the capabilities and behaviors of followers and also various other situational factors.
Transactional Leadership	People are motivated by reward and punishment. Social systems work best with a clear chain of command. When people have agreed to do a job, a part of the deal is that they cede all authority to their manager. The prime purpose of a subordinate is to do what their manager tells them to do.
Transformational Leadership	People will follow a person who inspires them. A person with vision and passion can achieve great things. The way to get things done is by injecting enthusiasm and energy.

Source: http://changingminds.org/disciplines/leadership/theories/leadership_theories. htm.

4. Cultural Intelligence (CQ) and Its Implication for Global Library Management

4.1. What is CQ?

Traditionally, people measure rational and logic-based verbal and quantitative intelligence by intelligence quotient (IQ) tests. Recently, leadership studies have placed Emotional Intelligence (EQ) as a prominent factor to determine success which can be measured by EQ tests. Nowadays, in addition to IQ and EQ, cultural intelligence (CQ), which can be measured by CQ tests, is now coming into existence. Studies have shown that people's facial expressions to show the emotions such as happiness, surprise, fear, sadness, anger, and disgust and so on, are based on their cultural background (Alon and Higgins, 2005). For example, Americans and Japanese may use quite different facial expressions to express the same feeling.

Earley and Ang (2003) defined Cultural Intelligence (CQ) as a "person's capability for successful adaptation to new cultural settings; that is, for unfamiliar settings attributable to cultural context" (p. 9). They described CQ in two types and three major categories. The two types of CQ are 1) Organizational Cultural Intelligence; and 2) Personal Cultural Intelligence—related to geographic/ethnic culture.

The three categories are:

- Cognitive (CQ from "head"): This refers to conceptual understanding differences among cultures; examples include asking questions about what motivate people in different environments.

- Physical (CQ from "body"): This refers to cultural differences reflected by observable physical actions; examples include how different cultures tolerate "touch"—a hug and kiss on cheeks between male and female colleagues in greeting each other may be okay in Latin America or France, but in other countries like U.S. might not be well-received or even be seen as sexual harassment.

- Emotional/motivational (CQ from "heart"): This may be the hardest or most complex component of cultural intelligence. It has the closest relationship with EQ, the Emotional (or Social) Intelligence; examples include understanding the dynamics in a diverse working group.

4.2. Cross-cultural management with Cultural Intelligence (CQ)

Cross-cultural management refers to the management practice in organizations with heterogeneous culture settings where cultural factors and sensitivities are being taken into primary consideration in organizational decision-making processes and frameworks.

In the growth of globalization in the business world, the increasingly dynamic change in conducting business globally will require leaders with the global aspect of functional business skill sets. The more important challenge is that as human resources and talents become commodities, it will require leaders to possess inter-cultural skills including CQ to conduct an effective cross-cultural management. The higher the CQ the leader possesses, the more capable the leader is in cross-cultural management.

4.3. Cross-cultural management in the library and information setting

Although the cross-cultural management concept and applications have grown popular in international or multi-national corporate business, it is a relatively new concept in the library management field. As libraries are going through the transition towards the global library, the cross-cultural management challenge is inevitably coming to library management.

One familiar application of cross-cultural management in library settings is managing diversity. Most definitions of diversity are mainly based on the following ideas: 1) people's diversity can add value to the organization if managed effectively; 2) diversity includes a lot of ways in which people differ from each other such as education, sexual orientation as well as gender, ethnicity, disability, etc.; 3) diversity is a primary concern in organizational culture and the working environment. Libraries have been a front runner in managing and promoting diversity.

The American Library Association (ALA) has declared that diversity is one of the five key actions areas to fulfill its mission to provide the best services to the patrons. ALA promotes equity in information access and library services for all library users. It also encourages libraries to recruit underrepresented groups and foster a diverse working environment in all libraries. ALA sets its diversity vision as follows:

> The American Library Association recognizes that in addition to race, creed, color, religion, gender, disability and national origin, there are multitude of differences (language origin, regional and geographic background, economic class, education, learning and communication styles, sexual orientation and personal lifestyle) that individuals bring to the workplace. It is this diversity that contributes a deeper level of understanding and competence to our daily work. The American Library Association envisions a richly, diverse workforce providing a high level of service to membership in an environment where respect, appreciation, equity and inclusion are core values. (ALA, http://www.ala.org/ala/diversity/diversity.htm)

In addition to the above example of managing the library workforce, examples also are found in library patron management. Lisa Norberg (2005) summarized some typical library-specific CQ-related issues in supporting American and international students.

- Language used in library service: to international students, "book check out" may mean to "examine" or to "pay for" the book.
- Nonverbal communication at the information or reference desk:
  - o Eye contact: American students look at people directly to indicate attention and respect. International student from other cultures may look away or down to show respect.
  - o Space: Middle Eastern students get very close and Japanese students keep a distance.
- Directness vs. indirectness in reference interview: American students are more direct and assertive than international students. Students from Asian countries may nod to indicate they understand, even when they do not understand, because they do not want to make you or themselves upset or embarrassed.

4.4. Cross-cultural management with an analysis using Chinese culture as an example

Rooted from its long history and rich civilization, Chinese culture carries many distinctive characteristics and has a deep impact on Chinese management philosophy. For example, individualism is considered as one of the main cultural characteristics in Western society; on the contrary, collectivism is regarded as a typical cultural characteristic for East Asian society such as Chinese society.

In cross-cultural management, one needs to be aware of the differences among various cultures. The challenge of cross-cultural management lies in the integration, understanding, and even tolerance of cultural differences. Effective cross-cultural management strives for maximization of adaptation and productivity among different cultures regardless of a manager's personal preference.

Individualism and collectivism are typical in the Western and Chinese cultures respectively. *Table 3* summarizes some management behavioral examples that are derived from individualism vs. collectivism in Western and Chinese society.

Table 3. Some typical business behavior in Western and Chinese organizations
(Ilan Alon, 2003).

Western	Chinese
Individualism	Collectivism
Individual self-control (through guilt)	Collective social control (through shame or *face*)
Governance through legal system	Personalistic governance through *guanxi*
Business relationship builds on contract	
Negotiation focuses on contract	Business relationship focus personal relation
Importance of efficiency and professionalism	Negotiation is contingent upon nature of relationship
Model is society	Importance of reciprocation, personal integrity, trust
Conversation focus is one's job	
Power through achievement	Model is family/community
Survival of the fittest	Conversation focus is on family
Personal interest/reward	Power through ascription
Short term, entry and exit strategies	Survival of those fitting
	Group interests
	Long term, family, wealth, welfare and succession

4.5. Library leadership development programs (LDPs) in the U.S. and China

With globalization, organizations have gone through tremendous changes, no matter whether they are large or small, for-profit or not-for-profit. Libraries are not exempted from such changes. Leadership is regarded as the most critical component of an effective organization which can adapt to changes quickly.

Although leadership development programs have been a popular management training topic in the business world, the leadership concept and theories did not begin to appear in the library literature until the 1980s (Mason & Wetherbee, 2004). Leadership was not even a subject heading or index term in the library literature. Don Riggs, in conducting his research for a book on library leadership, found only very few entries for librarianship and leaders in Library Literature for the years 1975–1981 (Riggs, 1998). Instead, some other subject headings were used in the place of leadership, such as "administration", "librarianship", "organizational behavior", "personnel" and specific type of subject headings such as TQM, etc.

In contrast, leadership exists as a subject heading in the major indexes for other professions, such as finance, accounting and nursing. This fact indicates that the lack of "leadership" as a subject heading is not only an access issue, but also a problem, which indicates that leadership as a concept in the profession of librarianship may have not been acknowledged as a legitimate discussion topic or entity, and has not been clearly defined and differentiated from other library management topics (Karp and Murdock, 1998).

Library leadership programs are one important way to address the library leadership issue and meet with the librarians' awareness of the need for leadership training. Mason and Wetherbee (2004) conducted a quite comprehensive review of thirty-one library leadership programs in the U.S. Six of them are mainly oriented towards academic librarians, as shown in *Table 4*. *Table 5* lists the information of three Chinese library leadership programs which are also targeted at academic librarians in China.

American libraries have pioneered in the field of library leadership development (LDP). Lessons learned from American libraries practices on LDP might be applied to libraries elsewhere.

American LDPs have been highly praised for their curriculum design, marketing/promotion, cross-segment coverage and so on. However, some major lessons learned in American LDPs can be valuable for others when they design LDPs.

- Lesson 1: Lack of well-designed and controlled, even consistent evaluation method made the assessment of efficacy of LDPs difficult. As Mason & Wetherbee (2004) pointed out, "very few published evaluations on library leadership training programs have been designed to yield stable and valid results about the impact of these programs on the abilities and careers of training program participants." There have been no consistent evaluation methods or processes identified for either the vertical segment or horizontal comparative segment LDPs.

- Lesson 2: Lack of a shared definition of leadership for librarians or library professionals constrained LDP programs' growth beyond traditional management development training. Without a shared definition of what leadership means to librarians, it is difficult to establish, develop and evaluate a set of consistent and desirable leadership qualities and traits for both existing and future library leaders. It is also difficult to outgrow the program in order to develop leaders in dealing with transformational changes in today's libraries.

Table 4. U.S. Library Leadership Program focus on Academic and Research Libraries

Name of Program	Target Audience	Selective admission	Primary Emphasis	Number of Participants	Moderators	First Offered (Number of days)	Continues (Y/N)
ACRL/ Harvard Leadership Institute	Academic library directors and associate directors	Yes	Leadership, organizational strategy, transformational leadership, planning	14	Harvard faculty, M. Sullivan, and others	1990 (5 days)	Yes
Association of Research Libraries and Career Development	Early and midcareer minority librarians in academic libraries	Yes	Encourage diversity in top leadership of academic libraries	20	Various	1997 (5 days+ off-site)	Yes
EDUCAUSE Leadership Institute	Information technology managers in higher education	Yes	Develop management skills focusing on motivation and deployment of staff	Unknown	Various	1998 (4-5 days)	Yes
Frye Leadership Institute	Higher education faculty, librarians, information technology professionals	Yes	Leadership skills for higher education leaders	40	Various	1999 (14+ days)	Yes
Stanford-California Institute	Mostly California librarians—the next generation of library leaders—most mid-career	Yes	Focus on topics including technology, library collections, organizational effectiveness, facilities planning, technology impacts	125-145	Various with Stanford faculty	2001 (unknown)	No
UCLA Senior Fellows Program	ARL directors or associate directors	Yes	Enhance leadership in North American libraries, particularly research libraries	15	Various	1982 (unknown)	Yes

(Mason & Wetherbee, 2004, pp. 197-202).

Table 5. Chinese Library Leadership Programs

Name of Program	Target Audience	Selective admission	Primary Emphasis	Number of Participants	Sponsors	Number of Days	Continues (Y/N)
National University Library Director Workshop	University Library directors or associate directors	Unknown	Application of new technology in academic libraries, library management	50-60	Steering Committee for Academic Libraries of China	Unknown	Yes
Hong Kong Asian Library Leadership Program	Academic librarians from Hong Kong, mainland China, Taiwan, Singapore, Japan, Korea, the Philippines and other countries in the region	Yes	1. To develop and enhance management and leadership qualities in academic and research librarians in the East Asia region, and 2. To enhance collaboration and foster relations among academic and research libraries in the region.	40	University of Hong Kong Libraries, University of Macau International Library and Hong Kong Joint University Librarians Advisory Committee	4 days	Yes
Chinese University Librarians Summer Workshop	Chinese librarians	Unknown	Leadership development, information sharing and collaboration, information technology and digital library	Unknown	UIUC (US) and Chinese Academy of Library Science	4 weeks	Yes

Note: The material reported here was gathered from various announcements, journals, emails, and reviews.

- Lesson 3: Lack of specially tailored curriculum for targeted audience and segment limited LDPs' potential to develop and attract library leaders who work in specialized library segment such as medical and corporate libraries.

Very little information can be found from deep web research on Chinese library LDPs. Those programs we have identified are still in the early development or experimental stage.

Cooperation and collaboration with Western libraries seems to be the main theme for Chinese library LDPs. Hong Kong libraries LDP is an example that closely followed ARL's practice, and they even brought in American facilitators for instruction. (http://lib.hku.hk/ leadership/) Another interesting program is the one which is jointly organized by the Chinese Academy of Library Science and University of Illinois (UIUC) Graduate School of Library and Information Science. (Lynn, 2006, http://www.news.uiuc.edu/news/06/0613librarians. html). Those two are good examples of special curricula and programs that were tailored to the needs of Chinese librarians. These are also good examples of international collaboration on library leadership training and development.

With accelerated globalization and the needs of developing future library leaders with global literacy, a special component of cross-cultural training needs to be added into LDP curriculum and program design. The international collaboration on LDP may be a feasible and effective way to address this issue.

5. Future Library and Information Services Leaders

5.1. The emerging demand of developing future library leaders

Librarianship as a profession entered an aging workforce, and library leadership is becoming more "graying". Fifty-eight percent of librarians in the U.S. are projected to reach the retirement age of 65 between 2005 and 2019, and 40 percent of library directors plan to retire in less than nine years (Department of Professional Employees, http://www.dpeaflcio. org/policy/factsheets/fs_2005_ library_workers.htm). Librarians, as a group, are much older than those in comparable professions. Moreover, they are also aging much faster. Currently only 12 percent of librarians are in the age range of 25-34, while the percentage in other professions is only about one-fourth (Lenzini, 2002).

There is also an international trend of "graying". In Australia, more than 52 percent of librarians are currently older than 45 years. If they will retire at the age of 60, then about half of the population of Australian librarians are expected to retire within the next 10 to 15 years. (Hutley and Solomons, 2004).

In the next 15-20 years, libraries will experience a loss of a large number of professional workers including leaders. Library leadership development becomes very important to ensure a new cohort of leaders, especially leaders with global vision ready to take over. Leadership development programs that focus on recruiting diverse backgrounds and ethnicities will be highly demanded. Librarians, as a profession, are forced to choose a strategically important decision on succession management.

5.2. Traits of future library leaders

In the emerging global library environment, library leaders must not only demonstrate all those conventional leadership qualities, but also be injected with new dimensions of leadership qualities that focus on cross-cultural management.

Successful library leaders will need to demonstrate "a blend of bold leadership, informed risk taking, widespread consultation, and consensus building. They will need keen analytical powers, abundant common sense, vibrant creativity, reasoned judgment, and a passionate commitment to the mission and goals of higher education" (Metz, 2001, p. 3).

Recent research in library leadership development summarized some key leadership traits or qualities for leaders in different library settings. *Table 6* listed key selective traits for ARL Directors.

Table 6. Leadership Qualities Important for Library Directors
including directors for ARL, non-ARL academic libraries and public libraries
(Hernon, Powell, and Young, 2003, pp. 115-116).

Leadership

- Ability to identify trends
- Ability to plan, implement and assess strategic goals
- Ability to work in collegial, networked environment
- Advocate for library
- Appreciates importance of marketing/public relations
- Articulates/communicates the vital role of the library to the community
- Brings issues of broad importance to the university community, fostering wide discussion and action when appropriate
- Builds a shared vision for the library
- Builds consensus in carrying out strategic directions
- Changes/shapes the library culture
- Collaborative skills (works collaboratively with campus colleagues)
- Commitment to (and record on) staff diversity (as well as comfortable with diverse populations and is culturally sensitive)
- Commitment to professional development of library personnel

- Create an environment that fosters accountability
- Demonstrates innovative leadership
- Demonstrates effective networking skills
- Develops a campus visibility for library
- Develops long-range plans in collaboration with library's community
- Develops various sources of funding
- Develop and fosters partnerships with groups and organizations on/off campus
- Encourages others (board and other community members) to be advocates for the library
- Exercises mature judgment
- Engages in fundraising and donor relations
- Manages/shapes change
- Is able to function in political environment
- Is an advocate for librarians' role in higher education
- Is collaborative
- Is entrepreneurial leader in a shared decision-making environment
- Keeps the library focused on its mission
- Leads and participates in consortia and cooperative endeavors
- Thinks "outside the box" (in new and creative ways applicable to the problem)

Individual or Personal Leadership Traits

- Able to ask the right questions
- Able to compromise
- Able to handle stress
- Accessible
- Articulates direction for the library
- Comfortable with ambiguity
- Committed to learning from mistakes
- Committed to set of values (integrity)
- Exercises good judgment
- Energetic
- Has organizational agility
- Has reasonable risk-taking skills
- Has team-building skills
- Intuitive
- Inspires trust
- Is innovative
- Is focused on change
- Is persuasive
- Is enthusiastic

- Is an enabler and facilitator
- Is committed to explaining decisions
- Optimistic
- Self-aware and confident
- Sense of humor
- Take initiatives
- Understands that one does not have all the answers

Cross-cultural management is more personal and relationship-oriented than mono-cultural management. Leaders in cross-cultural management settings require various approaches in order to deal with multiple cultures. Leaders who are skilled only in mono-cultural management will not succeed in today's global multi-cultural environment. Without a proper understanding of cultural norms, leaders can make fatal and embarrassing social mistakes while trying to manage their multi-cultural workforce.

Traditional leadership development does not emphasize traits in cross-cultural management. New sets of leadership traits that focus on cross-cultural management urgently need to be developed in order to train new leaders with the cross-cultural management ability.

The key component of cross-cultural management qualities is global literacy. "To be globally literate means seeing, thinking, acting, and mobilizing in culturally mindful ways" (Rosen & Digh, 2002, http://www1.sim.edu.sg/sim/pub/mag/sim_pub_mag_list.cfm?ID=961).

Table 7. Leadership Qualities for Library Directors in Cross-cultural Management

Leadership

- Is globally literate
- Is truly committed to ethnic, cultural, religion, ideology, gender, sexual-orientation diversity
- Is committed to the Intellectual Freedom Principles—freedom of inquiry and open access to ideas and information
- Self-awareness of one's own culture's biases
- Is sensitive to others' (from different cultures) feelings and reactions in making decisions
- Willing to change or modify decisions according to different cultures
- Willing to adjust one's behaviors according to different cultural settings
- Flexible to experience and adapt to new culture even beyond one's

comfort zone
- Willing to travel and live internationally
- Willing to learn new languages
- Awareness of global business and geo-politic environment
- Savvy on international relations, international economics, and international law issues

6. Conclusion

Globalization is an inevitable trend in all industries. The globalization tide brings great impact on the libraries and librarians. This paper introduces the new concept of the Global Library and describes its key characteristics and advantages as well as disadvantages. The authors believe that the end of the local library is unavoidable as more and more libraries are joining the global cooperation and collaboration in sharing collections, services and human talents. The Global Library will emerge as an effective model for future libraries around the world.

To be a successful leader in a global library environment, cultural intelligence (CQ) is very critical. One needs to manage employees with diverse cultural backgrounds and serve patrons from various cultures as well. CQ is an emerging and important leadership trait in cross-cultural management. The abilities to persistently adapt to diverse cultures and different ways of thinking and the skills to take the right responses in cross-cultural interpersonal and organizational relationships are prerequisites to successful global leadership.

Leadership, as a subject, has been neglected in the library field until the 1980s. As the library leaders are graying, libraries are facing an urgent need to educate and develop future library leaders. In the globalization age, library leadership development needs to add new dimensions, such as CQ in a cross-cultural management environment. In order to develop and train the next generation of library leaders, the libraries must either develop their leaders with global literary and high CQ or they need to select leaders with the appropriate skills.

One of the effective ways to develop a leadership program in a cross-cultural environment is to develop LDPs via international collaboration. With more participants and facilitators coming from different countries and cultures, cross-cultural engagement and learning experience can be achieved effectively.

Globalization is everywhere. The Global Library is emerging, and it is time we ask ourselves if we are ready to seize this opportunity, and if our leaders are ready to take such a challenge!

References

1 Alon, Ilan. (2003). Chinese Culture, Organizational Behavior, and International Business Management. London: Praeger.

2 Alon, Ilan and Higgins, James M. (2005). Global leadership success through emotional and cultural intelligences. *Business Horizons*, 48, 501-502.

3 American Library Association. Http://www.ala.org.

4 ChangingMinds.org. http://changingminds.org/index.htm.

5 Covey, Stephen R. (2004). The 8th Habit: From Effectiveness to Greatness. New York: Free Express.

6 Department for Professional Employees, AFL-CIO. (2005). Fact Sheet 2005: Library Workers. Retrieved on June 12, 2006 at: http://www. dpeaflcio.org/policy/factsheets/fs_2005_library_ workers.htm.

7 Earley, P. Christopher and Ang, Soon. (2003). Cultural Intelligence: Individual Interactions Across Cultures. Stanford, California: Stanford Business Books.

8 Friedman, Thomas. (2006). The World Is Flat. New York: Farrar, Straus and Giroux.

9 Global Library Initiative (http://www.globallibrary.org/en/index.php).

10 Hernon, P., Powell, R. and Young, A. (2003). The Next Library Leadership: Attributes of academic and public library directors.

11 Heye, Dennie. (2004). Library Globalization Study in Shell Exploration and Production. Retrieved on May 20, 2006 at: http://www.online-information.co.uk/2004proceedings/thursam/ heye_d.pdf.

12 HKU Libraries Leadership Institute. http://lib.hku.hk/leadership/.

13 Hutley, Sue and Solomons, Terena. (2004). Generational change in Australian librarianship: viewpoints from Generation X. Paper presented at ALIA 2004. Retrieved on June 12, 2006 at: http://www.library.uq.edu.au/papers/generational_change_in_australian_librarianship.pdf.

14 Karp, Rashelle S. and Murdock, Cindy. (1998). Leadership in librarianship. In Mech, Terrence R. and McCabe, Gerard B. eds., Leadership and Academic Librarians, pp. 251-264, Westport, Connecticut: Greenwood Press.

15 Kouzes, James M., and Posner, Barry Z. (2002). The Leadership Challenges. San Francisco: Jossey-Bass.

16 Lenzini, Rebecca T. (2002). The graying of the library profession: a survey

of our professional association and their responses. Searcher, vol. 10, no. 7, July/Aug 2002. Retrieved on June 12, 2006 at: http://www.infotoday. com/searcher/jul02/refs.

17 Log in to Learn. http://www.logintolearn.com/nextdistance.html.

18 Lynn, Andrea. (2006). Chinese Librarians Coming to U. of I. to Study 'Library Futures'. Retrieved on June 15, 2006 at: http://www.news.uiuc. edu/news/06/0613librarians.html.

19 Maxwell, John C. (1999). The 21 Indispensable Qualities of a Leader: Becoming the Person That People Will Want to Follow. Nashville: Thomas Nelson Publisher.

20 Metz, Terry. (2001) Wanted: library leaders for a discontinuous future. Library Issues 21, no. 3 (Jan. 2001), 2-3.

21 Norberg, Lisa. (2005). Instruction and Outreach in Support of a Global Curriculum. Retrieved on June 11, 2006 from: www.lib.unc.edu/instruct/ worldview/presentations/Instruction_and_ Outreach. pdf.

22 OCLC virtual reference QuestionPoint. http://www.oclc.org/questionpoint/ about/default.htm.

23 Rikowski, Ruth. (2005). Globalisation, Information and Libraries: The Implications of the World Trade Organisation's GATS and TRIPS Agreements. Oxford: Chandos Publishing.

24 Riggs, Donald E. (1998). Chapter 4. Visionary leadership. In Mech, Terrence R. and McCabe, Gerard B. ed., Leadership and Academic Librarians, pp. 55-65, Westport, Connecticut: Greenwood Press.

25 Rosen, Robert and Digh, Patricia. (2002). Developing Globally Literate Leaders. Retrieved on June 15, 2006 at: http://www1.sim.edu.sg/sim/pub/ mag/sim_pub_mag_list.cfm?ID=961.

Part V

Information Technology and
Library Management and Marketing

The Library and Cultural Patterns in Lending Statistics

Maja Coltura and Bart Vercruyssen
VCOB (Flemish Centre for Public Libraries)

Abstract

After a year of serious data cleaning and preparation, factor and cluster analysis revealed 11 (5 nonfiction types and 6 fiction) distinctive user segments that reflect the real and underlying drivers of the users. Because plenty of background variables (such as age, education, cultural interest, media preference) were taken in account, the user data reveals that library use is closely related to cultural interests and background.

Upon this segmentation a marketing strategy is designed that starts from how, why and when different segments use the library. The market strategy focuses on both the re-entering of young families and avoiding the drop-out (retention). Therefore five domains of marketing activity are at stake:

1. From a children's section to a family library.

2. From organization-driven cooperation to customer-driven cooperation (not the interests of the organization, but the interests of the customers is the start).

3. From a general communication to specific communication. Using the customer's interest to attract attention.

4. From lending software to databased marketing. Daily integration of loan statistics in marketing strategy.

5. From a warehouse to a public-friendly building. Using the customers' interest profiles to set up a library.

1. One Culture, Different Faces?

Through emerging communication systems and global trading, continents, cultures and people are closer to each other than ever before. Multiculturalism is mostly described as the living together (or clash) of different cultures. Culture in this definition is closely related to origin, and the included values and attitudes.

From this point of view cultures are seen as internally homogeneous and externally heterogeneous. All members of, e.g., western culture share a common set of values and attitudes, which are different from those of other cultures (e.g., Arabic). Multiculturalism becomes then the way how these different cultures (can) live together in one geographical area.

Closer investigation reveals that the idea of a homogeneous western culture is as convenient as it is misleading. Indeed, in-depth studies show that one culture is in fact a sum of different underlying cultures. The latter are predominant in how and which choices are made by people, including choices related to library use.

A commonly accepted view is that western society can be divided into high and low culture. Sociologists working in this field even refined this dichotomous model with a much broader variety of different cultures. In this approach culture is not related to a regional or racial determinant, but refers to how people use the (cultural) artifacts (clothing, newspapers and media, music, etc.) to express themselves and shape their cultural identity. Applied by marketers, these cultures are given the name of lifestyles.

Although this form of "multiculturalism" does not start from geographical or racial background, it doesn't exclude them. Studies showed that a majority of the people from non-western origin (easily) incorporated, applied and even shaped the existing western lifestyles.

At least it could be proven that this "lifestyle" approach of multiple cultures is very useful for analyzing and identifying user groups in the public library.

2. Analyzing Loan Statistics to Identify Cultural Patterns

In 2004 the Flemish centre for public libraries conducted a major investigation at 165 libraries. Over 32,000 people were selected randomly and surveyed, and their borrowing history was stored for about 6 months. The combination of the survey results and the continued borrowing gave insights that were completely new for the sector of public libraries.

The lending data, a huge data set with more than 150,000 records (=lendings) could be used to analyze patterns in:

• The amount of items borrowed

- The different materials borrowed (books, magazines, CDs, DVDs, . . .)
- The sort (genres) of fiction books and the type of non-fiction books that are borrowed together.

The first two types of analyses revealed interesting views on the use of the library in relation to the level of education of the users, as well on age and gender. From the last analysis a very detailed cultural pattern among the users was identified. Since the latter focuses on the central issue of this conference, less attention will be given to the former analysis.

2.1. Analyzing borrowed materials

By looking closer to who borrowed what items, it became obvious that gender, age and education were determinant factors.

A first analysis showed that elderly, lower-educated and men are under-represented in the library population, compared to their relative appearance in the Flemish population.

Detailed analysis on the other hand showed that older and lower-educated borrowers are more likely to be heavy users (more items borrowed).

It became also clear that they use the fiction collection much more.

So it can be said that although underrepresented in total numbers, older and lower-educated groups are overrepresented among the non-fiction users. It can also be said that they were less in number but higher in volume (amount of materials borrowed per capita).

Men on the other hand are higher-educated and more likely to be CD bor-rowers (and to a lesser extent non-fiction).

It led us to the conclusion that:

- Underrepresented groups are strongly interested in specific parts of the collection.
- It's due to its most basic materials that a library is attractive for older and lower-educated people. New materials, such as CDs and DVDs, attract higher-educated men, and this part of the collection can thus hardly be seen as popular (as in popular culture, attractive for large groups in society).

2.2. Analyzing the borrowed books

An analysis of the fiction genres and non-fiction genres showed that it's im-possible to construct one typology of all users of printed material. Reality showed that the first big division among library users is the one between fiction and non-fiction, or to stay closer to a functional approach, the use of the public library for information against the cultural (reading) recreational use.

Despite the fact that all books in Flemish libraries are evenly accessible, the study revealed underlying cultural behavior in people's selection of the genres and titles. Given this fact six fiction types and five non-fiction types could be identified.

2.2.1. Fiction

Given all the borrowed titles, thrillers is the most popular genre (37.4% of the borrowed fiction titles), followed by the romantic genre (18.3%). A-novels (11.7%), B-novels (popular) 8.1% and sci-fi 6% close the top five.

Upon this data a cluster analysis revealed six clusters. Using the data from the survey the background of these clusters could be revealed.

The sex clusters were:

- Fiction fearers
- Adrenaline addicts
- Young quality readers
- Voracious readers
- Older quality readers

2.2.1.1. The adrenaline addicts

This cluster is obsessed by thrillers and detective stories. Some of them also borrow a popular novel or a book on war.

There are more men in this group and they are medium-educated, but good earners.

They have a medium cultural background and interest in literature. Except for the books, they are not really interested in what else a library has to offer: they don't look around and don't use the catalogue.

2.2.1.2. Young quality readers

This segment chooses the "better books". 80% of them borrowed at least one A-novel, but also female books. Theater and poetry and essays are quite popular.

As the name suggests this is a younger group with a higher education. This group is stimulated in their youth to read and still have a very positive attitude on reading. To find their books they use more often the catalogue.

2.2.1.3. Romantics

As the name suggests these are the readers of the romantic books. A total of 97.5% of this group borrowed at least one romantic book during the reference period. Also the B-novel (popular) and thrillers are borrowed quite a lot.

This is a very "female" group, and just a bit older (over middle age), with a lower education. They were not that much stimulated to read in their childhood.

Nevertheless in amounts of visits they are "hard-core users". They visit the library more often for their children.

To find books they walk through the library, leaving the catalogue for what it is.

2.2.1.4. Voracious readers

There are only few genres that this segment doesn't take home. Thrillers, romantic books, A-novels, B-novels, sci-fi, female books, historical novels . . . They seem to like it all.

They have a lot in common with the romantics but they are older (retired). They tend to be female, lower-educated with not much cultural stimulation during childhood.

They find all those books by wandering through the library.

2.2.1.5. The older quality readers

They can be seen as the older version of the young. They like the same genres but borrow them more.

They're also higher educated and were strongly stimulated to read during childhood.

Unlike their younger version they don't use the catalogue a lot.

2.2.1.6. The fiction readers

These are in fact non-fiction readers who accidentally take a fiction book with them, not really a particular genre.

These are the higher educated male visitors. They don't come often to the library and when they do it is for a short time. They go immediately to what they need or search in the catalogue.

2.2.2. Non-fiction types

Just as we did with the fiction, the same could be done for non-fiction.

The fact that only five clusters are needed to describe the non-fiction borrowers, we can say that the underlying cultural patterns defining people's choices are less heterogeneous. One can argue that because of its more functional nature the non-fiction collection expresses less the underlying cultural patterns.

The five types are:

- Home and garden
- Spiritualists

- Self-taught
- The travel birds
- Non-fiction lovers

2.2.2.1. Home and garden

As the name suggests the home and garden books are most popular among this group. This group is more female (not if compared to the average library user) and middle-aged. This is a very family-oriented group.

2.2.2.2. Spiritualists

In the choice of non-fiction books this group is looking for equilibrium between body and soul. Books on psychology and philosophy as well as books on medicine and body are borrowed frequently.

The group is younger, very female and higher-educated, or still studying.

2.2.2.3. Self-taught

This segment visits the library to learn more on (local) history. They are called self-taught because these mostly older men are not highly educated. They also say that they visit the library to learn. They are hard-core library users.

2.2.2.4. The travel birds

Only one type of non-fiction books is taken home by this group: travel guides. They are middle-aged, higher-educated and more male. Because it is obvious that they visit the library for travel purposes, they are not frequently seen in the library.

2.2.2.5. The non-fiction lovers

This group has a very broad horizon of interest since they take home books from every category.

It is a higher-educated group that has not more or fewer older people than men among them.

3. From Theory to Practice

The marketing strategy of public libraries in Flanders and Brussels focuses on keeping the customer satisfied and on attracting new customers. We try to make the ideas less theoretical by showing you some of the projects that fit in the marketing strategy.

3.1. The week of the public library

The yearly Week of the Public Library works on both premises: keeping and attracting customers. Keeping customers is a job that suits the local libraries well. They know their customers. They see it when someone is getting mad and wants to give up his membership. If a loyal customer doesn't come around any longer, they can send him a letter, since they have his address and also know what his interests are, thanks to the survey.

In the Week of the Public Library the local libraries organize all kinds of treats for their loyal customers, from a cup of coffee and a piece of cake to a free DVD with every five DVDs you borrow.

If we want to attract new customers, we have to make a campaign that suits our new target group. And therefore we need to know who those targeted people are, what they like, which newspaper they read, what television program they watch, and where they spend their free time and would be able to notice our campaign posters. The survey gives us all the answers we need to know. We are convinced that lots of other young families can be persuaded to go (back) to the library and have the same experiences as the ones who already found their way back in.

3.1.1. Target group: young mothers

These young mothers used to be library members, and are coming back now, for one reason: their children. Apparently they have nice memories of their former library time, and they want to share that experience with their own family. They are also convinced that going to a library is part of a good and balanced education. The library is a place where the kids and the young mothers get wiser and spend a nice time.

When the young mothers in our survey find some spare time, they like to read women's magazines. In the evening, when the kids are asleep, they love to watch Eén, the family channel of the public television. That gives us already an idea of the look and feel we should use in our campaign. If we look at the books those young mothers borrow, we see literature and romantic stories for the fiction collection. Their interests in non-fiction books concentrate around life style, cooking, gardening, creating a nice home, and being healthy in a physical and a psychological way.

Famous Belgians attract, and certainly when they plead for a good cause, such as the public library. Therefore our campaign for the Week of the Public Library shows Marc Reynebeau, a famous Belgian known for his overall knowledge and intellect, but also for his clumsiness—someone who doesn't need a library, you would think. But even Marc Reynebeau gets wiser in the library, because he finds books that help him find the right stylish clothes. The book cover we use refers to the interests of our target group: life style. And based on women's magazines Marc Reynebeau is "well appreciated" by our target group.

3.1.2. Campaign

The Week of the Public Library works on three levels: Flanders national, the smaller regions and the local public library. The national campaign focuses on visibility with a website, posters, folders, flyers and funny booklet guides throughout Flanders and Brussels, and cooperation with national press. The regional campaign gains newcomers with a library contest and focuses on the regional press. Local libraries treat their loyal customers with a National Library Treat Day full of surprising activities and inform the local press. These three levels make the Week of the Public Library visible throughout Flanders and Brussels.

3.2. Poetry day

Flemish libraries attract lots of new members, but lose many at the same time. The balance stays. Stopping the outflow would already make a big difference. Therefore we created a project to stop members from leaving.

A Dutch investigation showed that you can write a personal letter to a member that stays away. If you write the letter within six months of his last visit, 20% of them come back. Promising a little gift makes the results even better.

At national Poetry Day, VCOB, the support centre for all public libraries in Flanders and Brussels, made mementos that libraries could order with us. We wrote a step-by-step manual to get all the members that stay away to return and gave an example of a letter you might send. A few libraries tested the project and the results were astonishing: 20 percent came back, and kept on coming back.

After this testing phase, we want to make promotional material for all libraries, so that every one can stop the outflow of library members.

3.3. Bibdating

Lots of libraries have reading groups, where one particular book is read and then discussed. Reading groups are fun, and attract mostly older women. Also younger people want to share their reading experiences but don't necessarily want to be a member of a reading group. And experienced reading groups are looking for a new fresh way of working. And thus, Bibdating was born.

3.3.1. What is bibdating?

Bibdating is inspired by speed dating, a trend in the world of singles. But instead of talking about just anything with your "blind date", you talk about books and reading experiences. Indeed, what you read tells a lot about who you are.

A bibdate starts with the right atmosphere: candles, colourful napkins and comfortable chairs set in pairs. The master of ceremonies welcomes everyone with a little drink, gives everyone a red or a green name tag to put on and explains what's about to happen. Everyone puts his favorite book on the table.

Because no one knows the others, we start with "ice breakers". Those are little questions the participants can ask another: do you buy or borrow your books, do you write in your books, do you always finish a book you have started, what is your favourite place to read . . . After they know the answer, both participants continue.

When the ice has been broken, bibdating can start. Everyone takes his book.

The red tags (or women, or youngsters, or . . .) sit down. The green tags join a red tag and start a conversation about the books, their experiences. After 5 minutes a nice tango music sounds: time to move on. The green tags move on to the next red tag, and so on.

When bibdating is over, all participants put their books back on the table. Everyone gets to put a few notes in a book of the person you want to communicate with. What to write on the paper? "Thanks for the nice book suggestion", "If you like this author, you might also like xxx", or in the best case: "A new bibdate next week, just the two of us? We'll meet in the library . . ."

3.3.2. A tailored bibdate

Library members have different profiles, and different interests. A bibdate tailored for specific interests and needs is possible with the insights of the survey. We took 6 profiles that are common and put them on a grid with two dimensions: "reading interest and patterns" on one hand, and "emotion" on the other hand.

3.3.2.1. Reading interest and patterns

40% of the borrowed books are fiction, 23% non-fiction. There is no such thing as the fiction reader and the non-fiction reader, but we can still make this group a bit more specific:

Fiction = more women, older, lower education, visits library often, browses to find books, isn't much into culture. Non-Fiction = more men, younger, higher education, visits less often, finds through catalogue, much into culture.

3.3.2.2. Emotion

Today life can be very stressful. People look for ways to de-stress, and we find two types of de-stressing. One type is the more "manly" type, which is more material, aggressive, extravert and adventurous. The more "feminine" type is emotional, tender, introvert and safe.

By crossing these two dimensions, we get four quadrants: fiction/manly, fiction/feminine, non-fiction/manly, non-fiction/feminine. All six profiles have their place on the axis. With a little test (as in women's magazines) participants can find out what kind of a reader they are. And that can be the start of a conversation with another like-minded person, or with someone who has a totally different profile.

3.4. Vlieg je mee—Fly with us

Vlieg je mee (fly with us) is a campaign that wants to bring children closer to culture. *Vlieg* (Fly) is a little icon that stands for "family and children-friendly culture." The survey tells us that the library and families go well together. *Vlieg* and libraries match. Therefore we started a campaign this summer: *De Leeszomer van Vlieg* (The Reading Summer of Fly). Lots of children stop going to the library during school breaks. That means two months of no reading. In September, at the beginning of the new school year, reading seems hard. But during summer vacation children have lots of spare time to read and discover how much fun reading can be.

The campaign starts at school. Teachers and parents get a library letter that tells them what happens after two months of not reading. All children get a funny poster to plan their two months. A poster and letter give more information on the campaign: go to the library in July and August and win! In fact, when children go to the library they get a post card where they can gather stamps: one for each book they have read. After three stamps they get a funny *Vlieg*-magnet to put on the refrigerator.

When children and their parents come to the library, we try to persuade the parents to take a book, DVD, or CD as well. That makes two flies at the same time: children read during holidays and parents get persuaded to become a member of the library.

Using the Feedback Loop to Create a Marketing Campaign

Jill Cousins

The European Library

Abstract

This paper will look at how The European Library has used several feedback loops to inform its marketing campaigns so far, what it will do in the future and how libraries generally might benefit from this approach.

The European Library is a purely digital resource. Allowing the user to access the deep web collections of the National Libraries of Europe, it was launched as a service in March 2005.

The site has made use of user feedback, both in terms of what users do on the site and what they are searching for to inform its marketing campaign. The more frequently used search words have been used in Google Ad word campaigns and for search engine optimization. These words have been used to inform the libraries on what to prioritize for digitization but have also provided clues for more targeted marketing. The creation of a linking campaign to get all the university libraries in the world to link to us is no small task so anything that focuses and prioritizes the campaign, such as subjects that are being searched, is helpful.

To dig further into this knowledge of what the user is looking for and how we might use it to market and develop the site, The European Library is developing a database of registered users. An analysis of the log files against the information given by individuals in this database should tell us more about whether the history professor is looking for something different from the history student and if they use the site differently. A constant feedback loop enables us to target our scarce resources to get maximum marketing coverage. Marketing is also an applicable term for enticing users through your site because for them to maximize it as a resource they need to be presented with what is in it and hence you need to know what they are seeking.

The experiences and knowledge gained by The European Library, particularly given its multicultural (45 national libraries) complexity might be of interest to other libraries aiming to create and market similar portals and networks. The paper will cover an approach to marketing that uses what the users are demanding.

1. What Is a Feedback Loop in Marketing

All marketing budgets are smaller than we would like so we have to maximize the effect for the money. One of the best ways of doing this is to use the feedback loops that are available to us. There are feedback loops in the more traditional methods of marketing such as posters, brochures, mail-outs etc., but the quantifiable aspect is quite rudimentary and the only real measurement you have is redemption, i.e., numbers of people who take up an offer, but these numbers do not tell you whether people looked at your brochure or if they filed or binned it. It is difficult to get any feeling of what has worked or whether this campaign was better than that one and what its real return on investment was. There are some industry norms, e.g., above 2% redemption on an offer is seen to be very good in traditional marketing, but this doesn't tell you about the ones who got away. Web marketing is much more measurable. The big advantage of the web and marketing via the web is that not only can you narrowcast market (one to one) but you can also see who liked what and what they did or didn't do on an individual basis. This is a far more effective feedback loop. With this information you can target your next campaign and therefore utilize scarce human and monetary resources more directly.

2. How Feedback Is Used in the European Library

Our main purpose in marketing The European Library is to achieve more relevant traffic to the site and therefore to our partner sites.

In the next section I propose to cover the areas where we are using feedback gained from the various activities to inform our next steps. It is less of a loop and more of a spider's web as one thing feeds into and informs another.

- Google Ad words
- Search Engine Optimisation
- Linking Programme

- Log File analysis
- Registered Users Database
- User Knowledge
- Site Development

The idea is that we use the knowledge we gain from advertising on Google to decide what pages we should optimize. This also tells us what people are searching on and an analysis of our collections against this knowledge tells us what we should be promoting. Our web analytics also tell us the origins of our users, this helps prioritise our linking programme. To further develop the ability to know what people want and do on the site we are in the process of changing our log files to capture relevant data and building a registered users database. The power of analyzing these two sets of data together for quantifiable, non-qualitative data will become apparent as together with a qualitative user survey we can assess what the stumbling blocks are for different user groups on our site and how therefore to present better the information it contains to them. The aim is always to get a good return on our marketing investment both monetary and human.

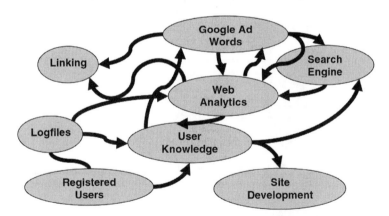

Figure 1: Web Marketing Feedback

2.1. Google ad words

There are several ways to find out what users looked for to get them to the website in the first place and one of the quickest is the use of Google advertisement words. This might appear a little extravagant on our 80,000 euro per year marketing budget, which has to cover all collateral such as brochures, letterhead and marketing in 43 countries, but it is a very effective way of knowing what the outside world is looking for and rates as important.

Google has a keyword tool, so you can pick words that will find subjects on your site and Google will suggest others, including synonyms and antonyms. Google tells you how many times a particular word or phrase has been searched on over the last month and you can choose your list of ad words for testing. It is also possible to use keyword inventory tools such as Overture/Yahoo! http://inventory.uk.overture.com to find this information for free, but the next step in the process of what people actually click on to get to your site is missing in this part of the loop. It is however a good way of finding some alternative keywords.

Figure 2: The keyword assistant on Yahoo!

You submit a set of keywords in a bidding process for a position and frequency according to your budget. The advertisement pops up when the user searches for those keywords, and only when the user clicks on the advert do you pay.

Once you have chosen your ad words the campaign is launched on Google and you only pay for click-throughs. So someone types in <Music manuscripts> and your ad appears, they click through the ad onto your site and hopefully continue to search for relevant information. This tells you what people have used to get to your site and using your web analytics packages on your log files you can then go further and see which of these ad words actually lead to someone doing something on your site. We have around 50% bouncers at the moment, i.e., people coming into the site and spending under 30 seconds on it before exiting. I would prefer this number to be nearer 35 so we will change the ad words that are producing the bouncers for others to test their efficacy.

Number of visits: 37808 - Average: 332 s	Number of visits	Percent
0s-30s	18160	48 %
30s-2mn	7544	19.9 %
2mn-5mn	4876	12.8 %
5mn-15mn	3495	9.2 %
15mn-30mn	1472	3.8 %
30mn-1h	1458	3.8 %
1h+	745	1.9 %
Unknown	58	0.1 %

Figure 3: Visits duration in May 2006 on The European Library

Relevant traffic is more important than sheer volume increases, but the effect of the Google Ad campaign on The European Library in the first 3 months of 2006 was quite dramatic, with traffic doubling every month and dropping very quickly when we stopped doing it in April while negotiating our budget.

The click-through on these chosen ad words tells us what people are searching on. This in turn gives feedback on the interest areas. This can inform digitization programmes as well as the next steps in marketing. The real feedback though is to use this knowledge to decide what search engine optimization pages to create. These are for free, more or less. Optimally you can have 20 search engine optimized pages in your root directory. Therefore you want to make sure these are the most useful.

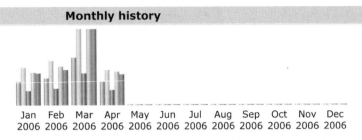

Month	Unique visitors	Number of visits	Pages	Hits	Bandwidth
Jan 2006	21108	34408	770163	1764919	7.14 MB
Feb 2006	24620	41321	911829	2095586	7.88 MB
Mar 2006	43737	70256	1708692	4118222	17.03 MB
Apr 2006	21143	32407	808227	1822595	6.86 MB

Figure 4: Traffic in response to the Google Ad campaign, first quarter 2006

2.2. Search engine optimisation

The aim with search engine optimization is to use the content of your site with your page rank to ensure that your results occur in the first 2 pages of search engine results.

Search engine optimization is a little more complicated than picking the ad words that generated the most traffic. For instance 'online library' was one of our early keyword advertisements and in May the ad was shown on Google 30,960 times because the words 'online library' were searched for by users that often; however the click-throughs on the ad were quite low, at 2309, compared to the ad for 'out of print books,' with 892 click-throughs on 8630—a 10.3% return on investment compared to 7.5% for 'online library.' This means that we might be more likely to write a search engine optimization page for out of print books than online library. However other factors come into play, such as competition. At The European Library we have a high page rank at 7/10 which helps push our results higher up the Google results pages, but competitors have equally high or higher rankings and appear higher in the results. There is no point aiming for a position that you will not get because the competition is so stiff. Competitors here need not be other virtual libraries but could even be a library shelving company promoting their library capabilities online. Other considerations include not optimizing for 'books,' as the competition is extreme and it is a very common keyword, but we have optimized for 'books online,' where the competition is not so high. However while 'books online' will give us good traffic ratings it will not necessarily be quality traffic, whereas rare books could attract this quality because it is more targeted at the group of people we are aiming for.

Two frequent mistakes are to aim for a keyword that won't give a position in the first 3 or 4 pages of results because the competition is so fierce and diverse or to target very common keywords which may generate a fair amount of visitors but will not convert to action. Getting the traffic from search engines is only useful if visitors don't bounce.

We played with various ad words, assessing their click-through rates, direct relevance to the site and their longevity, i.e., are they worth writing landing pages for. Below is the original set of keywords submitted for advertisements on Google.

	Keyword	Indication			Keyword	Indication
1	books online	6.677		22	music collections	365
1	book online	6.643		23	London library	334
2	catalogs	2.985		24	antique book	292
3	libraries	2.212		25	old book	238
4	music score	2.154		26	book education	223
5	rare books	1.926		27	classic books	159
6	British library	1875		28	book library	150
7	children's literature	1.583		29	literature online	130
8	antique maps	1.502		30	literature study	127
9	English literature	1.130		31	library books	121
10	music scores	1.123		32	national library	116
11	old maps	975		33	education study	103
12	atlases	838		34	education resource	93
13	online library	739		35	library catalogue	84
14	antique books	734		36	libraries book	59
15	old books	699		37	educational resource	59
16	literary	498		38	classic literature	57
17	manuscripts	450		39	book collection	47
18	educational books	434		40	books collection	46
19	rare book	431		41	online libraries	40
20	reference books	398		42	national libraries	6
21	manuscript	385				

Figure 5: Keywords used to advertise content in
The European Library on Google

From these keywords we took the following to create landing pages:

> antique books
> antique maps
> Atlases
> books online
> catalogs
> children's literature
> educational books
> libraries
> manuscript
> manuscripts
> music collections
> music score
> music scores
> old books
> old maps
> online library
> rare book
> rare books
> treasures
> treasures

Figure 6: Words used for search engine
optimization texts

As mentioned, it is possible to do this without payment via yahoo! but it will take longer to find out if the keywords really work for you. However this method is truly for free: you look up your keywords and decide if they will generate a decent response and then write your optimized pages.

For each keyword or words you need to write a landing page for the crawlers to crawl and index and for the user to initially land on after following a link from a search engine. This content can be updated regularly but not so often that it becomes burdensome. The creation of these pages is particularly useful in a site where the content is not accessible by crawlers, and this is true of most library-related sites. Content is in the OPACs or non-crawl-able/harvestable databases.

In writing these pages some attention has to be paid to brand, as it is the page the user first lands on having clicked through from the search engine and as enticement or advertisement at the point they are browsing the results of their searches in Google or Yahoo, etc. However it also worth remembering that few users read very much at all!

A landing page looks like the following example for Rare Books:

Figure 7: Example of a landing page for a search engine user having searched for rare books and clicked through to The European Library.

You can straight away see the difference from our usual homepage.

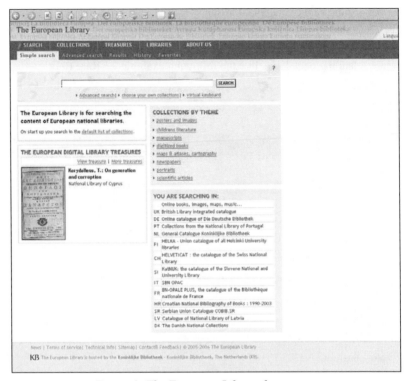

Figure 8: The European Library home page

There is a technique to writing landing pages whereby you write quite a lot of copy for each keyword so that many search combinations can be made for that keyword. These combinations are indexed by the search engines. This means visitors come into the site having searched on the various keyword combinations you have created; see figure 9.

Writing landing pages requires some attention to your brand, but can also be used to manoeuvre the user into correct use of the site. For instance we know from our latest user survey that most users have no concept of what a collection is and certainly do not choose collections before conducting their searches. This is a big problem for any portal site. The Google habitué expects to get results on a two-word search, not to pick or search for collections first. So for the odd person who actually reads the opening sentences of a site we are using the landing page as a means of pushing them to choose the relevant collections, as illustrated in figure 10.

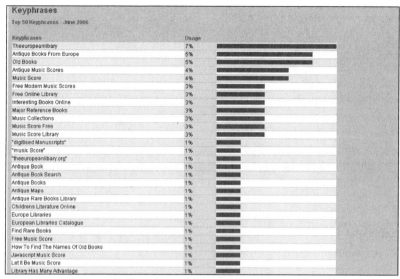

Figure 9: Search combinations leading to visitors

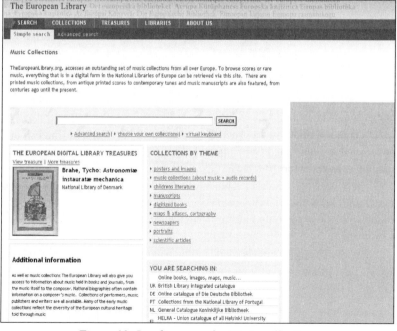

Figure 10: Landing page for Music collections

We hope that the first sentence will encourage the user to click on <music collections> and therefore 'choose' their collections and be searching in the music ones, not the default ones, and so get much better results, such as this search in the music collections on volksmuziek:

Figure 11: From the 'Music Collections' of The European Library

Search optimization has been executed for 25 keywords in English and has started in French and German and Italian. Eventually we would like to do this for at least the top 10 relevant search words for each language.

These pages go on working when you are sleeping. All the search engines crawl and index them every month and users search globally every minute of every day, but you only have to make a search optimization once for each search term.

The search engine crawls each landing page and indexes the information, which then becomes visible in their results. So the search on rare books in Google will now show up:

Figure 12: Rare Books search on Google

And clicking through takes you to the landing page shown in figure 7 above.

2.3. Linking programme

This is slightly tangential to the main theme but we also use feedback here to prioritise our programme. We are aiming to link to all relevant sites in the world. This is partly to ensure distribution of the site and hence is marketing in itself but also to help keep and improve our ranking in the search engine results. However 'all the relevant sites' is an enormous task, so we look at ways to prioritise our workload. We can use what people are searching on to inform this, but also where our users are coming from, so we target more of the same. Are they academics from research institutions or universities, are they students or hobbyists? Not surprisingly our best users are academics and researchers or librarians researching on someone else's behalf. Common sense would probably tell us that we should link to the academic libraries and institutions first, but we can use our web analytics to tell us which countries we should be concentrating on. If we already have a lot of academic traffic from a country we could demote it in our linking programme. A comparison of March and May country of origin stats shows us that our linking programme in Italy has had considerable effect on the traffic gained from that site. It also tells us that we need to work on some of our partner countries more; Denmark and Slovenia should be doing better than Canada for example.

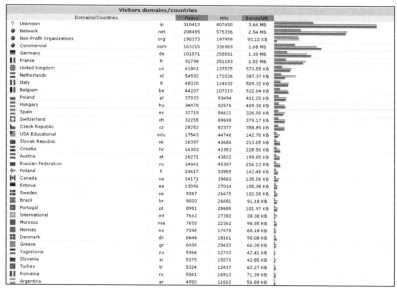

Figure 13: Visitors' to The European Library country of origin, March

Visitors domains/countries				
Domains/Countries		Pages	Hits	Bandwidth
? Unknown	ip	310413	807650	3.64 MB
Network	net	208485	575336	2.54 MB
Non-Profit Organizations	org	190373	197958	90.18 KB
Commercial	com	163215	336989	1.68 MB
Germany	de	101871	258881	1.30 MB
France	fr	92798	251183	1.02 MB
United Kingdom	uk	61841	137575	573.55 KB
Netherlands	nl	54592	172036	387.37 KB
Italy	it	48320	114632	509.32 KB
Belgium	be	44207	107219	522.04 KB
Poland	pl	37033	93494	411.20 KB
Hungary	hu	34478	82576	409.38 KB
Spain	es	32719	86621	326.90 KB
Switzerland	ch	32255	89698	379.17 KB
Czech Republic	cz	28252	82377	358.89 KB
USA Educational	edu	17543	44746	142.70 KB
Slovak Republic	sk	16397	43686	213.05 KB
Croatia	hr	16303	42353	228.50 KB
Austria	at	16271	43822	199.85 KB
Russian Federation	ru	14841	45397	216.13 KB
Finland	fi	14617	33955	142.48 KB
Canada	ca	14171	39660	135.06 KB
Estonia	ee	13096	27014	105.38 KB
Sweden	se	9387	26475	102.08 KB
Brazil	br	9000	26681	91.18 KB
Portugal	pt	8951	28685	101.97 KB
International	int	7662	27382	38.38 KB
Morocco	ma	7658	22362	98.85 KB
Norway	no	7394	17478	68.18 KB
Denmark	dk	6644	18161	90.08 KB
Greece	gr	6404	20433	66.30 KB
Yugoslavia	yu	5964	12733	42.41 KB
Slovenia	si	5375	15576	42.85 KB
Turkey	tr	5324	12437	62.27 KB
Romania	ro	5041	16913	71.39 KB
Argentina	ar	4950	11610	56.80 KB

Figure 14: Visitors' to The European Library country of origin, May

2.4. Log files

This is an area where we know what we want but have yet to achieve it. We are working with some Delos network partners, Gerhard Weikum of the Max Planck Inst. and Maristella Agosti, Giorgio Maria Di Nunzio and Alberto Niero of the University of Padova to be able to create log files that will then give us useful feedback on what our users are doing and what they want.

We have log files for the search part of the portal and for the website itself. These log files tell us what people are searching. They also tell us if they find it and where they have gone on the site. Do they leave after the first page, do they sift through the results, do they download an item? Knowing what the user is doing is useful for site development and to target our marketing. If we know that the history professor spends time looking through the collections and downloading references then we can promote this aspect of the site on historical society websites, but we can also personalize the site so that the pages presented to the history professor relate to his or her preferences. Equally if we know that the history student is largely looking for images then we can make links with the various new learning environments such as blackboard that emphasize this aspect of the site, but also ensure that the images are presented to the history student when he or she is using The European Library. Such personalization should have a direct result on the numbers of people bookmarking and returning to the site.

However, in order to really know that the person searching for Erasmus's influence is indeed the history professor and not the history student, we need more than just the log files. This is the main purpose of our registered users database, that comes on stream in July. With it we can cross-analyse what a particular sort of person is doing on the site and therefore what they want to do.

For the July 2006 release we will create a registered users database. This is not to force people to log in to be able to use the site, but to be able to give those who want it updates via email alerts for new content and saved searches. To receive these alerts a user will have to give his or her email, country, and profession, optional will be information on age and institution. The take-up rate for such emails is normally quite high and helps enormously to keep your site in the vision field of the user.

Such knowledge of individuals' search requirements helps us retarget our linking programmes and also tells us what people are looking for currently that we could create ads or search engine optimization pages for. And so we are back at the beginning of the loop—where users are telling us what we should be promoting at any one point in time.

3. The Future for the European Library:
Using the Content Itself to Market

To really make our content work for us we are encouraging libraries to produce OAI compliant metadata, which can then be crawled by us and enriched
for the big search engines. This means a user searching for Shanghai would
actually be able to find articles from the German Library Exile Press,

Figure 15: Search on Shanghai in Exilepress

or old maps of China in the Maritime Atlases of the Koninklijke Bibliotheek.

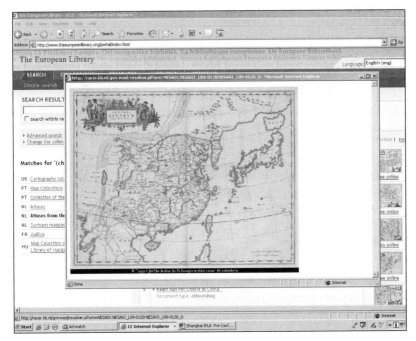

Figure 16: Search on China in the Map Collections

4. Conclusions

The use of the quantifiable information that can be derived from web logs and online marketing makes the return on investment calculable. It can be seen what does and does not work. This means you can direct your efforts towards the most effective marketing. The creation of brochures selling library services are probably the poorest return on investment you could do. We know people take them and file them with no interim step of reading. With the use of online marketing you are putting the information in front of the person at the point of need.

References

1   Weikum, Agosti, Di Nunzio and Alberto Niero. Max Planck and University of Padova, for work on The European Library logfiles, as yet unpublished.

2   Tribal Internet Marketing B.V. www.tribal-im.com, for work on search engine promotion for The European Library.

Performance Measurement of Metadata Management

Leon Zhao
System and Network Center, Shanghai Library, China

Abstract

As a buzz word nowadays, metadata management is ubiquitous but sparsely defined explicitly in research papers of library science. According to West-brooks's definition, Metadata management is the sum of activities designed to create, preserve, describe, maintain access, and manipulate metadata, that may be owned, aggregated, or distributed by the managing institution. In other words, metadata management is less "technical" than "organizational".

By looking into the environmental issues in detail of the current meta-data applications in the library community, which is decentralized and with many standards and more new technologies, the paper discusses the general problems and issues in metadata management. Metadata management is more than a management life cycle of itself, but an organizational and intellectual process required physical resources, financial commitment, and policy planning, which composes the whole framework of metadata management. The most important issue is the performance measurement of the process. By using the methodology adapted from widely accepted measurement tools, an entire framework is proposed to measure the performance of metadata activities in a library environment from four perspectives: financial, customer, internal business process, and learning and growth. These perspectives should be tailored to the environment of metadata management, to assure the measurement tool's usefulness and effectiveness. The paper also discusses some details of using the method and adapting the tool for a real metadata management environment. For example, the customer perspective should be focused on the usage requirements of metadata from the user, to see if the metadata is really helpful for the user to find, locate, access and evaluate the resources they exactly need. In addition, the internal business process focuses on the workflow of the metadata creation, preservation, maintaining and accessing, which should be measured if it is being organized and managed well enough from the organizational perspective. In the paper, ten indexes and weight for them about four perspectives will also be introduced to make people involved in metadata management fully understand the measurement process. In the conclusion, the paper discusses some considerations and difficulties about performance measurement of metadata management.

1. Introduction

Metadata management is known as one of the most serious issue in today's library community. The major problem of it is evaluation of the performance of metadata management. With not only a design and discussion of an approach to implementing a balanced scorecard, but also a survey of all the metrics discussed here, this paper gives us a new approach of metadata management performance measurement.

2. Metadata Management

As a buzz word nowadays, metadata management is ubiquitous but sparsely defined explicitly in research papers of library science. One of the extensive definitions comes from Kurth, Ruddy, and Rupp in their article "Repurposing MARC metadata: using digital project experience to develop a metadata management design". They defined metadata management as coordination of the "intellectual activity and physical resources required to create and manipulate metadata" (Kurth et al, 2004). In "Distributing and synchronizing heterogeneous metadata in geospatial information repositories for access", Westbrooks proposed the following definition of metadata management: "In a broad sense . . . metadata management implies the implementation of a metadata policy (i.e. principles that form the guiding framework within which metadata exists) and adherence to metadata standards" (Westbrooks, 2004). And in a literature review of metadata management, Westbrooks noted that Diane Hillmann, metadata coordinator for the National Science Digital Library (NSDL), provided a definition that is implicit and brief, but she explicitly stated, "metadata management is less a 'technical' process than an 'organizational' one" (Westbrooks, 2005).

Also in this literature review, Westbrooks gives a prescribed definition: "Metadata management is the sum of activities designed to create, preserve, describe, maintain access, and manipulate metadata, MARC and otherwise, that may be owned, aggregated, or distributed by the managing institution. These organizational and intellectual activities require the physical resources (web services, scripts and cross-walks), financial commitment (much like that already invested into OPACs), and policy planning that codifies the guiding framework within which metadata exists" (Westbrooks, 2005).

All those definitions introduce the key components of what metadata management can be, and Westbrooks formulated a good definition of what metadata management should be. In my opinion, metadata management is not only a critical lifecycle process of metadata, but also more a managerial task than a technical job. Because it is a managerial job, performance measurement becomes the key issue of it.

Nowadays, library staffs have a long history to manage all library metadata processes in an environment that is complicated by decentralization. The decentralized situation in which libraries find themselves parallels that in all automated work environments following the emergence of relational databases, desktop workstations, and client-server architectures. And using multiple metadata schemes, including MARC or non-MARC, magnifies the decentralization and complexity common to automated workplaces (Kurth et al, 2004). Thus metadata management has become a serious problem we have to face due to the number of records and the many different types of metadata standards in the future. Though it's easier said than done, with the help of modern technology and a managerial tool such as a balanced scoreboard, we now have many means to solve it.

3. Balanced Scorecard

The concept of balanced scorecard was introduced by Kaplan and Norton in 1992. As an innovative performance measurement tool, the balanced scorecard (BSC) evolved to a comprehensive strategic management device. Kaplan and Norton themselves stated that *"The Balanced Scorecard* translates an organization's mission and strategy into a comprehensive set of performance measures and provides the framework for strategic measurement and Management"* (Kaplan and Norton, 1996b). This simple overview is accurate, but does not clarify fully the radical approach that the BSC provides. The BSC defines and assesses the critical success factors considered necessary to fulfill the corporate goal(s) to ensure future success. This is achieved by close understanding of cause and effect relationships. By measuring organizational performance across *four balanced perspectives*, the balanced scorecard complements traditional financial indicators with measures for customers, internal processes, and learning and growth activities.

Though being used by and developed originally for the business sector, the BSC approach has been adapted to the activities and conditions of the public services such as governmental and non-profit organizations, including libraries. In 2001 the Association of Research Libraries (ARL) and OCLC sponsored a three-day workshop on performance measures, which focused on the balanced scorecard (Association of Research Libraries, 2001). The German Research Association is sponsoring a balanced scorecard initiative among several German libraries (Poll, 2001). In early 2001 the University of Virginia Library began implementation of the balanced scorecard. The adoption of the scorecard has forced the library to focus its assessment and statistical activities, and to identity and develop those measurements that actually make a difference (Self, 2003).

The balanced scorecard approach is to investigate cause and effect relationships in organizational activities and bring some balanced measure between traditional financial criteria and performance from three additional perspectives: customer, internal processes, and learning and growth.

Firstly, the customer perspective captures the ability of the organization to provide quality goods and services, the effectiveness of their delivery, and overall customer service and satisfaction. Many organizations today have a mission focused on the customer, and how an organization is performing from its customers' perspective has become a priority for top management (Kaplan and Norton, 1992). In a public organization model, the principal driver of performance is different from that in a commercial environment; namely customer and stakeholder interests take prominence over financial results.

Secondly, the internal business processes perspective is primarily an analysis of the organization's internal processes. Internal business processes are the mechanisms through which performance expectations are achieved. This perspective focuses on the internal business results that lead to financial success and satisfied customers' expectations. Therefore, managers need to focus on those critical internal operations that enable them to satisfy customer needs (Kaplan and Norton, 1992).

Thirdly, the customer and internal business process measures identify the parameters that the organization considers most important for competitive success. The targets for success keep changing, and intense competition requires that organizations make continual improvements to their existing products and processes and have the ability to introduce entirely new processes with expansion capabilities (Kaplan and Norton, 1992). The learning and growth perspective looks at such issues, which include the ability of employees, the quality of information systems, and the effects of organizational alignment in supporting accomplishment of organizational goals.

Fourthly, financial performance measures indicate whether the organization's strategy, implementation, and execution are contributing to bottom-line improvement. It shows the results of the strategic choices made in the other perspectives. By making fundamental improvements in their operations, the financial numbers will take care of themselves, according to Kaplan and Norton (1992). In the public arena, the "financial" perspective differs from that of the traditional private sector. Private sector financial objectives generally represent clear long-range targets for profit-seeking organizations, operating in a purely commercial environment. Financial considerations for public organizations should be measured by how effectively and efficiently they meet the needs of their stakeholders. Therefore, in the government, the financial perspective emphasizes cost efficiency, i.e., ability to deliver maximum value to the customer.

4. Research Design and Metrics

As I stated before, metadata management is more than a management life cycle of itself, but an organizational and intellectual process requiring physical resources, financial commitment, and policy planning, which composes the whole framework of metadata management. The most important issue of metadata management is performance management. Since the balanced scorecard is an effective tool for performance measurement of activities of an organization such as metadata management, an entire framework is proposed to measure the performance of metadata activities in a library environment. According to Kaplan and Norton (1996a) a typical balanced scorecard may employ 20-25 measures. However, in almost all cases, when developing a balanced scorecard the people involved in the process end up with a huge list of measures. By summarizing these discussion about key issues of metadata management from (Kurth et al, 2004), (Westbrooks, 2005) and (IGGI, 2004), I put up a relatively simple suggestion with thirteen measures and thirty-one target metrics balanced scorecard framework as a starting point for this research design. By conducting a survey with dozens of experienced librarians to see which metrics should take more weight in this measurement, the experiment of this design got some interesting results.

Let's look at all the measures by four perspectives roughly in figure 1.

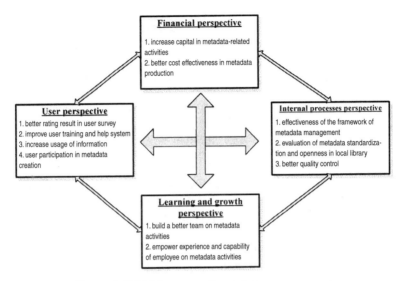

Figure 1. BSC Measures of metadata management

A better illustration of this balanced scorecard design is listed here with four tables in four perspectives with all the metrics. These tables showed us the rational of design with more detailed information.

User perspective	
1. Better rating result in user survey	1.1 Quality rating in user survey
	1.2 Convenience rating in user survey
2. Improve user training and help system	2.1 Times of user training
	2.2 Evaluation of help system
3. Increase usage of information	3.1 Frequency survey of usage on user average
4. User participation in metadata creation	4.1 User rating of metadata quality
	4.2 Proportion of user created content in metadata

Table 1. Metrics from the user perspective

Internal process perspective	
1. Effectiveness of the framework of metadata management	1.1 Effectiveness rating of the process of design, production, use and preservation of metadata
	1.2 Rating of effective balance between centralized and decentralized metadata management model
	1.3 Coverage survey of applying open standard in metadata management
	1.4 Governance in metadata management
2. Evaluation of metadata standardization and openness in local library	2.1 Standardization evaluation of application profiles used
	2.2 Standardization evaluation of design process of application profiles
	2.3 Interoperability between local metadata schema
	2.4 Interoperability between local and other systems' metadata
3. Better quality control	3.1 Standardized workflow in metadata design
	3.2 Standardized workflow in metadata production
	3.3 Quality control milestone in design and production process

Table 2. Metrics from the internal process perspective

Financial perspective	
1. Increase capital in metadata related activities	1.1 Increase of expenditures of total metadata related activities compare to last year
	1.2 Metadata related expenditures as a proportion of total content production
2. Better cost effectiveness in metadata production	2.1 Unit cost of metadata production
	2.2 Unit cost of metadata use

Table 3. Metrics from the financial perspective

Learning and growth perspective	
1. Build a better team on metadata activities	1.1 Reasonable ratio overall different types metadata employees
	1.2 Recruit amount of high productive, qualified metadata employees yearly
2. Empower experience and capability of employee on metadata activities	2.1 Understanding on metadata standards
	2.2 Understanding on metadata management framework and policy
	2.3 Ability of metadata design
	2.4 Ability of metadata creation
	2.5 Ability of metadata research (total numbers of metadata research project)
3. Evaluation of training	3.1 Evaluation of training course
	3.2 Attendance in training

Table 4. Metrics from learning and growth perspective

5. Metrics Survey

Metrics play an important role in the balanced scorecard device and should be more specific and measurable so that an observer can say with certainty whether the organization was successful with a given metric. There is another critical concern about weight in metrics, which tells us about the importance of every metric in the whole performance-measuring system. By conducting a small survey about weight of each metric, we got results from thirty-seven experienced librarians. Every librarian in our survey gives his/her rating about the weight of every metric. We got some useful and interesting information about these metrics. The top five and bottom five average rating metrics are listed in Table 5 and Table 6.

Perspective	Metrics	Average rating
User	Quality rating in user survey	4.62
	Convenience rating in user survey	4.41
Internal Process	Interoperability between local and other systems' metadata	4.38
	Quality control milestone in design and production process	4.30
	Interoperability between local metadata schema	4.08

Table 5. Top five average rating metrics

Perspective	Metrics	Average rating
Internal Process	Coverage survey of applying open standard in metadata management	3.38
	Rating of effective balance between centralized and decentralized metadata management model	3.19
Financial	Increase of expenditures of total metadata related activities compared to last year	3.16
User	Times of user training	3.00
Learning and growth	Employee attendance in training	2.70

Table 6. Bottom five average rating metrics

From Tables 5 and 6, we learn that librarians gave much attention to user service, that is, user perspective, but comparatively little to finance, internal processes, or learning and growth. Quality and usability in user service got most attention from librarians. It is no surprise that quality control and interoperability are regarded as important metrics in metadata management performance. For me, it does not mean that because training for both user and employee or financial supporting etc. as metrics got the least attention they were of less importance. In addition, scorecard metrics need to show balance including a mix of outcomes and performance drivers.

6. Conclusions

There is an old saying that what gets measured, gets managed. As a hard task we are facing today, metadata management needs to be measured to get better performance. The balanced scorecard is a practical and innovative tool which can fulfil the objectives in metadata management. By designing this metrics framework as a starting point, we find a new way for solving the problems of performance measure for metadata management, which was mostly favored in our survey from thirty-seven professionals. Next, we need to focus more attention on how to put this design into practice.

References

1   Kurth, M., Ruddy, D. and Rupp, N. (2004). "Repurposing MARC metadata: using digital project experience to develop a metadata management design", Library Hi Tech, Vol. 20 No. 2, pp. 153-65.

2   Westbrooks, E.L. (2004). "Distributing and synchronizing heterogeneous metadata in geospatial information repositories for access", in Hillmann, D. and Westbrooks, E.L. (Eds), Metadata in Practice, APA, Chicago, IL.

3   Westbrooks, E. L. (2005). "Remarks on Metadata Management". OCLC Systems & Services: International Digital Library Perspectives 21, no.1, pp. 5-7.

4   Kaplan, R.S. and Norton, D.P. (1996b). "The Balanced Scorecard: Translating Strategy into Action", Harvard Business School Press, Cambridge, MA.

5   Self, J. (2003). "From values to metrics: implementation of the balanced scorecard at a university library", Performance Measurement and Metries, Vol. 4 No. 2, pp. 57-63.

6   Poll, R. (2001). "Performance, processes and costs: managing service quality with the balanced scorecard", Library Trends, Vol. 49 No. 4, pp. 709-17.

7   Kaplan, R.S. and Norton, D.P. (1992). "The balanced score card—measures that drive performance", Harvard Business Review, January-February, pp. 171-9.

8   Kaplan, R.S. and Norton, D.P. (1996a). "The Balanced Scorecard", Harvard Business School Press, Boston, MA.

9   Intra-governmental Group on Geographic Information (IGGI). (2004). "The Principles of Good Metadata Management", Office of the Deputy Prime Minister: London, 2nd ed.

The Knowledge Society of Digital Librarians' Blogging Information Management

Xiaowen Ding

Library of Jiangsu Provincial Party Institute, Nanjing, P.R. China

Abstract

This paper analyzes the situation in which digital library blogging is applied, and arrives at the conclusion that digital librarians are an increasing managing power as an agency of the "blogging link". Meanwhile, digital librarians are taking advantage of new technology and new concepts to promote the service of blogging mainly in the form of the "link", which is the basis of individuated and concerted information service and makes it possible for information to be available. For the supervisors of the activity—librarians—the positioning of "blogging" information management should be given priority and concern.

1. Introduction

Blogging is a new application of the Internet that is rapidly developing and transforming, a new way of airing one's views which can be updated continually. The experts believe that the employment of blogging in the digital library could reveal the depth of the information and offer an orientation of links. Up to now, digital librarians in different countries advocate the service similar to that of blogging, and innovate the service of information, with which the rudiments of digital libraries' blogging websites could be seen.

As digital library blogging is a new concept in library science, the positioning of relevant blogging information is still under study. With regard to it, the searching of the positioning method and emphasizing the management on an application basis are remarkably important.

2. The Positioning of Digital Library Blogging Information

Since the moment the Internet and Web 2.0 became available, the participation of users, the spirit of interaction, and the combination of the techniques and content with links are particularly stressed. Web 2.0 works this way. The content of libraries developed from Web 2.0 works this way as well. The application of blogging in the Web 2.0 environment encourages "being open" and "being shared" and makes them the presentation of the creativity of digital library links. And the service patterns, the content, the system, and the techniques of digital library blogging could help to take shape.

As to the induction and positioning of the information management of digital library blogging, we may get at the same point of view with the following concepts.

2.1. Collective management of the "double link"

"Internet is the medium of all media." Not only the employed media in the past are a part of Internet, but also people who use the Internet.(2) According to the latest concept and technique of the Internet, digital librarians could make use of their intrinsic derivation assembling ability to put the changing information essence of blogging to use in the background of the service of opening a digital library by collective links and make the link users of the digital library play two roles—transmitter as well as receiver. With this, the acquisition of information from the open digital library is not confined by the preference of the librarians and the link users are entitled to decide what information they order and accept, which means link users and librarians act as key decision-makers at the same time.

2.2. "Talmud" file management

"Double links", as the nature of digital libraries' blogging, is very similar to the nature of ancient Rabbinic writings, the Talmud.(3) The works consist of texts and footnotes of later generations. More and more footnotes are compiled into the works and the texts are "open" instead of "read only". New texts are available for links, thus forming a special way of delivering information. By contrasting and analyzing, with Web 2.0, the information of the digital library for presentation, links, and expression could be accessible in this way. The power of links of hypertext in files and the value of links of the digital library can be perceived.

The management of blogging relies on the links of information resources, and the management of links derives from links. The collaboration of two sides might form a new collective way, which is different from the traditional library. The main concern of the management of digital library blogging information is diverting the link user's attention to itself. And with existent and potential links, information can be shared with others, which enables the information used to be information producers. Knowing the nature of management and the features of Internet links—multi-genres, standardized, and transcending time—we can use many ways of information management and knowledge management to classify information in an effective way. We should control disordered information, irregular information distribution, and dynamic information with sorting.

3. The Procedures of the Information Management of the Digital Librarian

Web 2.0 techniques simplify the procedures of information management and distribution, lessen intervention, and improve automation, which is the result of blogging management. The techniques of digital library blogging emphasize that spontaneous technique expansion and the acquisition of source codes are the new way of blogging information management. Up to now, many Web OPAC possessed the distributing ability of RSS, and more and more databases as well as secondary files servers begin to offer dynamic link service. Henceforth, digital librarians should make link activities the center of management procedures and direct information from "closed state" and "read only" to "open state". The key details of digital library blogging management should be the new and innovative steps of logging in, information ordering, information collecting, information quoting and path design.

3.1. Alignment procedures of interactive blogging information management

The organization of digital library information is acquired on a chronological basis. New ideas, academic theories, monographs and administration of departments are issued or arranged in chronological order. Users' links are not confined to "periods" of information collection, processing and transmission and time could direct the users in links so that users might receive the searching and positioning function of others' information and sent messages to others directly or indirectly. This way of management is often employed in new books issue and new books storage in the digital library.

3.2. Cascade procedures of acquisition of blogging information management

Under the guidance of innovative service patterns, such as the selection of WebPages and the reservation of RSS, information could be issued from one level to subordinate levels in different categories and areas. Links might be of many levels, many dimensions. The state of blogging could be stored, and searching could be shifted in second- or third-level pages, so that information resources could be best made use of. This way of management is often employed in links of library topics and subject selection.

4. The Practical Use of Digital Library Blogging Information

There are variations in the use of digital library blogging. Some emphasize RSS management, such as the New York Public Library, in which there are seven RSS links offered, and dynamic content in every special service area is issued which can be seen once updated. Some emphasize standard service patterns, such as http://www.rcpl. Info/services/liblog.htm, and some emphasize the open acquisition of linked content. We might say that our main concern is the digital library website suitable for the open acquisition of links. Many digital libraries have attempted to offer information service on the third- or fourth-level WebPages which contains a lot of originality. Digital librarians could provide the users with bloggers' news programs, reading programs, academic programs, communication programs, and navigation service that could be realized by information conveying and storing. The information stored (including titles, abstracts, and content) could be sent to the users according to their requirements, thus forming "humanized" service patterns with the expansion of information. And herewith, we turn to the ZhouBoTong RSS reading machine and the information flow process of 52KS web abstract. It mainly contains the key serving factors, the converging of websites, storing of Web-Pages, and the classifying of titles, which are important link steps in blogging information management.

4.1. The management of information expansion

The ZhouBoTong RSS reading machine is one of the most prevalent in Chinese, with friendly interfaces and simple operations, in which hundreds of sources of information are placed. Users can read the news they like instantly without opening the web pages. It has many other advantages as well: users can add RSS addresses on the web pages to their media list conveniently; it also supports RSS0.92, RSS1.0 and ATOM; users can share exclusive RSS media; users can upload their RSS media to the servers and offer instant searching of local information; users can book Baidu key words searching service; users can blog offline.

4.2. Bloggers' selection of links

52KS web abstract is unique. It is as convenient as other net bookmarks, capable of collecting websites, titles, content, pictures, and Flash, even forming abstracts automatically. Technically, it is combined with the right-button menu of Internet Explorer, which means users only need to Ctrl+A the part of information they want to store, then press the right button of the mouse in IE, click and "add it to my web abstract". In the whole process, users are not required to open the websites; instead, they could store the files anytime, anywhere. With the assistance of 52KS web abstract, users can classify, combine and revise web abstracts easily and conveniently.

Up to now, the research of digital library blogging is launched, to a large extent, on the platform of digital librarians' personal bloggings. Therefore, cultivating the digital librarians' awareness, guiding their thoughts, promoting professional service from the "information shared" level to the "knowledge shared" level, and instructing the librarians to find the proper positions in management and links are very important in perfecting digital libraries and fulfilling the librarians' occupation duties in the IT age.

Reference

1 baidu or google. "library blog".
2 Paul Levinson. Digital Mcluhan, a guide to the information millennium. Routledge Press, 1999.
3 http://www.blogchina.com/idea/blog-book/ (2006/5/30).
4 http://www.52ks.com/user0/158/html/1194.html (2006/5/30).

K · G · Saur Verlag

IFLA Publications
Edited by Sjoerd Koopman

The *International Federation of Library Associations and Institutions* (IFLA) is the leading international body representing the interests of library and information services and their users. It is the global voice of the information profession.

120/121
Management, Marketing and Promotion of Library Services. Based on Statistics, Analyses and Evaluation
Edited by Trine Kolderup Flaten
2006. 462 pages. Hardbound
€ 128.00 (for IFLA members: € 96.00)
ISBN 978-3-598-21848-4

122
Newspapers of the World Online: U.S. and International Perspectives. Proceedings of Conferences in Salt Lake City and Seoul, 2006
Edited by Hartmut Walravens
2006. 195 pages. Hardbound
€ 78.00 (for IFLA members: € 58.00)
ISBN 978-3-598-21849-1

123
Changing Roles of NGOs in the Creation, Storage, and Dissemination of Information in Developing Countries
Edited by Steve W. Witt
2006. 146 pages. Hardbound
€ 78.00 (for IFLA members: € 58.00)
ISBN 978-3-598-22030-2

124
Librarianship as a Bridge to an Information and Knowledge Society in Africa
Edited by Alli Mcharazo and Sjoerd Koopman
2007. 248 pages. Hardbound
€ 78.00 (for IFLA members: € 58.00)
ISBN 978-3-598-22031-9

www.saur.de

K · G · Saur Verlag

IFLA Series on Bibliographic Control

Edited by Sjoerd Koopman

IFLA Series on Bibliographic Control publications provide detailed information on bibliographic standards and norms, the cultivation and development of which has become indispensable to the exchange of national bibliographic information on an international level. The IFLA Series on Bibliographic Control publications also give a comprehensive and accurate overview of a wide range of national bibliographic services on offer.

www.saur.de